# *Network Distributed Computing*

# Network Distributed Computing

## Computing

### Fitscapes and Fallacies

Max K. Goff

PRENTICE HALL
Professional Technical Reference
Upper Saddle River, NJ 07458
www.phptr.com

For information regarding corporate and government bulk discounts please contact: Corporate and Government Sales (800) 382-3419 or corpsales@pearsontechgroup.com. Or write: Prentice Hall PTR. Corporate Sales Dept., One Lake Street, Upper Saddle River, NJ 07458.

Sun Microsystems Press Publisher: Myrna Rivera

Executive Editor: Greg Doench

Marketing Manager: Chris Guzikowski

Manufacturing Buyer: Alexis Heydt-Long

Cover Design Director: Jerry Votta

Cover Design: Anthony Gemmellaro

Compositor: G & S Typesetters, Inc.

Editorial/Production Supervision: Jamie Armstrong

Full-Service Production Manager: Anne Garcia

10  9  8  7  6  5  4  3  2  1

ISBN 0-13-100152-3

**Sun Microsystems Press**
A Prentice Hall Title

For Libby, Jim, Else, and Dustin

# About Prentice Hall Professional Technical Reference

With origins reaching back to the industry's first computer science publishing program in the 1960s, and formally launched as its own imprint in 1986, Prentice Hall Professional Technical Reference (PH PTR) has developed into the leading provider of technical books in the world today. Our editors now publish over 200 books annually, authored by leaders in the fields of computing, engineering, and business.

Our roots are firmly planted in the soil that gave rise to the technical revolution. Our bookshelf contains many of the industry's computing and engineering classics: Kernighan and Ritchie's *C Programming Language*, Nemeth's *UNIX System Administration Handbook*, Horstmann's *Core Java*, and Johnson's *High-Speed Digital Design.*

PH PTR acknowledges its auspicious beginnings while it looks to the future for inspiration. We continue to evolve and break new ground in publishing by providing today's professionals with tomorrow's solutions.

PRENTICE
HALL
PTR

# Contents

# Foreword

Our notion of network computing is changing. We don't go to a single machine hoping that it can meet our needs. We use collaborating federations of sometimes invisible computers to access the services we want. As the network changes from client-server to multitier to interacting stacks of multitier networks and beyond, the way we interact with it also changes. Where once a single access point was the entrance to a particular network, the fractal future networks promise that every machine is an edge of a heterogeneous network without an easily defined boundary.

This book on Network Distributed Computing (NDC) isn't a destination—it too is an edge. It is a node in a fascinating ongoing discussion and discovery process. It is an entry point to a network of people and their ideas. You'll find a wealth of information culled from writings and history of computer science, biology, mathematics, philosophy, and other fields that prepares you for further exploration.

All the while, Max Goff keeps his focus on people and ideas. As he says, "Biologists are much more interested in microbes than in microscopes. Computers are tools at best and annoyances otherwise; for too long software developers have dwelt on the discipline-specific minutiae while ignoring big-picture implications that NDC finally presses to our noses, demanding resolution. If the computer industry itself is to be more than just a passing fad, outside-the-box visionaries must be given a fair hearing."

I met Max Goff at a JavaOne BOF (Birds of a Feather) session that I led on Swarm computing. You can think of the popular wasp analogy. No wasp knows how to build a nest and yet collectively they do it. Simon Phipps suggests a metaphor of collaborating devices. Suppose, he says, that you are late for a breakfast meeting. Your PDA knows what time it is and what time your meeting is scheduled and where. Your GSA knows where you are, and so your GSA and PDA can together figure out that you're not going to make the meeting on time. They get your cell phone to contact your office computer and the machines of those you are meeting to reschedule the appointment.

Max contributed to the session with great questions and interesting scenarios. We kept bumping into each other at the rest of JavaOne. He was at the Jini community meeting and a ton of other sessions. Each time we'd meet up, he'd suggest another book that I should read. You'll find these recommendations and more in the reference material for this book.

I'm struck not just by what Max knows but also by his relentless quest to learn more. He's constantly looking around to see what's happening everywhere, driven by the admonition contained in Joy's Law that "Innovation occurs elsewhere." As Max explains in the text, "No matter who you are, regardless of locale, financial well-being, intellectual property owned or clarity of vision, there are innovations occurring in other places, produced by entities beyond your own, which have impact upon the markets you serve and the work you do. Given the connected nature of a knowledge economy, any firm that denies the inevitability of innovations occurring elsewhere is doomed to fail."

Network distributed computing requires that we change our notion of how to write programs. We need to think differently about what we can control as well as about what we can accomplish. We interact with computers without being aware of their presence and contributions.

While being excited by the promise of new technologies, Max keeps his eye on the ball. He quotes Weiser's principles of pervasive computing, reminding us that "the computer should extend your unconscious and technology should create calm."

After all of the books that Max has recommended I read, I am happy to recommend his book to you. He is a technologist who loves to communicate his passion and understanding. Communication doesn't mean writing or talking any more than teaching means standing up in front of a class a lecturing. I can't resist one more quote from this interesting book that you hold. Max understands that "Communication . . . represents not only the transmission of information but the receipt and ultimate understanding of it as well." Welcome to the discussion.

Daniel H. Steinberg
Director of Java Offerings
DIM SUM Thinking
and
Editor of java.net and ONJava.com

# Preface

The problems that exist in the world today cannot
be solved by the level of thinking that created them.
— Albert Einstein

The first time a baby breathes, systems designed to ease
the transition from one life-support stage to the next
kick in, and a mandatory cry launches the baby's lungs
on their new mission: breathing air instead of "breathing" amniotic fluid. This sort of systemic state transition, fundamental to so many biological phenomena, is
also critical to complex adaptive systems of other kinds,
including networks of computers. It is within this shared
context that I ask you to consider this volume.

When I initially proposed some of the ideas for this book, my intent was to provide a balanced overview of network distributed computing (NDC) frameworks for software developers, including comparisons between them from the perspective of L. Peter Deutsch's Eight Fallacies of distributed computing. But as with most complex endeavors, the work evolved as it progressed. In particular, the notion of a *fitscape* became a common thread. I have Greg Doench of Prentice Hall PTR to thank for blessing the term and recognizing the strength of the metaphor as such.

From a Darwinian perspective, a complex adaptive system harboring autonomous agents competing for resources can be called a "fitness landscape." As these agents become more fit for the landscape over successive generations, the landscape itself is modified in the process. I use the term "fitscape" to refer to any complex system incorporating such competitive, adaptive agents—for example, an economy at any level, a biosphere at any level, a community of interest. While the term "ecosystem" is traditionally used as a descriptive metaphor for such systems, we do often find ourselves talking about preservation of the earth's ecosystem at all costs. Hence, the implication of the word "ecosystem" seems to beg the question in that some level of stasis is implied. A fitscape, by contrast, is always in flux. It does not represent a delicate balance requiring husbandry but is rather a system in which change, based on adaptive fitness, is applauded.

Software too is created and exists within fitscapes. In particular, as NDC frameworks increasingly become fitscapes in their own right, hyperproductive competition is leading to a rate of innovation that equals in each passing year the sum of all previous years. As exhilarating as it is daunting, the future of NDC remains filled with promise, despite economic and social perturbations; even the threat of war stimulates this continual exploration of novelty.

I am an unapologetic proponent of technology. Sun Microsystems, my former employer, is one of few firms that has historically exhibited the sensibilities and ethics of the Network Age now upon us. As a technology evangelist for Sun from 1997 to 2002, I had the opportunity to commune with software developers from all over the world. These conversations have given me an even deeper appreciation of the difficult challenges we face in distributed computing. But they have also reinforced my otherwise optimistic nature.

Despite a touch of early 21st-century ennui, my mantra has remained constant: if there's hope for humanity, it's in software. And it is equally true that if there is hope for software, it's in our humanity. An examination of the past, present, and future of NDC illuminates many possible directions in which we might progress as we seek to fulfill this hope. By offering foundational comparisons between NDC frameworks, with a filter supplied by Deutsch and using a descriptive mechanism suggested by Stuart Kauffman, I seek to provide assistance to the software developers on whom so much depends.

Admittedly, my tour of duty with Sun has left me with residual platform biases. I have, in fact, illustrated most concepts using examples from Sun's offerings. But I also believe the observations and principles contained herein transcend any specific company agenda or approach; the Church-Turing thesis applies to NDC too.

# Acknowledgments

I had little appreciation for the amount of work, the extent of the commitment, or the demands of faith that would be required to complete this book when I first submitted a proposal to Sun Press on the topic of distributed computing. At the time, in the fall of 2000, the world seemed to me far different than it does today, as I'm sure is the case for much of America if not humanity. Since then, world events and the unfolding of circumstances in my own life have forced a personal reevaluation of so many notions I may have held dear at the time. But some things have remained constant, not the least of which is my gratitude to those who have influenced and contributed to this work.

My decade (1994–2003) working for Sun Microsystems was rewarding in so many ways. The opportunity to serve and learn at the feet of such giants as Bill Joy and James Gosling allowed me to grow in ways I can only appreciate in retrospect. Now that I have left and passed through a period of separation anxiety, I have had time to reflect on that period and my gratitude for that time has only grown. Conversations with James were especially influential in preparation of this book.

I am also appreciative of my evangelism cohorts at Sun: Bill, Rags, Rima, Reggie, Renita, John, Matt, Sang, Doris, Peter, Carol, Sridhar, Srikanth, Jason, Doug, Gary, and Saloni . . . keen minds, committed souls, and elegant engineers all. And, of course, the profound influence that is Jim Waldo cannot be understated. Simon Ritter deserves special mention for his heroic effort reviewing an early copy of this work. Technology evangelism is as much an engineering discipline as it is a faith-based calling, and my respect for those who are called as such is prodigious. My thanks also extend to Greg Doench of Prentice Hall, for going the distance when, at times, the journey seemed impossible. Thanks too to Jamie at G & S Typesetters and to Mary Lou for exercising prudence and sound judgment in the final preparation of this text.

My gratitude extends to other writers who have influenced me in the preparation of this work: Ray Kurzweil, David Gelernter, James Gleick, and Stuart Kauffman are all near the top of my list. But most especially to my wife, Elizabeth Harwell Goff, whose own experience and accomplishments as an author grounded me when I needed it, encouraged me when I wanted it, and had faith in me when I doubted it. In an age of uncertainty, I have no doubt that I could not have completed this without her.

Max K. Goff
New Albany, Mississippi
January 2004

# CHAPTER 1

# Fitscapes and Fallacies

The vast majority of all computing today is distributed. Local computing, which forms the roots of computer science and is itself still evolving, has become the exception rather than the rule.

In the summer of 1969, the first manned moon landing connected all humanity through televised images from our nearest celestial neighbor. That spring, James Lovelock had first presented his "Gaia hypothesis," which placed humanity (along with all terrestrial life) within a self-regulating, adaptive, interdependent biosphere we now call home. Autumn was witness to the beginning of the Internet, which now connects us ever more closely by computer surrogates. 1969 was a seminal year.

## The Age of the Network—The Age of Paradox

Computer science is both very young and very old. When I enrolled as a freshman at the University of Utah in the fall of 1969, there were few if any computer science departments in the entire world. But that is not to say that people were not studying computer science or that it was new at the time. In fact, we've been studying computer science since ancient Greece—if pattern matching, logic, and mathematics are considered part of the science of computing, as indeed they should be.

Some would argue that modern computer science began with Charles Babbage and the invention of his Analytical machine in the early 19th century, while others would insist on Alan Turing, with his theoretical Turing machine. Still others might honor the prodigy John Von Neumann. Regardless of its genesis, computer science has unleashed profound and undeniable changes on our shared planet over the past 35 years or so, affecting almost every aspect of our lives. There is nothing that software does not touch today—no art, science, discipline, economy, study, leisure activity, or human concern—that is not materially and essentially impacted by the growing science of computation and its implementations. And if you can manage to think of a human arena in which computer science doesn't yet play a role, be assured we will be there tomorrow.

Once it became clear that computers had great potential for many different applications, it was also apparent that interconnecting computers increased their potential. Despite Thomas Watson's oft-quoted misjudgment—"I think there is a world market for maybe five computers"[1]—there seems to be no end in sight for the novel purposes that computer science, coupled with boundless human ingenuity, can ultimately fulfill. Thanks almost entirely to computers that are hooked together and chattering away in networks, patterns of human interaction are changing more rapidly than at any time in human history. Indeed, the rate of this change is quickly accelerating.

Many terms might be used to describe this phase of our development: the Information Age, the Network Age, the Integral Age; the Decline of Western Civilization, the Death of Capitalism; the New Economy, the New New Economy. . . . Clearly, we are at a turning point in human history. Cultural changes as profound and as painful as those that marked the transition from the Dark Ages to the Enlightenment in the West some 500 years ago are now visited upon us, motivated and facilitated by computer science.

In fact, one word in particular lends itself to describing this epoch: paradox. What once appeared easily discernible through our sciences seems to have become profoundly counterintuitive. As we explore nature more deeply, as Einstein implored, with tools made sharper and eyes made keener by computer science, nature changes around us; the mindsets that gave rise to the very sciences that posit reality now are challenged by their own discoveries. For example, physics now teaches not only a fundamental uncertainty, not only a relativistic universe bound only to perspective and the speed of light, but a local universe that is merely a segment of a greater multiversal fruit, composed only of one-dimensional strings tightly enfolded and firmly packed, strings that give rise to a strange quantum reality which manifests as immediate, limited, relativistic, unlimited, and not really here at all upon deeper inspection.[2] This view seems so greatly at odds with what most of us have learned about the universe we inhabit that even accepting it is difficult, never mind comprehending it.

Becoming comfortable with the fundamentally paradoxical nature of our universe will be one of the greatest challenges we face in the early 21st century. And while computer science may drive the examination of paradox in other quarters, we practitioners of that science are not immune! Distributed computing is probably the clearest example of the many paradoxical challenges we face in computer science today.

## Processing of Information

So what is distributed computing anyway? How is it different from local computing? To understand what distributed computing is, we need to understand what it isn't, and that requires discussion of a few rudimentary concepts. Let's start simply and at the beginning so that complexity emerges.

Generally speaking, a computer is made of two elements: hardware and software. The hardware element is composed of stuff—plastic, copper, silicon doped with rare earth elements, perhaps a bit of rubber and some other material. Hardware, once designed and built, is usually fixed—a static collection of atoms that are subject only to the universal laws of entropy and the occasional user-induced trauma. To perform the everyday magic that computers give us, we need to add the software element. That's where programmers come in.

Software is, most simply, the set of instructions a computer needs in order to do something useful. An analogy might be a musical instrument, such as a clarinet. A clarinet is made of stuff, which is fixed. The musician who plays the clarinet provides the instructions the clarinet needs to make music: which holes and valves to open and close when, the amount, timing, and intensity of the air to be forced past the reed, the interruptions of the reed's vibrations caused by the tongue. Computer software is to the computer as the musician is to the clarinet. Computers, very much like clarinets, will follow precisely the instructions given them, regardless of the correctness or intent of the musician. If the musician is a good one, the clarinet makes music. If not, noise is the best we can expect. The same is true of computers and software.

Unlike musical instruments, computers store instructions, which become available when the computer is turned on; it's as if the clarinet could remember the exact sequence of events that made it play and was able to reproduce those events when properly motivated, resulting in the song or songs originally played by the musician but reproduced exactly as though it were played again live. Data is stored on computers by all sorts of methods: on hard disks and floppy disks, in nonvolatile RAM. . . . Indeed, this data is held in a computer's short-term memory as well, which is usually a thousand times faster to access than any long-term storage.

Computer programs—their instructions—are stored like any other kind of data. The browser on your computer is a program, a set of instructions. The image or icon that represents your browser is not a program; it's data that must be interpreted by a program (in this case, the operating system).

Programs, stored in so-called files, provide the data used as instructions for operating the computer. Other kinds of data are also stored in files but are apt to be more like a structured document; one program or another will likely know what to do with a data file, provided the file is not damaged or corrupted. An operating system (as a rule) is a program that manages the resources on the computer. All the devices, memory locations, program files, and data files are managed and enabled by the operating system. To extend our analogy, the operating system is the musician who ultimately controls the clarinet. But the musician must know what to play; sheet music is often involved. The sheet music is like a program running under the operating system (musician) on the hardware (clarinet) in question. So the operating system manages things, decides if and when another program should be loaded into fast memory for processing, how much time the program should take, how much disk space is available for the program to consume, and much more.

Most computers host many other programs in addition to an operating system. Each program functions and is governed by a set of rules, which the operating system (in conjunction with the hardware) provides, and a program must follow its instructions blindly, having no knowledge of whether it is operating with any degree of "correctness."

The basic meaning of instructions is similar on most computer systems. There are differences in *syntax* between different languages—different languages offer different features and approaches to solving different kinds of problems—but in the end, there is a great deal of common ground from one system to the next and from one language to the next. Computers, like people who play the clarinet, share much in common, despite their apparent differences.

## Organizing Information

Despite these simple structures that govern computer systems, things get very complicated very quickly. To build a manageable framework within which to understand computers and computer programming, we must organize information in such a way as to provide both a human processing model upon which we can all agree, and one that computers can also use in common, once the model is properly programmed within that framework. Some very rudimentary but useful tools for organizing information are part and parcel of every beginning computer science class. Among them are things like problem analysis charts (flow charts), pseudocode, and the simple input-processing-output (IPO) model shown in Figure 1.1.

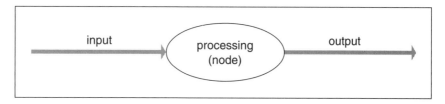

Figure 1.1 IPO model

For the programmer, the IPO model provides a simple but effective approach to organizing any local computing problem.

To understand that statement, let's first define *local computing* to be a program that runs on one and only one node. A *node* is a computer that provides a unified operating system interface. (This includes computers containing several CPUs that may run several different operating systems or several images of a single operating system, or the equivalent of an operating system on a I/O board.) A *node,* for the purposes of this book, however, is any system that offers a single unified interface to the programs that run on it.

Now, the IPO model helps organize information and describe the flow of data through this local computer system; this is the primary task in local computing. (It's useful at this juncture to note that both storage devices, such as hard disks, and human users are sources of input as well as targets for output.) The IPO process is directed by software but performed by hardware. If all we ever wanted or needed was one computer operating all by itself, alone in a world separate from all other systems, this model would suffice for organizing any programming need.

Clearly, however, that is not today's computing reality, despite programming models that appear to assume otherwise. And while many computers are still sold for which this model will suffice—things like calculators, for example, or your wrist watch (if it isn't a smart one!)—most computing devices produced today are a part of, or want to be part of, a network of other devices. The IPO model remains of some use, especially for those first learning to organize information for purposes of computer programming, but its simplifying assumptions are fundamentally flawed once a program leaves the local computing nest. Unintended but costly consequences easily arise from this fundamental misapplication.

An obvious example lies in the vast majority of computer viruses in the world today. Typically, when personal computers were first released, the IPO model guided their programming, on the assumption that each computer would stand alone. Our PCs are still vulnerable to the nuisance of viruses because of that flawed early assumption, which was *necessary* for useful programming to occur but not *complete* given the explosion of networked uses today for PCs and other intelligent devices. This is typical of many of the pitfalls that await in the land of distributed computing.

# Distributed Computing Model

So how does distributed computing differ from local computing? Distributed computing comes in several forms, each of which requires a different set of considerations when it comes to constructing a reasonable programming model; that is, one for which its architects mindfully consider aspects not covered by the IPO model for software deployment on the system. Table 1.1 presents a simple taxonomy of distributed computing (DC) systems, which naturally includes networked distributed computing systems.

Table 1.1    Taxonomy of distributed computing systems

| Family | Type | Typical Use |
| --- | --- | --- |
| Local (embedded, e.g., an automobile) | private DC | single user |
| Local (single room to campuswide) | clustered DC | multi-multiuser |
| Networked (private LAN) | private NDC | multi-multiuser |
| Networked (private WAN) | private NDC | multiuser |
| Networked (public LAN) | public NDC | multiuser |
| Networked (Internet) | public NDC | embedded/single/multiuser |

Distributed systems can be embedded in a single device or can operate within a cluster of devices in which the nodes work together to appear as a single node, offering a unified view of system resources to the application. Such clustered systems are usually connected to a fixed, high-speed datacom line, rather than a public network, and can share space in a single room, a building, a campus, or even a community, depending on the use and quality of the connection among the nodes. By the same token, a collection of embedded processors tightly bound by a proprietary datacom protocol can just as easily represent a cluster. *The distinction between DC and NDC is one of datacom, with NDC bound to standard networking protocols rather than to a private data connection.*

Networked distributed computing adds another layer of complexity to the task of programming applications, especially those that run "in the wild" or outside a private local area network (LAN) or private wide area network (WAN), in environments such as the public Internet. In general

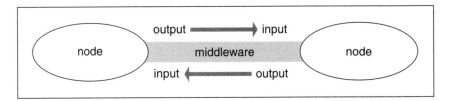

Figure 1.2  Simple NDC model

terms, the simple model for understanding and organizing information and the flow of information in the NDC environment borrows from the IPO model but adds a layer of complexity, as shown in Figure 1.2.

In this simple NDC model, the output of one node becomes the input to another node. The communication, however, need not always be in one direction. Indeed, as the model indicates, information can and usually does flow bidirectionally. But the flow of information the type and reliability of the information and the directionality of the information may acquire any number of patterns, depending on the context of deployment. Information flow, and therefore programming constraints, will always depend on the context in which the nodes operate—which leads to an important and often unstated rule of engineering, software or otherwise.

---

*Goff's axiom:* For any engineering question, there is one answer that is always correct—"It depends on context."

---

Note the thick line between nodes labeled *middleware* in the simple NDC model. This insidious term is used in our times to indicate a vast array of confusing, competing, often contentious layers of software—things like protocols, filters, converters, and firewalls. Middleware is a central NDC concept, perhaps the most important of all. Information flow through the middleware is an aspect of NDC programming that does not apply for less connected generations of applications. Strictly speaking, middleware can be thought of as software that connects two or more otherwise separate applications or separate products, serving as the glue between the applications. It is sometimes called plumbing because it connects applications, passing data between them. Note that middleware is orthogonal to NDC, which is to say that middleware is often utilized on a solitary node, facilitating local application chatter. But the focus here is NDC and the inherent pitfalls when utilizing middleware therein.

# "A Note on Distributed Computing": A Discourse on Pitfalls

Despite the growth of NDC over the past twenty years or more, many of the pitfalls inherent in NDC programming have not been widely documented. While excellent university-level texts and a vast array of research have focused on principles and paradigms for distributed systems, little has been explicitly said regarding the essential differences between local and remote computing in the wild, even as demands for a post-client-server architecture mount in this Internet-fueled era.

In 1994, a paper innocuously entitled, "A Note on Distributed Computing" was published by four engineers from Sun Microsystems.[3] This oft-cited paper introduces several important observations for programmers creating NDC applications, including four key differences between local computing and remote (or distributed) computing. (While the paper focuses on object-oriented computing paradigms, these differences are just as applicable to other programming models.) The four key differences are as follows:

- ◆ Latency
- ◆ Memory access
- ◆ Concurrency
- ◆ Partial failure

At least two of these differences should be obvious: latency and memory access.

If Einstein is correct, the speed of light is a universal limit that we cannot ignore.[4] Although the speed of light as a constraint may not be of acute interest to a single node today,[5] it most certainly has an impact across an arbitrary network within which data transfer time, which is measured in milliseconds at best and which is a million times longer than the nanoseconds in which intranode latency is measured.

Memory maps will clearly differ from one node to the next, even if both nodes run identical operating systems on identical hardware. As such, memory access that is arbitrated through abstraction layers is both useful and utilized. Note that among other features, interface definition languages (IDLs) also function as intermediaries to memory; such approaches sometimes allow for a reasonable masking of fundamental memory differences between NDC nodes, depending on use and context.

The third and fourth key differences might not be so obvious but are nevertheless real.

Concurrency, strictly speaking, is the illusion a single node gives to multiple users: that their applications are running in a dedicated CPU environment. The terms *multitasking, multiprocessing, multiprogramming, concurrency,* and *process scheduling* all refer to techniques used by operating systems to share a single processor among several independent jobs.

Concurrency in a given node implies the existence of a system process that behaves like a "scheduler," which suspends the currently running task after it has run for its time period (a "time slice"). The scheduler is also responsible for selecting the next task to run and (re)starting it.

A multiuser operating system generally provides some degree of protection of each task from others, to prevent tasks from interacting in unexpected and unplanned ways (such as accidentally modifying the contents of an unrelated process' memory area). When such an event occurs, it is generally classified as a *bug.* The processes in a multiuser or multitasking system can belong to one or many users, as opposed to parallel processing by which one user can run several tasks on several processors.

Multithreading is a kind of multitasking with low overheads and no protection of tasks from each other; all threads share the same memory. Multithreading applications are also part of the general topic of concurrency, as by implication are the concepts surrounding the sequence of execution of various threads.

The differences in a framework's ability to ensure predictable concurrency attributes in local and remote environments are a close cousin to the fourth key difference: the inevitability of a partial failure.

In a single node, either components in the system are working or they are not, and a *central authority* (i.e., an operating system) governs all resources. The multiple nodes of a distributed system provide potentially greater resources, but the lack of a central authority increases resource ambiguity. This problem, according to "A Note on Distributed Computing," is as inevitable as it is unwise to ignore, as some approaches to distributed computing would seem to advise. In a single node, either a given transaction occurred, which can be known, or it did not, which can also be known; on a network, there is the added possibility that it might have occurred but a partial failure prevents us from finding out. For example, either the remote node expired before the transaction was complete, or it completed the transaction and then expired but couldn't confirm the transaction before it expired. This circumstance gives rise to an *indeterminacy* in the NDC model that is not present in the local model, due almost entirely to the *lack of a central authority.*

Because concurrency in NDC may involve the simultaneous execution of tasks or threads over multiple nodes or a sequencing of execution otherwise, it is also impacted by the lack of a central authority and is thus inherently different from assurances of concurrency, which are available on an isolated node.

## Eight Fallacies of Distributed Computing

Peter Deutsch, now retired from Sun Microsystems, is often credited for having articulated the Eight Fallacies of Distributed Computing, which are related to the paper previously cited. According to James Gosling, Deutsch originally articulated only four or five of the fallacies. The rest were added (by Deutsch or others) to the list over time. Regardless of the origin of the fallacies, Deutsch is credited with listing them, all of which are obvious and insightful. And all are likely to be ignored, not only by novice NDC programmers but sometimes by major frameworks that attempt to solve myriad middleware problems in order to allow NDC developers to ignore the differences between local and distributed computing.

Deutsch wrote:

> Essentially everyone, when they first build a distributed application, makes the following eight assumptions. All prove to be false in the long run and all cause big trouble and painful learning experiences.[6]
>
> The eight fallacies are
>
> 1.  The network is reliable
> 2.  Latency is zero
> 3.  Bandwidth is infinite
> 4.  The network is secure
> 5.  Topology doesn't change
> 6.  There is one administrator
> 7.  Transport cost is zero
> 8.  The network is homogeneous

Any reasonable examination of NDC must clearly acknowledge the fallaciousness of these assumptions.

If we juxtapose the key differences cited in *A Note on Distributed Computing* with the Deutsch Fallacies, it is clear that the lack of a central authority is responsible for many of the dissimilarities between local and distributed computing, as shown in Table 1.2.

Table 1.2    Fallacies and key differences: Primary causes

| Key Differences | Deutsch's Fallacies | Primary cause |
|---|---|---|
| Partial failure, concurrency | The network is reliable | Implicit in network design/implementation |
| Latency | Latency is zero | Speed of light constraint |
| Concurrency | Bandwidth is infinite | Implicit in network design/implementation |
| | The network is secure | Lack of central authority |
| Partial failure, concurrency | Topology doesn't change | Lack of central authority |
| | Single administrator | Lack of central authority |
| Concurrency | Transport cost is zero | Implicit in datacom design/implementation |
| Memory access | Network homogeneity | Implicit in network design/implementation |

It is generally deemed impossible to engineer around the fundamental NDC constraint of the absence of a central authority. So, to cope with the differences listed above—the speed of light limit, the inevitability of partial failure, and the tenuous-at-best assurance of concurrency—NDC must ignore the semantic assurances proffered by models that try to mask the differences. Instead, NDC must somehow learn to adapt to the inherent differences, either by exposing them to software developers or by masking them and hoping for the best. *A Note on Distributed Computing* makes this very point.

## NDC Context

In addition to an examination of the differences between local and remote computing—the context in which applications must operate—it is also useful to review the context in which programmers actually develop code. The metatrends that drive the computer industry have had and may continue to have a strong influence on design decisions, available tools, and economic constraints, all of which form an ecological framework in which programmers compete in order to make a living. The metatrends that have driven software development recently differ markedly from trends of previous development periods. Moore's law, for example, has been a well-documented trend that has impacted software development for at least two decades. The acceleration of that trend in recent years, however, when coupled with other, exponentially expressed, trends has given rise to a rapidly changing fitness landscape, or *fitscape,*[7] in which programs (and programmers) must continually compete anew.

## The Nth Laws

The three exponentially expressed metatrends are:

- Moore's law: The density of transistors doubles every 18–24 months.

- Gilder's law: Global communications bandwidth doubles every 6 months.

- Metcalfe's law: The potential value of a network is the number of nodes squared.

These three "Nth Laws"[8] can be viewed as metatrends because they shaped the current fitscape in which software must compete. As shapers of the fitscape, these laws are manifest in specific terms but are not directly measurable otherwise.

For example, Moore's law ensures that processor speeds will increase over time, in addition to providing more compute capability per average processor. It also ensures that memory (both silicon and disk) will increase in capacity just as rapidly; it also says that relative costs for computing resources will fall just as rapidly over time.

Gilder's law promised fat pipes approaching light speed as optoelectrical switching devices inevitably gave rise to pure optical devices, even as wireless technologies vied for mobile and last-mile connections to the fiber-optic backbone, which too was increasing in capacity. That is, of course, until the implosion of the telecom sector, beginning in the spring of 2000, with names like Global Crossing and WorldCom, once grand leaders of this burgeoning space, running afoul of both corporate prudence and financial viability. But despite economic shakeouts in telecommunications, which inevitably impacts investment capital, Gilder's law is likely to resume in full force in relatively short order. Why? The assets of a bankrupt firm are often sold at huge discounts. Thus, buyers of such assets are in a much better position to profitably capitalize them, enabling more cost-competitive products in the end. Ultimately, progress is a function of demand. As long as increased bandwidth correlates to increased

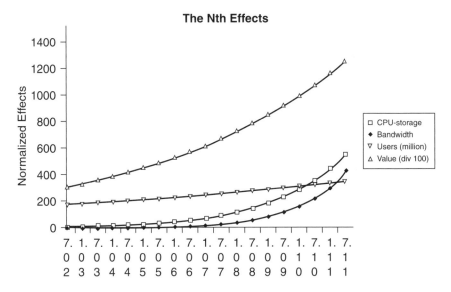

Figure 1.3 Moore's law, Gilder's law, and Metcalfe's law (pro forma)

productivity, some form of Gilder's law will remain a factor that software developers must consider.

At the same time, Metcalfe's law ensures that as technology adoption increases linearly, the potential value, or opportunity, represented by that adoption increases exponentially. Figure 1.3 illustrates the combination of these metatrends.

If these trends continue as they have in the past, then over the next nine years, the potential value of the network will increase dramatically even if there is only a modest growth (10 percent per annum) in the number of users over the same period. By the same token, aggregate bandwidth (normalized to 1 in 7/2002 in Figure 1.3) should easily keep pace with CPU-storage increases (normalized to 10 in 7/2002) and should surpass the ability of the average CPU-storage unit to assimilate fat pipes (in the aggregate) before the end of the decade.

This does not necessarily suggest that the "world wide wait" will be over; in fact, the timely availability of data-on-demand will likely be just as much a function of application design and the NDC frameworks those applications utilize as of aggregate bandwidth potential. Nor are these metatrends inevitable. Indeed, the collapse of significant telecom players may yet cool Gilder's enthusiasm. But in the spirit of optimism, significant growth, based on productivity-enhancing demand not only for more bandwidth but more of Moore and Metcalfe as well, is assumed.

More bandwidth, faster CPUs, and lots of storage won't make up for bad NDC design, however. The need to pay close attention to the fundamental differences between local and remote computing will be even more magnified in light of these Nth Laws if consumer expectations and experiences continue to shape the fitscape of technology adoption in the coming decade.

## Nth Laws Echoes

Two other trends that affect and shape the overall NDC fitscape bear mention as well. Probably an echo of the three Nth laws, these trends are more measurable:

- ◆ Decomposition and the drive to components: At some critical juncture, computing must be distributed even further. This is true at the macro and micro levels, driven by shrinking physical components, network growth, and other economic factors.

- ◆ Sedimentation and consolidation: Things that were once differentiators are now expected, fundamental pieces of a technology. An operating system, for example, may now embed applications, such as a browser.

## Zero Dollar Bill

Another derivative of the software fitscape deserves mention here—not a "law" as the three cited above, but rather more of a side effect of software itself. Since software is merely data, which is independent of substrate—bits can easily be transferred from one medium to another, from one communication modality to another, at relatively low cost—it can be said that the distribution of a unit of data is effectively free, given required storage and pervasive datacom capabilities.

In other words, once I have a PC with sufficient storage capability and an Internet connection of reasonable speed, theoretically any information on the network can be mine to download or share for free. From an NDC perspective, all software products (spreadsheets, word processors, database engines and the data that fills them), along with anything else that can be digitally represented (movies, music, news, weather, sports, telephony, books, and even education) can all be effectively free.

Figure 1.4 The Zero Dollar Bill: A metaphor for software economics

Inspired by a wall of currencies I studied while doing my laundry in Amsterdam in the summer of 1998, I started to speak of "the Zero Dollar Bill," shown in Figure 1.4. I have continued to promote this metaphor despite the implosion of the dotcom bubble because the concept is still germane to software development and deployment, which in turn is still germane to our economies.

World economics, in fact, is fundamentally disrupted by Zero Dollar Bill–derived software. As computer science continues to influence literally all aspects of human activities, accelerating rates of change across the board because of the Nth-Law cycles enabled by software, the disruptive influence of the Zero Dollar Bill has profound impact.

Indeed, software piracy alone is a huge issue. Microsoft's Windows XP operating system raison d'être is arguably one of a serious attempt at software piracy prevention. Will it stop illegal distribution? Probably not. Especially in light of the growth of Linux, which is effectively free, the idea of paying nonzero currencies for something like an operating system is beginning to seem more suspect than it might have been just a decade ago. Software piracy may therefore actually increase, despite Microsoft's attempts to preserve its historically successful business model.

Witness, too, the disruptive influence of Napster and other peer-to-peer technologies that encourage Internet users to enjoin groups designed with the expressed purpose of trading digital versions of material that is supposed to be licensed and controlled by entities other than the users themselves. The Zero Dollar Bill—a metaphor for the potential of software economics—will continue to challenge the basic assumptions of intellectual property, copyrights and licenses, and all the related institutions we remember from 20th century.

Indeed, all the assumptions and institutions that brought us here are fundamentally challenged by the work we do in computer science. The Zero Dollar Bill is a reminder of the disruptive nature of our work, a symbol of imminent egalitarian wealth as well as inevitable economic restructuring. Great change does not happen without pain.

## More Thoughts on a Fitscape

> I now discuss an algorithmic model of the real economic web, the one outside in the bustling world of the shopping mall, of mergers and acquisitions. While powerful, however, no algorithmic model is complete, for neither the biosphere nor the econosphere is finitely prestatable. Indeed, the effort to design and construct an algorithmic model of the real economic web will simultaneously help us see the weakness of any finite description. It all hangs on object-oriented programming . . .
> —Stuart Kauffman

Kauffman's *Investigations* is about a biologist who has been studying the emerging science of complexity from the confines of the Sante Fe Institute in New Mexico (by definition and charter cross-disciplinary). Kauffman offers a refreshing view of phenomena and our processes for understanding them, one we must consider if the promise of computer science is to be realized. As Einstein taught us, "The significant problems we face cannot be solved at the same level of thinking we were at when we created them." We sorely need new insights if we are to emerge from our current epoch enlightened if not fully intact.

### The Scientific Method

Science has an honored tradition. Indeed, were it not for the discipline of science, we likely would have never loosened the shackles of pre-Enlightenment thinking. In 1600, Renaissance writer and monk Giordano Bruno was burned at the stake for advocating the unthinkable idea that other worlds orbited other suns in our universe. The mindset that punished Bruno then might still be in vogue today were it not for science,

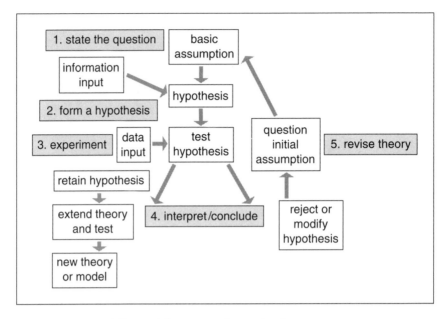

Figure 1.5  Logical flow of the scientific method

firmly rooted in mathematics and the discipline of the scientific method, which is summarized below and illustrated in Figure 1.5.

1. State the question.
2. Form a hypothesis.
3. Do experiments.
4. Interpret data and draw conclusions.
5. Revise theory (go back to step 2).

Leveraged from Aristotle, borrowed from Socrates, the scientific method is grounded in a Newtonian world view that is (a) linear, (b) finitely pre-statable (as in formation of a hypothesis), (c) observable, and (d) mathematically bound. The linear attribute is key to understanding science for the past 500 years. Indeed, before the maturation of computer science and the great solution-in-search-of-a-problem it has given us, science had no other choice.

As Kauffman and many others from traditionally reductionist quarters have begun to realize, all living systems, including our brains, reflect non-linear dynamics. The strategy of classical science, which has been to separate the elements of such systems in order to study the parts in isolated, controlled environments, was necessary before we dreamed of useful computer systems because of the mathematics involved. Such environments require the rounding-off of small differences to allow scientists the opportunity to examine the nature of causality in a simplified manner; either reduced to solvable linear equations or, when that was impossible, to a statistical analysis of averages.

It wasn't until the availability of computers that science could imagine kicking the habit of translating nonlinear equations into linear approximations. Once we began to perceive the universe through our silicon-adapted eyes, the presence of a more complex dynamic, which had previously been hidden, began to appear. The emerging science of complexity recognizes first and foremost the sensitive dependency on initial conditions that is the essence of complex systems. This awakening is still just beginning, its genesis coming sometime after the appearance of the first personal computer in the mid-1980s.[9]

Today we find ourselves confronted with a universe in which nonlinear interdependence is more the rule than the exception, and we are beginning to acknowledge that it is from a nonlinear standard that our models must proceed.

## Attributes of a Fitscape

Kauffman makes several important points which prudent NDC designers and programmers will be cognizant of, given the increasingly complex context of software development which now capture our collective imaginations:

- There is a fitscape that comprises the ecosphere in which the game is played. Whether it be a biosphere, an economy, a football league, or the fitscape of NDC development, complex, adaptive environments manifest fitscapes which will share abstract attributes with other fitscapes.

- Autonomous agents pursue competitive activities within their respective fitscapes to survive or "make a living."

- Autonomous agents persistently explore the "adjacent possible," giving rise to novelty (innovation).

- It is impossible to finitely prestate the adjacent possible. Whether it be the set of all possible protein molecules, life forms, economic models, legal systems, or computer programs, the derivatives and combinations of possibilities exceed our ability to express a finite set (which Step 2 in our scientific method requires).

♦ The rate of innovation cannot exceed the ability of the fitscape to adequately test the novelty without risking systemic collapse.

# Commentary

Of course, there is more, which is beyond the scope of this effort. But it is my view that if we are to move forward in NDC development in a manner that best suits the needs of all of humanity in these most interesting times, an appreciation of the concepts that Stuart Kauffman has articulated will be most useful. Indeed, Turing taught us with the Halting Problem that at least one class of prestatable conditions is indeed impossible for computer science. As direct heirs to Gödel's realizations (which overturned our assumptions about mathematics in the 20th century as dramatically as Einstein did our pre-20th-century assumptions regarding time), computer science is best positioned not only to lead the way to a richer, more complete understanding of our universe, but to help humanity comfortably embrace the paradoxes it will discover along the way.

## Notes

1. At the time of this writing, www.google.com found 6,440 references to the famous 1943 quotation by Thomas Watson, the IBM chairman. The reference for the purpose of this footnote will be to an FCC archived page. Given the U.S. government's penchant for long maintenance of archived materials, it is likely that this URL (http://www.fcc.gov/Speeches/Ness/spsn705.txt) will not fade any time soon. Clearly, what Watson forgot to add at the end of his famous sentence was "per person."

2. Brian Greene, *The Elegant Universe* (New York: Norton 1999).

3. Samuel C. Kendall, Jim Waldo, Ann Wollrath, and Geoff Wyant, http://research.sun.com/techrep/1994/abstract_29.html

4. Quantum entanglement may one day provide a means to ignore even this limit, although such an accomplishment would require not only engineering feats of unknown magnitude but a rather impressive modification of currently understood fundamental laws of the universe.

5. As clock speeds for processors increase, the speed of light may one day have an impact on local computing models as well, once memory access across a board or a bus takes orders of magnitude longer than on-chip cache.

6. The only known "original" reference is on James Gosling's Web site (java.sun.com/people/jag/Fallacies.html). I have taken the liberty of replicating Deutsch's fallacies on my own Web site (www.maxgoff.com/Fallacies.html) as well.

7. Stuart Kauffman discusses the concept of a "fitness landscape" in *Investigations* (New York: Oxford University Press, 2000). The term "fitscape" is meant to convey the abstract essence of a Darwinian fitness landscape, as described by Kauffman, complete with all the attributes cited herein.

8. Note that only Metcalfe's Law is firmly rooted in mathematics; Moore's and Gilder's laws are really observations of historical trends, the result of "virtuous cycles" which may or may not continue for any predictable period.

9. James Gleick, *Chaos: Making a New Science* (New York: Viking, 1987).

# CHAPTER 2

# Ten Technology Trends

All major technology trends both impact and are impacted by NDC development. The extent to which the Internet is bound to exponential growth phenomena is reflected by the innovations coming from the communities that have embraced it.

To identify a trend, we must establish a measurable threshold of participation by agents within a fitscape. The adoption of a given technology is a function of a complex set of relationships among agents, governed by economic principles and assumptions and measured accordingly.

All major technology trends today are either direct beneficiaries of the metatrends (the Nth Laws) cited in Chapter 1 or are cousins of those trends, and all have direct impact on NDC development. Each trend is also enabled by NDC, with community-building technologies greatly increasing productivity. The attributes of a fitscape apply to the communities that constitute the autonomous agents affecting each trend, institutional and individual.

In an effort to create a list of ten and only ten major technology trends, I've erred on the side of inclusion and lumped a few together. While this list is not meant to be complete, it suggests the scope and depth that accelerating metatrends engender.

1. Wireless and Mobile Computing
2. Web Services and the Semantic Web
3. Robotics
4. Genomics and Biotechnology
5. Material Science and Nanotechnology
6. Internet2, Pervasive and Ubiquitous Computing
7. Globalization, COTS, and Increasing Competition
8. Real-Time and Embedded Systems, Grid Computing, Clusters, and Composability
9. Security, Global Transparency, and Privacy
10. Competing NDC Frameworks, the Emerging Global OS, and Recombinant Software

Thorough exploration of each of the trends would require at least an essay, if not a small library. For our purposes, a terse note for each must suffice.

## Wireless and Mobile Computing

Wireless technologies are transforming the computer industry and the very concept of NDC. No longer bound by wires to homes and offices, wireless datacom promises not only freedom of movement for connected users but also increased likelihood of finding connections where hard-wired infrastructures are not yet globally competitive. Indeed, developing nations may find that skipping the copper phase of datacom growth in favor of wireless is not only faster but much less costly. Coupled with increasingly effective data compression, which allows greater quantities of information to be squeezed through limited bandwidths and space-based satellite networks to serve remote locations, the wireless/mobile trend in datacom is drawing high levels of investment, and therefore NDC developer interest, worldwide.

One near-term technology of consequence for high-speed wireless access is IEEE 802.11b, aka WiFi.[1] WiFi is a relatively short-range technology; a single base station may cover, say, a small building. But base stations are cheap—around US$100 each—making deployment of wireless Internet infrastructures relatively inexpensive given sufficient population density, as in most cities. Bill Gates has announced a commitment to WiFi going forward, and for better or for worse, when Bill Gates speaks, the industry listens. According to Gates:

> 802.11, we think, is a fundamental technology that every business, every home, every convention center is going to be wired up with high capacity 802.11. And that's finally the way that we'll have information wherever we want it.[2]

A number of problems remain to be solved before Gates' cut on WiFi becomes reality. For example, how does an ISP charge for services for network connections that are by definition short and transient? Will meta-ISPs emerge, aggregating services transparent to users, akin to the early cell phones providers in the United States? Will microtransactions be required for such services to work? Or is Microsoft itself planning on becoming the WiFi service provider of choice, which could spark yet another round of legal challenges for the Redmond giant? Clearly, once these kinds of problems are solved, the ability to provide wireless customers with a mobile Internet connection independent of cell service provider issues could trigger a renaissance in high-speed wireless access.

Another wireless technology of consequence to consider is Bluetooth.[3] Unlike WiFi, the Bluetooth specification includes both link layer and application layer definitions for product developers supporting data, voice, and content-centric applications. Radios that comply with the Bluetooth specification operate in the unlicensed 2.4 GHz radio spectrum—a situation that may one day become a problem if locale-specific band licensing becomes reality. Bluetooth radios use a spread-spectrum, frequency-hopping, full-duplex approach to provide a high degree of "interference immunity," that is, it should enable several personal Bluetooth devices to operate simultaneously without concern for interference from other local users. Bluetooth competes with WiFi but also complements it, being likely more appropriate as the personal area network (PAN) technology of choice, aggregating future personal NDC devices; for example, my PDA, wearable GPS system, implanted cardiovascular monitor, and Internet goggles all share data via Bluetooth with my WiFi connected cell phone, which also also functions as my personal web server and soul catcher!

WiFi and Bluetooth are just two examples of the investments currently being made in wireless and mobile technologies. Wireless and mobile datacom are changing technology usage patterns, the computer industry, and NDC development.

## Web Services and the Semantic Web

That Web Services is a trend should be obvious. A growing list of vendors, tools, press releases, and books is sufficient witness to that fact. But for the promises of Web Services to materialize, the Semantic Web must also be considered.

In the May 2001 edition of *Scientific American,* Tim Berners-Lee, James Hendler, and Ora Lassila articulated a succinct and impressive vision for the future of the Internet from the perspective of *meaningful information* and the impact it could have.

> The Semantic Web is not a separate Web but an extension of the current one, in which information is given well-defined meaning, better enabling computers and people to work in cooperation. The first steps in weaving the Semantic Web into the structure of the existing Web are already under way. In the near future, these developments will usher in significant new functionality as machines become much better able to process and understand the data that they merely display at present.[4]

In addition to the invention of the transistor in 1947 by William Shockley, John Bardeen, and Walter Brattain at Bell Labs, the publication of *The Mathematical Theory of Communication* by Claude E. Shannon (also of Bell Labs) the following year effectively enabled the unfolding era of computing in which we all now participate.[5] Information theory is as confusing to the nonmathematician as ANSI C code is to the nonprogrammer, with counterintuitive cuts on (nonthermodynamic) entropy, information content, and reversibility of information. A detailed discussion of information theory is beyond the scope of this effort; suffice it to say that

Shannon's work has enabled a highly mathematical and tractable approach to the idea of information and communication, and this approach has enabled modern datacom even as the transistor provided a basis for implementation of really cool computational devices.

Shannon effectively removed information from its substrate; once mathematically independent of physical constraints (such as matter and energy), information could flow over a wide array of "carrier" modalities as abstract and independent as mathematics itself. Arguably, the path to cybernetics[6] was paved with Shannon's information theory, which itself was perhaps another misunderstanding of the relationship between people and technology in the Einsteinian century of ethical relativity.

With the emergence of the Semantic Web, information is once again potentially grounded in meaning and therefore no longer divorced from context. Paradoxically, the Semantic Web is enabled by XML,[7] promising self-describing data, which metaphorically salutes information theory's illusion of separation even as it enables the emergence of inherent meaning, which can only be grounded in context, which can only be grasped by acknowledging the connectedness of the information. Thus, a fine paradox is embraced.

According to the aforementioned article in *Scientific American,*

> the Semantic Web can assist the evolution of human knowledge as a whole . . . [it] lets anyone express new concepts that they invent with minimal effort. Its unifying logical language will enable . . . concepts to be progressively linked into a universal Web. This structure will open up the knowledge and workings of humankind to meaningful analysis by software agents, providing a new class of tools by which we can live, work and learn together.

This idea has great potential and is a major technological trend (and challenge) that will have considerable impact on NDC programming. By the same token, for Web Services to rise to the hype, as it were, much will be required of the Semantic Web.

# Robotics

Computational power is to a mind what a locomotive engine is to a train. The train can't move if the engine is too small. But engine power is effective only if properly coupled to the load. Locomotive engines of the eighteenth century learned the relationship between speed, pulling power, engine size, and transmission ratios by trial and

> error, no doubt overturning many horsecart-derived intuitions. Two
> centuries later, robotics is learning analogous lessons.
> —Hans Moravec

Where did the idea of a robot begin? It depends on the context of the discussion. As early as the third century BC, a Greek engineer named Ctesibus made organs and water clocks with movable figures. Did that mark the beginning of modern-day robotics? Or was it even earlier, with the ancient Egyptian water clocks that purportedly foretold the future? Perhaps the mind-body problem as formulated by René Descartes at the beginning of the Enlightenment marked a turning point in the way we humans categorize the nature of being and the potential for "mind children"—as Moravec put it,[8] intelligent creatures created with our own hands and minds. Certainly, Mary Shelley gave us reason to pause with *Frankenstein* in the early 19th century. But then Isaac Asimov turned fear once again into hope in 1942 when he wrote "Runaround," the story that first stated his "Three Laws of Robotics":

- ◆ "A robot may not injure a human, or, through inaction, allow a human being to come to harm.

- ◆ "A robot must obey the orders it is given by human beings except where such orders would conflict with the First Law.

- ◆ "A robot must protect its own existence as long as such protection does not conflict with the First or Second Laws."[9]

In 1948, when Norbert Wiener published *Cybernetics,* affecting and affected by Shannon's work on information theory and sharing temporal influence with the invention of the transistor, the Information Age was born.[10] Perhaps that was indeed the year we became post-human and robotics found traction.

Key to any meaningful advance in robotics beyond that of Ctesibus and his clocks is computer science. Before the birth of the Information Age, robots or any serious notion of animated extrabiological forms was simply puppeteering, not robotics in the strictest sense. But with computer "intelligence," robots are now not only imaginable, they are becoming common.

Robots routinely aid in manufacturing today and have done so for the better part of the past decade, if not longer. As with the adoption of any technology, the early phase has been marked by slow, often stuttered, steps. At some point a "knee" is reached and the sky-pointing view of the

S-curve is achieved. Economic blue sky continues until market saturation occurs or at least until another technology comes along that promises less cost, more utility, or both.

Have you driven or been a passenger in a car that was built since 1998? That automobile was built by processes that involved quite a few robots. And since robots work with a much greater level of predictability than we humans do, have far fewer sick days, require no vacation or overtime pay, and are generally not prone to join labor unions, in the long term, robots have the clear edge when it comes to the manufacturing job market. Eventually, too, even the lowest paid sweat-shop workers will find themselves unable to compete with their robotic counterparts; the metatrends and the ever-mutating world economic fitscape ensure that technology will one day make slave-wage humans redundant too.

The implication for NDC developers? All those robots will be needing a whole lot of code going forward. Supervised and controlled by networks, as upgradeable as the next version of code they host, robots and NDC developers will find an increasingly greater need for each other over this next decade, and probably well beyond—at least until we too are made redundant by robots better able to program themselves by the very software frameworks and computer science we are today exploring. But perhaps by then we will have worked out this interesting economic paradox that is so clearly implicit in the metatrends.

## Genomics and Biotechnology

Yes, we cracked the human genome, and that too was enabled by computer science. But it was just the beginning; biotechnology will revolutionize our view of living organisms as we continue to learn to engineer DNA. Of all the major technology trends, the revolutionary effects of biotechnology may be the most shocking that we will encounter over the next decade. Collective breakthroughs in biology and medicine, including a complete rethinking of geriatrics, may improve both the quality and the length of human life, even as engineering of our environment reaches unprecedented levels of intervention and granularity of control.

What is the impact of hyper-biotech on NDC development? Enormous! What if you knew your potential lifespan was approaching 500 years? Would that have an impact on your day-to-day activities? Might you behave differently? Perhaps write a little better code? Study harder? Might the short-term fluctuations of the stock market seem as insignificant as they really are once the broader view is adopted? Might education and respect for others improve?

Game theory teaches us that the optimal strategy for success depends on an assumed frequency of interaction—if I know our encounters will be many, which I can logically assume if our lives encompass centuries, then I must also know that cooperation is the optimal strategy for my own personal success. And since we all share virtually all information, you would know that too.

These ideas don't touch on the application development opportunities inherent in the data-intensive, CPU-intensive demands of neo-biotech. As venture capital seeks the obvious rewards of innovating the cure for aging, for example, many dollars will be spent on NDC applications (and NDC application developers). And in what other ways will cracking the human genome be of value?

DNA analysis machines and chip-based systems can potentially accelerate the proliferation of genetic analysis practices, improve drug search capabilities, and enable biological sensors. The genomes of plants (from food crops to new forms of fuel) and animals (from bacteria such as anthrax to mammals) will continue to be decoded and understood. To the extent that genes determine function and behavior, extensive genetic profiling could provide an ability to better diagnose human health problems, provide designer drugs based on individual problems, and provide better predictive capabilities for genetically bound diseases.

Genetic profiling could also have a significant effect on security and law enforcement. DNA identification may complement existing biometrics technologies (such as retinal scans) for granting access to secure systems and eventually become the norm, eliminating the need for credit cards and drivers' licenses. Biosensors (some genetically engineered) may also aid in detecting biological threats, improving food and water testing, providing continuous health monitoring, and executing medical laboratory analyses. Such capabilities could permanently change the way health services are rendered by greatly improving disease diagnosis and monitoring capabilities.

These incredible possibilities are not unfolding without issue, however. Just mention cloning or genetically modified food at your next cocktail party and watch the sparks fly. Numerous ethical, legal, environmental, and safety concerns will demand resolution as humanity comes to grip with the potential effect of the incredible biological revolution that is now immediately upon us—a revolution seasoned and blessed by myriad incantations from the magic of computer science.

# Material Science and Nanotechnology

In 1959, Dr. Richard Feynman gave a talk at the annual meeting of the American Physical Society at the California Institute of Technology that is considered by most nanotechnology researchers to be the inspiration for their work.[11] But it wasn't until K. Eric Drexler published *Engines of Creation: The Coming Era of Nanotechnology* in 1986 that the general public began to get wind of this promising approach to materials and technology.[12]

Imagine, for example, the respirocyte.[13] The respirocyte is a hypothetical device, about 1 micron in diameter, designed to efficiently bind with $CO_2$ and oxygen. Approximately 5 cubic centimeters of respirocytes will replace every red blood cell in your body and do a better job of facilitating a metabolism that has taken millions of years to evolve. With respirocytes, you'll live longer, breathe easier, and generally feel a whole lot better. The respirocyte doesn't exist—yet. We may be 10 years away from respirocytes, or 20. But we are most certainly moving very quickly in a direction that will ultimately bring respirocytes to a pharmacy near you and that brings up a number of interesting questions.

Will respirocytes be considered a prescription drug? A therapy? A prosthesis? If I ingest respirocytes and you don't, are we physiologically different? Are there ethical implications? What if my potential life span increases by at least 100 years simply by my taking respirocyte therapy, but the cost of respirocyte treatments are such that only the wealthiest 2 percent of world citizens can afford it? What happens then? And this is just one example of the unimaginable array of applications for material science as modified by the creations of applied nanotechnology.

Composite materials design uses computing power (sometimes together with massive parallel experimentation) to screen different materials possibilities in order to optimize properties for specific applications like catalysts, drugs, ceramics, polymers, and ultimately the assembly of very small devices like the respirocyte.

Nanoscale materials (those with properties that can be controlled at submicron or nanometer levels) are an increasingly active area of research; properties in regimes of these sizes are fundamentally different from those of ordinary materials. Examples include carbon nanotubes, quantum dots, and biological molecules. We are discovering that these materials can be prepared either by purification methods or by tailored fabrication methods, both of which require copious computer control mechanisms and computational resources.

Nanotechnology too promises quantum computing, which lives at the bleeding edge of research. With nanoscale engineering, at the very least Moore's law should continue unabated until at least 2015, by which time computing may very well become fully ubiquitous. In the near term, it is likely that by the time this book reaches shelves (or becomes available on virtual shelves) some nanoscale materials may have found their way into next-generation PCs and other computing devices.[14]

I still recall my first real job writing code for a fledgling UNIX startup in Park City, Utah, in 1983, when there were literally hundreds of UNIX startups around the world. In that small shop, I typically developed code on a small system with maybe 256 KB of memory (as I recall) and a 2- or 3-MB hard disk drive, best case; such systems I would routinely share with at least two other developers. That was our typical shared environment for writing code, and we were lucky to have it. Tonight I'm writing this paragraph in my home office on Sun's UltraSPARC 10 workstation, which boasts 256 MB of RAM and an 8-GB hard drive. I've had this system for at least three years now, so it may be a little behind the times.

Next to my trusty UltraSPARC workstation is a newer Toshiba Tecra 8200 laptop, which has 512 MB of RAM and a 20-GB internal drive . . . oh, and hooked to it is a 32-GB external drive that I bought last year to store WAV and MP3 files for when I produce my own audio presentations for the Web. There are two other older laptops on my home LAN, both of which serve ancillary functions like handling the parallel printer or accommodating the occasional visitor who would surf the Web while I work. And that's not counting the Apple iMac that is on back-order for my last birthday present, the two Apple systems my wife uses in her studio in the basement, or the myriad embedded processors we routinely use each day whenever we watch cable television, heat coffee in the microwave, or answer the phone.

The point is, in less than 20 years, my personal access to computing systems has increased at least 1000-fold and I'm no longer required to share any of those basic productivity resources. Oh, and I've got all those systems on the Internet now too. The footprint for all the systems I have at home is considerably less than the typical shared system we used in Park City way back when. And the cost for all these systems today is maybe half of what it was in actual dollars, and is less than a quarter of what it would be if inflation is considered. That's how dramatically things have changed since 1983.

The systems I use today, which allow me to be considerably more productive than I might have been in 1983, will seem just as antiquated and provincial in 2015 as that modest shared system in 1983 does today. Nanotechnology ensures that the rate of change between now and 2015, as promised by Moore's law, will inevitably continue. NDC programmers need to be well aware not only of the dramatic increase in computing resources but also of the dramatic proliferation of computing systems they will want to network with going forward.

## Internet2, Pervasive and Ubiquitous Computing

> The most profound technologies are those that disappear.
> They weave themselves into the fabric of everyday life until they
> are indistinguishable from it.
> —Mark Weiser

When the seminal article on ubiquitous computing was first published in Scientific American in 1991,[15] it was as visionary and important to the genesis of "ubiquitous computing" as Feynman's 1959 speech was to the genesis of nanotechnology. But Mark Weiser's article didn't take nearly as long to germinate traction and active participation by a significant portion of the research community.

What is pervasive or ubiquitous computing? It's a lot more than simply the appearance of computing resources everywhere. Processors have become so small and inexpensive that the idea of embedding a processor in your shoe is no longer far-fetched.[16] But what good are processors everywhere if some ensemble of systems cannot or does not produce something actually usable from a human perspective?

Weiser has articulated several principles that we need to consider as we embark upon the mission of providing intelligence in just about anything you can think of. This is, on the surface, the teleology of ubiquitous or pervasive computing. But as with so many other aspects of learning, superficial characteristics often mask deeper organization or meaning. Consider Weiser's principles of pervasive computing:

- ♦ The purpose of a computer is to help you do something else.
- ♦ The best computer is a quiet, invisible servant.
- ♦ The more you can do by intuition, the smarter you are; the computer should extend your unconscious.
- ♦ Technology should create calm.

The era of pervasive computing is one is which computers should simply disappear. The challenges such a proposition presents to NDC developers are considerable, to say the least.

At the same time, if we consider the possibilities, benefits, and challenges of providing integrated intelligence everywhere, the potential of a next-generation network enters the equation. Internet2 is a collaborative effort that today involves at least 200 universities and businesses, all working toward a network capable of providing bandwidth several orders of magnitude greater than what even the best Internet connections can provide today.

At the heart of Internet2 are optical transmission technologies—theoretically capable of delivering a data stream that can approach a limit of 30 terabits per second per fiber once an all-optical network is in place (based on optical switching and routing devices that are envisioned but not yet commercially real).[17] With the Internet2 project come visions of a future that includes telepresence, extremely high bandwidth collaborative processes, personal broadcasts of HDTV-quality video, and more . . . the possibilities of extremely high bandwidth make even the StarTrek holodeck seem possible within the next decade.

To provide not just sheer bandwidth but some assurance of quality of service (QoS), researchers involved in Internet2 have found it necessary to consider issues of middleware, one of the themes of this book. The ideas that are surfacing regarding a future middleware that might provide more reasonable assurances of QoS for Internet2 are discussed throughout the book.

The implications of ubiquitous, pervasive computing for future NDC development are very clear because this technology will be entirely dependent on NDC.

## Globalization, COTS, and Increasing Competition

> Global economic integration will be the means by which the consequences of overpopulation in the Third World are generalized to the globe as a whole.
> —Herman E. Daly

If you are reading this book, one fact can be assumed: you know how to read. We live on a planet, according to UNESCO, where the assumption of adult literacy is not entirely valid. UNESCO estimates that there are about 1 billion nonliterate adults on earth today—more than 25 percent of the world's adult population. Two-thirds of all nonliterate are women; 98 percent live in developing countries. In the least developed countries, half the adult population cannot read.

Global economic integration is an undeniable fact today. Some argue that integration is a regional rather than a global phenomenon. I'm hard-pressed to understand how this could be so, given the proliferation of computers around our planet. The economics of the computer industry have increasingly taken on a global flavor in the past 20 years; clearly, the sourcing of computer components transcends regional boundaries, as does the assembly of systems, the creation of software, and the integration of services through networks. I believe the same is true of the automotive industry. While some segments may remain local or regional, much of the world's economy is now truly a world economy.

The utilization of commercially available, off-the-shelf (COTS) technologies has also been a trend in economic sectors where procurement was once accomplished through well-defined supplier "silos." Military, mission-critical, and real-time implementations[18] (which include the largest consumer of computer chips in the world, the automotive industry) have all become adopters of COTS technologies over the past decade. Why? Economic pressures.

In a global economy, capital generally flows to those places in which the costs of doing a particular business are the lowest. Once it was good enough to be the best (which often means the most efficient) purveyor on your block of whatever product or service you may provide. But as transportation and communication capabilities improve, the reach of your service or product can extend into your immediate town, then to your county, then to your state or nation, then to your region. It naturally follows that extending transportation and communication capabilities to a global reach will give rise to a globally integrated economy, one in which competition must increase as a result of a wider competitive framework.

The inevitabilities of a global economy serve the trend of ephemeralization—doing more with less—just as they are disruptive to economic relationships based on preglobal models. The impact on NDC developers should be quite clear: we will be integrating COTS components into larger applications, and we will be competing with other NDC developers from literally all corners of the globe in doing so. By the same token, our products and services will need to address potentially a global audience.

## Real-Time and Embedded Systems, Grid Computing, Clusters, and Composability

To remain competitive in a global economy, any firm (except perhaps a monopoly) must employ one of two fundamental strategies:

1. Become the lowest-cost (bargain) provider.
2. Provide added value through continuous innovation.

All marketing, branding, sex appeal, e-nonsense, and lies aside, one or the other of these strategies, or a combination of the two, is the basic teleological assumption of any business competing in world markets today. Any other approach can be categorized as a function of one of these two. The lowest-cost strategy requires doing more with less (ephemeralization)—production costs must continue to fall in order to survive fitscape pressures. The added-value strategy requires continuous investment in knowledge-based processes to create that value, the requirements for which are also dictated by the fitscape.

Earlier we spoke of the automobile sold in 1998, built in some part by robotic labor. That same automobile also enclosed you in an EmNet, a network of embedded computers, some of which were *real time,* which means that one very important aspect of the system's performance profile is predictable execution with respect to time. In fact, probably most or all automobiles manufactured in the 1990s featured a growing list of EmNet components as well as a growing pool of robotic laborers. Through the research I've done in the real-time space, it has become clear to me that the automotive industry has had to be an early and eager adopter of COTS technologies to compete in the emerging global economy. The "world car" has been a concept firmly entrenched in business education since I labored over case studies in the early 1990s.

The average automobile today (with the clear exception of SUVs[19]) weighs less, is more fuel efficient, is made of smarter composite materials, and provides a safer driving experience than the equivalent automobile sold just 10 years ago. This improvement is due both to the influences of the metatrends cited earlier and to the interaction of these two basic business strategies in the global fitscape that rules automobile production practices. In this dynamic system, the fitscape itself is altered by the metatrends as it drives the two strategic pressures to the benefit of the automobile consumer.

In this sense, automobile manufacturing is indicative of the direction in which all industry, being affected by the same globalizing trends and forces, must proceed. COTS technologies, embraced by fitscape pressures, will inevitably be enthusiastically adopted by NDC development going forward. Indeed, other aspects of real-time and EmNet adoption in a changing fitscape will ultimately be reflected in NDC development as well.

## Composability

Consider the notion of composability. Remember our musician with her clarinet? Let's use her as an example here. She may be well versed in reading sheet music and very well practiced, able to play well in any ensemble. But for her to "constructively integrate" in an ensemble, she must be cognizant of (a) those with whom she is playing, (b) her part in the whole of the composition with respect to volume, timing, tone, and timbre, and (c) the overall timing of the piece. In other words, the *context* of her performance is just as important as her ability to read, understand, and play the composition, which itself must be well constructed in all its parts.

A composable software architecture is something like that ensemble of musicians (which may also include a conductor, depending on the complexity and demands of the piece in question). In the NDC space, composability is still an alien creature—not yet seriously recognized as a need, and hence not seriously considered as a requirement for frameworks that would facilitate the development and deployment of useful and reliable NDC programs. But if indeed real-time and embedded computer research and practice is a harbinger of things to come, NDC will one day too reflect a composability requirement in order to survive fitscape pressures.

## Grid Computing and Clusters

Another trend in this category (and an argument for NDC composability) is the emergence of an organizing principle called *grid computing,* which is actually a form of NDC. The topic of grid computing is more properly included in the discussion of competing NDC frameworks, later in this chapter. But a brief mention here is useful in further illustrating the concept of composability.[20]

Grid computing shares many attributes with the concept of computer clusters. Both approaches would harness the capabilities of multiple systems with increasingly COTS components (that is, integrated hardware/ software commodity systems) which communicate through a network (private or public) to present a unified view of compute resources to an arbitrary application. From a composability perspective, research in grid computing echoes the needs now recognized in the real-time and EmNet worlds.

## Connections

To remain competitive given the three metatrends, the two primary business strategies and the inevitable consequences of globalization, composable architecture, regardless of the difficulties in achieving it, will soon be a requirement in our future. Research in many aspects of computer science, including real-time, mission-critical, and grid-computing systems, reflects that realization today.

# Security, Global Transparency, and Privacy

Just two decades ago, computer security was a specialized field that seemed important only to a small percentage of customers, most of whom represented governmental agencies. For others, nothing more than a password or a simple encryption scheme was deemed necessary. Indeed, the U.S. government has long had export restrictions on encryption technologies, restrictions that have relaxed to some extent over the past few years but that still affect those who are engaged in next-generation encryption research and development.

Today, however, the need for high-quality security is much better understood by a growing population of computer users. In an age when Internet-distributed computer viruses, denial-of-service attacks, and bad hacker[21] cultures abound, to say nothing of the impact that one dark day in 2001 had on global zeitgeist, it is not surprising that many who have ignored the need for serious computer security are now vocally supporting such efforts. Deutsch's Fourth Fallacy (The network is secure) cannot be ignored any longer by NDC developers, as even those companies so willing to gain "features" at the expense of proper functional awareness in a networked world seem to be coming to the table.

Juxtaposed with security is the notion of global transparency, which has at least three meanings:

1. Global business transparency (how do we avoid future Enron-type debacles in a global economy without standardized practices and disclosures?)

2. Global data transparency (grid computing requires data-set name transparency, data location transparency, access protocol transparency, and so on)

3. Global activity transparency (increasing satellite capabilities, proliferation of COTS networked cameras, and so on)

Global transparency is often at odds with security requirements. Security demands that information be protected; transparency demands that information be disclosed. The threat to personal and organizational privacy is clearly evident in the trend toward global transparency.

Another paradox looms in any discussion of security, global transparency, and privacy, however, especially insofar as computer science and computer systems are concerned. Consider "A Globalization Paradox."

---

### A Globalization Paradox

The more integrated the globalized economy becomes, the more dependent it becomes on transportation, communication, and computer-based, productivity-enhancing methodologies.

The more computer systems we implement and integrate, the more dependent we become on the ensemble of connected, intelligent devices; hence, the more vulnerable we become to attacks on the systems upon which we depend.

The more vulnerable we become to attacks on the computer systems upon which we depend, the more likely we are to adopt highly secure systems and processes in order to defend ourselves, and the less likely we are to trust (and do business with) regions, cultures, nations, organizations, or individuals that are not tightly bound to our computer systems, processes, and security approaches.

The more likely we are to distrust regions, cultures, nations, organizations or individuals that are not tightly bound to our computer systems and processes, the less likely global economic integration becomes.

---

Perhaps this observation is too simplistic to express the forces and dynamics that might more adequately describe a world fitscape. But the prudent NDC developer will at least note the superficial validity of the logic above and perhaps weigh design implications and market impact accordingly.

# Competing NDC Frameworks, the Emerging Global OS, and Recombinant Software

> Entia non sunt multiplicanda praeter necessitatem
> [Entities should not be multiplied unnecessarily]
> —"Occam's Razor"
> William of Occam, 1285–1349

Ernst Mach (for whom supersonic travel was named, and perhaps even the CMU microkernel) was a contemporary of Einstein's who advocated a version of Occam's Razor which he called "the Principle of Economy." This principle basically stated that scientists should always use the simplest means of doing their work and exclude everything not perceived by the senses. Taken to its logical conclusion, this approach becomes "positivism," which is the belief that there is no difference between something that exists but is not observable and something that does not exist. Mach influenced Einstein when he argued that space and time are not absolute, but he also applied the positivist approach to molecules—claiming that molecules were metaphysical because they were too small to detect directly.

The moral of Mach's story is that Occam's Razor should not be wielded without qualification, lest we cut away the potential for a more complete understanding of our universe, regardless of the discipline involved. Certainly the same argument applies to computer science.

Attempts to measure complexity are by their nature complex. In mathematics, economics, biology, physics, chemistry, cognitive psychology, geography, games, groups, and computer science, complexity measures range from simplifying linear assumptions to hands-in-the-air prayer. The emerging science of complexity may one day yield formal methods for expressing universal organizing principles which we can intuitively appreciate but not fully yet comprehend. Stephen Wolfram has documented as much in *A New Kind of Science*.[22] Mathematics has aptly named simple expressions that seem to betray an innate order we cannot yet fully comprehend as transcendental; nonalgebraic, nonrational, yet as essential as any more comprehensible expression. There is clearly an underlying order in our universe that we are still only beginning to appreciate, despite Mach's advice to the contrary. Indeed, computer science is helping us understand and extend the very senses Mach would venerate.

But for computer scientists, especially those tasked with the day-to-day need to create valuable NDC applications that compete in real-world fitscapes, managing growing complexity is a daily chore and not a philosophical diversion. We must, therefore, do something to enhance our capabilities. Last, therefore, in this incomplete list of major technology trends is a discussion of NDC software frameworks and likely directions we may take in attempting to cope with network expansion and ever-increasing complexity.

## Competing NDC Frameworks

As previously noted, considerable investments have been and are being made by many firms today in the general area of Web Services. Suffice it to say at this juncture that competing NDC frameworks already existing, address the growing complexities we face in different ways.

More importantly for this discussion, today's competing NDC frameworks also shed light on the data and software legacy we will be facing a decade from now. On the surface, if we would embrace the observations of "A Note on Distributed Computing" in toto as well as the often good advice of Occam's Razor, the idea of a global or networkwide operating system would be dismissed out of hand; no central authority we can imagine can viably be implemented on any network that would introduce communication-induced indeterminacy. Yet we have in existence proof of efforts to thwart the very conclusions we would reach a priori.

## Global Operating Systems

Projects that allude to a "global operating system" include efforts by Microsoft, IBM, the University of Virginia, the University of California at Berkeley, and others.[23] If efforts like these bear fruit, it may be that within 10 years, operating systems will have characteristics that can facilitate worldwide scalability, within which one logical system may be partitioned across any number of nodes on an arbitrary network. And perhaps seamless, transparent distribution as well, in which an operating system decides where data resides and where computation occurs agnostic to the geographic or organizational location of compute resources. NDC fault tolerance and self-configuration are also implied by these approaches. The lack of a central authority may become less limiting than previously believed. But then again, research does not always yield viable implementations. Time will tell.

## Recombinant Software

As complexity in NDC continues to rise, we may find it necessary to adopt radically new approaches for software development. "Growing" applications, as opposed to designing them, may become the only strategy that makes sense, as the level of complexity exceeds that which even the most devoted groups of experts can adequately comprehend. *Recombinant software* refers in a general sense to research in computer science that does not specify particular ends before a given experiment is launched. This approach suggests, "Let's see what happens if I try this," deriving lessons from the results, which again, strictly speaking, turns a blind eye to the scientific method.

Genetic algorithms are a part of "evolutionary computing," which is a growing area of research in artificial intelligence. Simply stated, a solution to a problem solved by a genetic algorithm is evolved rather than designed. The idea of evolutionary computing was introduced in the 1960s by I. Rechenberg in his work *Evolution Strategies.*[24] His idea was then developed by other researchers, including John Holland, who invented and developed genetic algorithms.

Holland's approach, which incorporates genetic algorithms and autonomous digital agents, has demonstrated that, "such systems are particularly prone to exhibiting emergent phenomena."[25]

Might such systems, when their digital autonomous agents properly motivated and rewarded, behave in a manner akin to Kauffman's fitscape? Moreover, will such an approach finally bring artificial intelligence to a place beyond the oxymoron category it has inhabited since it was envisioned? As with every other question that faces NDC development and engineering in general, Goff's axiom applies: it all depends on context.

# Commentary: The Context of Context

There are a number of other contextual considerations going forward if prudent we would be. One aspect of our work that we must acknowledge is that of the unintended consequences of human activities, especially technology. To that end please consider my own view regarding the context of our work in the following paragraphs.

Technological advances have always borne consequences which were not envisioned or intended at the moment of innovation. Euclid could not have envisioned the utilization of large prime numbers to encrypt and decrypt data. Gutenberg, I'm sure, did not labor to enable pornography.

While Einstein may have seen the potential for nuclear weapons as part of his legacy, did he also predict the ethical left turn the relativistic 20th century would take? If all points of view are equally valid, then doesn't it also follow that "anything goes?" Perhaps not . . . but the consequences of technology and innovation clearly cannot be predicted. The fitscape, as Kauffman suggests, cannot be finitely prestated, regardless of Newton's assurances to the contrary.[26]

One of the best metaphors we have today for unintended consequences is the hole in the ozone layer, as shown in Figure 2.1, which is now believed to be due to the ignorant release of excessive chlorofluorocarbons as a by-product of refrigeration technologies. The hole as metaphor reminds us of unintended consequences, of friction and heat loss (metaphorically speaking) due to inefficiencies in resource utilization, of our lack of understanding, and of the care we must take in the work in which we are engaged. This one ambiguous hole serves to silently communicate both the warning and the wonder we must acknowledge in these most interesting times.

What is the purpose of software if not to remedy inefficiencies in processes and improve resource utilization? What developer of software hasn't recognized the need to optimize in some fashion, for pure speed, or memory utilization, or code maintainability? What is the ultimate aim of software if not to "do more with less"?

Figure 2.1  The ozone hole: a metaphor for unintended consequences
and poor utilization of resources

Buckminster Fuller gave us our term for this grand trend: ephemeralization. Human beings have been ephemeralizing since the invention of the wheel. How many ancients left large stone reminders of generations of labor, entire civilizations devoted to developing the simple predictive capabilities of an ordinary calendar? These are trivialities today.

How wealthy would you be if the laser printer everybody now has access to were at your disposal in a pre-Gutenberg era? How many men do you imagine died laying the first copper cables beneath the Atlantic to facilitate communications in the early 20th century, which then cost the equivalent of billions of dollars in today's funds? A quarter-ton satellite carries so much more data at a fraction of the cost.

We didn't invent ephemeralization with software; but we may very well be perfecting it. Such is the legacy and opportunity, the elation and the terror which is especially ours as computer scientists and software developers in the early 21st century.

The hole, in form, is also a reminder of the Zero Dollar Bill, infinity paradoxically expressed on the low end, where we might not expect to find it; is nanotechnology also implied here? The hole is also our goad then, if we would be ritually mindful of the complexities we face when studying complex NDC systems; a significant theme in the context of the study of context.

One final point: If Metcalfe's law is to be believed, if the potential value of any network is a function exponentially related to the number of nodes on the network, then clearly our networks will not approach a maximum potential value until all nodes are connected. Which is another way of saying we need to include everyone. Paradoxically, it is only by including everyone that we operate in our own best self-interest. These are interesting times indeed.

## Notes

1. grouper.ieee.org/groups/802/11/

2. www.microsoft.com/billgates/speeches/2001/11-30mvp.asp

3. www.bluetooth.com, www.bluetooth.org

4. www.sciam.com/2001/0501issue/0501berners-lee.html

5. Claude Elwood Shannon, *The Mathematical Theory of Communication* (Urbana: University of Illinois Press, 1949).

6. Strictly speaking, *cybernetics* is the comparative study of the internal workings of organic and machine processes, to understand

their similarities and differences. Cybernetics often refers to machines that imitate human behavior, for example, robots. For an interesting and informative view of the history of cybernetics and its relationship of information theory see *How We Became Posthuman: Virtual Bodies in Cybernetics, Literature, and Informatics* by N. Katherine Hayles (Chicago, IL: University of Chicago Press, 1999).

7.  Extensible Markup Language (XML) is the universal format for structured documents and data on the Web, enabling self-describing data that is not bound to a particular platform or language. See www.w3c.org/XML/.

8.  Hans Moravec, *Robot* (New York: Oxford University Press, 1999), p. 51.

9.  Isaac Asimov, *Runaround* (New York: Faucett Crest, 1942).

10. Norbert Wiener, *Cybernetics: Control and Communication in the Animal and the Machine* (New York: Wiley, 1948).

11. Transcript at www.zyvex.com/nanotech/feynman.html

12. *Engines of Creation* was originally published in hardcover by Anchor Books in 1986.

13. www.foresight.org/Nanomedicine/Respirocytes.html

14. www.techreview.com/articles/rotman0302.asp

15. Mark Weiser, "The Computer for the Twenty-First Century," *Scientific American,* 265 (September 1991), pp. 94–104.

16. Neil Gershenfeld, *When Things Start to Think* (New York: Henry Holt, 1999).

17. David D. Nolte, *Mind at Light Speed: A New Kind of Intelligence* (New York: Free Press, 2001), p. 118.

18. www.rtcgroup.com/cotsjournal/index.shtml provides just one example of COTS technologies creeping into implementations that were once thought to be immune from the otherwise indeterminate nature of commercial products.

19. The popularity of SUVs in the United States is, in my view, a function of sociology and an interesting ecological/economic denial, which perhaps too is a reaction to the creeping globalization that has occurred over the past 20 years.

20. While it may be intuitively obvious why the problems associated with composable components need to be addressed if viable grid

computing architectures are to emerge, it would be helpful to consider the inevitability of partial failure in any networked configuration. Because components of the grid will inevitably fail, to provide for a robust grid solution, facilitate dynamic recovery, and achieve maximum availability, composability of components on some level must be addressed. This is not to say that composability itself is germane only to grid computing or that grid computing is the only domain in which composability must be addressed. But it should be clear that the problems associated with composable components must, at some level, be addressed as part of the grid computing problem space.

21. When I began programming, the term *hacker* meant something different from what it does today. While I personally dislike the use of the term to describe those who would maliciously or illegally abuse computer systems owned by others, the general use of the term is more or less accepted by a broad range of people.

22. Stephen Wolfram, *A New Kind of Science* (Champaign, IL: Wolfram Media, 2002).

23. research.microsoft.com/sn/Farsite/; www.research.ibm.com/bluegene/; legion.virginia.edu/; endeavour.cs.berkeley.edu/.

24. I. Rechenberg, *Evolutionsstrategie: Optimierung technischer Systeme und Prinzipien der biologischen Evolution* (Stuttgart: Frommann-Holzboog, 1973).

25. John H. Holland, *Emergence* (New York: Perseus Books, 1998), p. 184.

26. Stuart Kauffman, *Investigations* (New York: Oxford University Press, 2000), p. 125.

# CHAPTER 3

# The Scope of NDC

Since December 1969, when the ARPANET project created the first modern packet-switched network—the genesis of today's Internet—the challenge and promise of NDC has resulted in an explosion of investment, research, and software development. Ensuing efforts encompass nearly all aspects of computer science today.

The scope of NDC is quite impressive. No other single aspect of computer science research and development quite compares with the myriad problem spaces enjoined when computers communicate, swap data, and share processing responsibilities. This chapter presents an overview of some of the many relevant areas of NDC research and development today.

Each of these areas is a moving target, in that while progress is being made in each area and rapid improvement may sometimes be achieved, a complete examination or solution in any of these areas is not likely in the short term. In fact, to the extent that each represents a community of autonomous agents, general fitscape attributes apply. Other categories of NDC will emerge over time, as new technologies converge and evolve and as innovative technology adoption patterns continue to manifest themselves in consumer-driven economic fitscapes worldwide.

The categories here, which I call fitscapes, reflect many of the topical areas of the IEEE Computer Society's Distributed Systems Online journal, which itself is a constantly changing resource that tracks the branching processes so evident in the exploration of NDC today.[1] The categories are derived as well from other fitscapes: ongoing activities of the W3C, for example, and traditional areas of development that may be closely related but are nevertheless subtly different (for example, grid computing versus massively parallel computing).

Table 3.1 lists (in alphabetical order) the general areas of NDC R&D that are explored in this chapter, representing a sampling of the general categories of NDC R&D. Each category is ripe with potential, rich in detail and nuance, and deserving of extensive examination well beyond the scope of this volume.

Table 3.1    Some NDC research and development areas

| cluster concepts | distributed storage | peer-to-peer |
|---|---|---|
| collaborative computing | grid computing | pervasive computing |
| dependable systems | languages | real time and embedded |
| distributed agents | massively parallel systems | security |
| distributed algorithms | middleware | Semantic Web |
| distributed databases | mobile and wireless | spaces computing |
| distributed filesystems | network protocols | ubiquitous computing |
| distributed media | operating systems | Web Services |

This list does not represent all R&D fitscapes within NDC. One obvious area not covered here is that of systems and network management, a pioneering technology in areas like distributed agents and network protocols. Since the management of systems and networks is encompassed in a number of the 24 categories cited in this chapter, it's left out of the overviews in this chapter. Also not considered here are many of the rapidly evolving edge-related aspects of NDC, including user interfaces. As some of the areas considered in this chapter converge over time, that consolidation will give impetus to the NDC edge-computing fitscapes. The fitscapes presented here represent those that are either historically ripe, currently in vogue, or of sufficient industry interest to attract levels of investment beyond one or two research institutions.

There are clear connections between and among these areas—relationships that are presumably recognized by many of the participants engaged in the exploration of each. For example, NDC security is germane to all other categories of NDC development. Distributed agents share ground and influence with at least pervasive and ubiquitous computing and the Semantic Web, and probably others as well. A random clump of these fitscapes chaotically thrown against the wall, with relationships mapped, might appear as in Figure 3.1.

The purpose of this map is not to present a canonical listing of relations and dependencies; indeed, only the most obvious ones are noted here. Every aspect of NDC is directly related in some way to almost every other aspect of NDC, thus making the map moot as an exercise, so don't bother trying to follow the relationships or memorize the dependencies. The point of the map is to illustrate the level of complexity inherent in our efforts to simply articulate the relationships among the areas of research in NDC, never mind the more profound complexities inherent within each.

Imagine the complexities you encounter in keeping track of all the influences and discoveries if, for example, your role is one of conceptualizing distributed agents. How can your work, dependent on NDC-related work in—at least—middleware, security, distributed databases, and possibly operating systems, proceed concurrently with work in those areas? How can you, with many other potential advances also dependent on you, confidently progress? Clearly, not everything can proceed in lock-step. By the same token, it may not be obvious, nor is it reasonable, to stage an ordered process whereby advances in subdisciplines of NDC research can proceed. A complex fitscape governs each subdiscipline from which a broader, much more complex, fitscape of overall NDC R&D emerges.

It may be reasonable, however, to estimate possible dependencies that one category of exploration might have on another over time. Work in

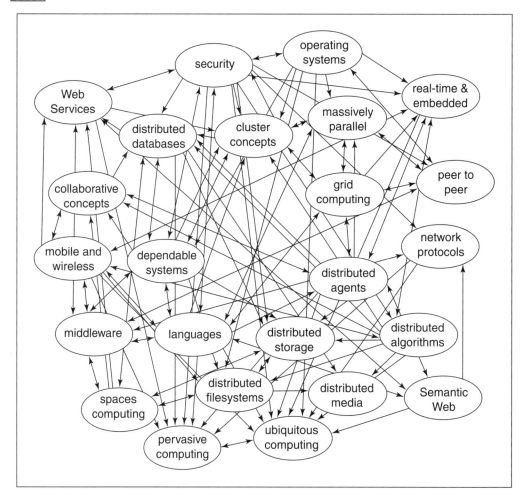

Figure 3.1  NDC R&D fitscapes

some areas will certainly mature more quickly than others, driven by levels of investment, which in turn are driven by technology adoption patterns, and governed by the complexity of the computer sciences issues that must be solved.

The chart in Figure 3.2 offers conjecture with respect to a maturity order of the 24 categories, evolving such as to provide basic solutions upon which NDC developers can build. The *y* axis, *degree of decoupling,* captures component decomposition as well as the movement of intelligence closer to the "edge" of networks; the impact of Moore's law over time, upon which various categories of NDC development will build, is also implied here and will accommodate an even greater decoupling.

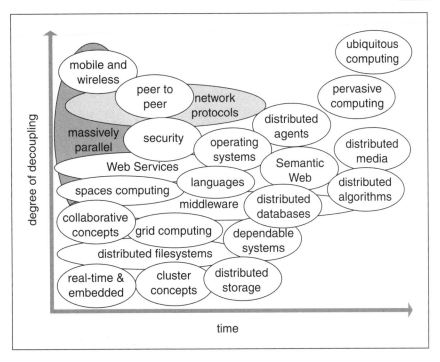

Figure 3.2  Evolution of NDC over time (pro forma)

Given an accelerating rate of innovation in the major technology trends cited earlier (some of which are themselves fitscapes of NDC), it is a given that any estimates of future developments, relationships, or dependencies among these should be viewed as speculative. The odds are perhaps not as high as those against walking into the Atlantis Hotel and Casino in Reno, Nevada, placing a $3 bet in the MegaBucks machine, pulling the handle, and winning the jackpot in one try. But futures in NDC are nevertheless speculative.

I will say more about the Atlantis Casino later in the context of real-world implementation, which, as you may know, is not always by design. Nor is implementation research, strictly speaking by design; implementations are less erudite and much dirtier than speculation, research, or theory would have us believe. But for now, an overview of many of the current NDC R&D fitscapes is in order.

## Ubiquitous Computing

In a well-connected network, we can begin with any node and theoretically find our way to each of the others by following links along the way.

Begin with an end in mind, and you'll find lofty ideals touted by an inspired fitscape. The teleological vector of technology,[2] at least that which is heir to Turing's mind child, is ubiquitous computing. Pervasive computing would make information available everywhere; ubiquitous computing would *require* information everywhere. There is a subtle but certain difference, one that will provide NDC challenges for years beyond the near-future, pervasive-computing world that we might soon imagine.

Buildings need to be smart, down to the rivet. Electrical systems need to be smart, down to the light bulb. Monetary systems need to be smart, down to the penny. And all those systems and more need to be connected and available down to the network if the ultimate in ephemeralization is ever to be approached. Are continuing productivity increases necessary? Goff's axiom may apply here as well. What do we call economies that do not grow? The essence of economic growth is increasing productivity. Unless we are prepared both to forgo economic organizational assumptions altogether and begin anew, as it were, with other approaches (which may be even more painful to consider than economic stagnation) and to decline given current assumptions, we cannot turn away from the path of ephemeralization. There is no other direction, therefore, than eagerly toward ubiquitous computing.

Many authors do not distinguish between "pervasive" and "ubiquitous" when it comes to computing visions; even Mark Weiser used the terms synonymously. But I think it's important to be cognizant of the differences and argue that we will enjoy the fruits of one even as we continue to pursue the other. Indeed, we are beginning to see early signs of pervasive computing today. Any city in which I can easily find an "information field," in which dynamic network connections can be enjoined via a mobile computing device, is one in which pervasive computing potential has emerged. Arguably, any place where an I-mode phone can function is a place of pervasive computing. But until all possible computing applications are explored and every niche for network intelligence fully exploited, ubiquitous computing will remain the unseen terminal of a teleological vector.

Once computers disappear and dynamic, ad hoc ensembles of software swarm about like beneficent organisms to serve our every whim, utilizing resources with previously unimaginable efficiencies, a miraculous invisible network may then emerge which is as unfathomable to our early 21st-century minds as a wireless Internet-connected device would have been to a pre-Copernican vision. The Network Age is the age of magic. NDC developers, by virtue of the myriad fitscapes in which we all play, are the magicians of this new age. Ubiquitous computing is our shared Nirvana—whether we realize it or not.

# Web Services

There is nothing either good or bad but thinking makes it so.
—William Shakespeare, *Hamlet*

From the sublime to the ridiculous, the first two NDC fitscapes reveal an interesting yin/yang: the transcendent hope of ubiquitous computing versus the gritty reality of Web Services. Arg![3] Reaching Nirvana through the church of Web Services may be a long journey indeed.

I am not a fervent evangelist of the vanilla Web Services approach to NDC. My own biases are drawn to the more *organic* approaches, embodied in spaces computing, mixed with the sensibilities of real-time and embedded computing. In my view, the advent of SOAP was not the brightest day in world of Internet standards. Alas, my personal views are not germane to a reasoned discussion of NDC in a larger sense, so I'll attempt to not color this commentary accordingly—at least not just yet.

Web Services are based on several XML-derived concepts, designed to facilitate standardized, portable exchange of "component" data in NDC enviroments. In the fall of 2001, Microsoft and IBM jointly announced the Global XML Web Services Architecture, which includes XML, SOAP, and UDDI.[4]

 ♦ XML: eXtensible Markup Language

 ♦ SOAP: Simple Object Access Protocol

 ♦ UDDI: Universal Directory and Discovery Interface

 ♦ WSDL: Web Services Description Language

The Global XML Web Services architecture would also define specification principles that, in tandem with aspects of the Semantic Web, would give one day give rise to an NDC framework that would be

 ♦ Modular—Composable modules that can be combined as needed to deliver end-to-end capabilities (new modular elements enjoined into ensembles as needs arise);

 ♦ General purpose—Designed to meet a wide range of XML Web Services scenarios, ranging from business-to-business and enterprise application integration solutions to peer-to-peer applications and business-to-consumer services;

♦ Federated—Fully distributed, designed to support XML Web Services that cross organizational and trust boundaries, requiring no centralized servers or administrative functions;

♦ Standards based—Based on protocols that are submitted to "appropriate standards bodies."

Component reuse, one holy grail of software development, may potentially be realized if both the Web Services and Semantic Web visions are viable and embraced. Indeed, promises from Microsoft and IBM in the Web Services arena would clearly indicate that component composability is not only within reach, it is imminent. The promise of component reuse and composability is to software what COTS VLSI chips were to hardware; once enabled by NDC, the joint visions of the Semantic Web and Web Services promise a composable NDC architecture. The operative word is *promise*. Composability is nontrivial in any environment that involves distributed systems, and is especially so in NDC. Much like the clarinet player, a component needs more than sheet music and a functioning instrument if a viable orchestration is to be achieved.

## The Semantic Web

> The Semantic Web will bring structure to the meaningful content of Web pages, creating an environment where software agents, roaming from page to page can readily carry out sophisticated tasks for users.
> —Tim Berners-Lee, et al.

Homo sapiens is a culture-creating species. Our social expressions serve to reduce our needs, individually and institutionally. A hierarchy of needs, identified by Abraham Maslow,[5] is as applicable to institutions as it is to individuals, as a benchmark of cultural provisioning. Language, traditions, economics, and social and political arrangements, all reflect need-reduction epistemologies, which run the gamut from physical survival at the bottom of the pyramid to self-actualization at the summit. Each successive step in the virtuous climb toward a shared peak involves creation of a shared meaning, which itself constitutes an abstract fitscape: culture and meaning.

According to clinical psychologist Paul Watzlawick, the question of whether there is order in our shared reality has one of three possible answers:

1. There is no order, in which case reality is tantamount to confusion and chaos, and life is a psychotic nightmare.

2. We relieve our existential state of *disinformation* by inventing an order, forgetting that we have invented it and experiencing it as something "out there" that we call reality.

3. There is an order. It is the creation of some higher Being on whom we depend but who Himself is quite independent of us. *Communication* with this Being, therefore, becomes man's most important goal.[6]

Either there is order or there is not. If there is not, we perceptively impose order. If there is, we discern it. But in either case, the point Watzlawick makes should be clear with respect to semantics: meaning too is either something we create by perception or something we similarly discern. Regardless, there is a cultural imperative to articulate meaning in such a manner as to facilitate communication.

Although human communication mechanisms are highly redundant and equally ambiguous, the paradoxical nature of communication itself, the handmaiden of culture, never seems to prevent heroic attempts to engineer to its essence. The Semantic Web is perhaps the most ambitious of such efforts to date.[7]

Semantic Web activities, chartered by the W3C, proffer and articulate the following general layers of software, which would ostensibly lead to a meaningful realization of the vision:

♦ XML—eXtensible Markup Language

♦ RDF—Resource Description Framework

♦ Ontologies—Formal definitions of relationship

♦ Agent—An agent language providing for exchange of proofs (i.e., trust)

In specifying data that can self-describe, XML provides data portability. It was proposed in 1996 by John Bosak of Sun Microsystems and accepted for standardization by the W3C, partially in response to proprietary extensions to HTML that resulted from the now-historic browser conflict of that era.[8] As a language describing language for portability, XML is misnamed. The language would more accurately be described by its ability to provide a basis for the creation of portable metadata—stories about the stories that data would tell.

RDF builds upon XML, providing a framework for representing that metadata. RDF does not require XML, per se. The specification for RDF is not bound to XML, though XML can (and likely will) be used for implementation of the RDF model. The ultimate goal of RDF is to enable the automation of activities (such as discovery) that are germane to dynamic, ad hoc assemblies of data and behavior.

A standardized metadata framework is not yet enough. Once we can portably express meaning, meaning must be meaningfully expressed as ontologies. Ontologies are collections of information that provide an organizational basis for expression.

---

The term *ontology,* borrowed from philosophy and referring to a theory regarding the nature of existence, implies a study and classification of that which exists. AI research uses the word to mean a collection of formally defined relations among terms, the most common being a set of inference rules and a taxonomy therein. (A taxonomy specifies classes of objects and relations among them; for example, an address may contain a street, a street number, a city, a zone, a nation, and so on.)

---

Once data can be represented in a standard manner and organized to provide a basis for common semantic agreement, we can realize the potential of NDC by dynamically knitting together meaningful collections of information, thereby yielding levels of services heretofore only imagined. Widespread, standardized, distributed agents can become viable. Knowledge management, edge-to-edge services, integrated information pools—with the realization of the Semantic Web, the foundation of ubiquitous computing itself is theoretically in place.

# Spaces Computing

A Mirror World is some huge institution's moving, true-to-life mirror image trapped inside a computer—where you can see and grasp it whole. The thick, dense, busy sub-world that encompasses you is *also,* now, an object in your hands. A brand new equilibrium is born.
—David Gelernter

Biologists are much more interested in microbes than in microscopes. Computers are tools at best and annoyances otherwise; for too long, software developers have dwelt on the discipline-specific minutiae while ignoring the big-picture implications that NDC finally forces before our eyes, demanding resolution. If the computer industry itself is to be more than just a passing fad, outside-the-box visions must be heeded. Spaces computing is one of those visions.

David Gelernter of Yale University published *Mirror Worlds* in 1991, well before the general public had heard of the Internet, let alone acquired an email address.[9] In the Mirror World, a software framework could contain all elements of reality we would deign to measure, track, transport, or number; reality could be reflected in software in real time—as could all the relationships among myriad mirrored images. This vision was manifested in the implementation Gelernter pioneered, a system called "Linda," which tendered *tuple-spaces*, a simple persistent storage that transcended nodes and networks, the mirror in which levels of reality could begin to reflect.

With *Mirror Worlds*, Gelernter was hailed as one of the most brilliant computer scientists of the modern era—so celebrated, in fact, that he was victimized by one David Kaczynski, aka the Unabomber, in June of '93, toward the end of the neo-Luddite's anonymous reign of terror. Gelernter was consumed by a lengthy recovery the next several years, the period which saw URLs emerge from obscurity to emblems of the then nascent dotcom mania. Gelernter's vision, however, needed no therapy.

## A Sun Implementation

Let's look at JavaSpaces. Sun Microsystems demonstrated JavaSpaces in the spring of 1998 at the JavaOne conference, the annual worldwide gathering of Java devotees in San Francisco's Moscone Center. JavaSpaces was the first commercially viable instantiation of Gelernter's seminal vision, a Mirror World framework, which was enabled by the Write Once, Run Anywhere promise of the Java platform. Built upon Jini network technology protocols, JavaSpaces was demonstrated at the conference by the 14,000 Java Rings given away to conference attendees.

The rings, as shown in Figure 3.3, featured a small embedded processor[10] that ran the smallest of Java virtual machines, a Java SmartCard-specified device that defines a WORA engine for credit-card sized devices.

Figure 3.3  The Java Ring, JavaOne 1998

Once the ring was registered in a central database, each ring bearer's name and coffee preference were stored in their own ring as persistent data that could be accessed upon subsequent connections to the serial readers that were interfaces for such devices. Demonstrations were then made available at coffee-dispensing stations around the event facilities. Espresso, cappuccino, or regular coffee? Decaffeinated? Tea, perhaps? The stored preference on each ring determined the beverage of choice.

But another demonstration of Java Ring technology proved to be even more interesting.

What if all those rings could be used to solve a large problem? What if 14,000 asynchronous, independent, intermittently connected CPUs could be harnessed to serve the needs of one problem? Would that, conceptually, hold value? What other kinds of applications might also be so served? Conference attendees were encouraged to periodically take a few moments, connect their rings briefly to the network, and allow the ring CPU to be used to compute a small part of a large problem.

The fractal mathematics necessary to compute the location and color of each pixel in the 64K image, as shown in Figure 3.4, that emerged over the course of the four days of the event was hosted on those rings. Over a conference period, the image slowly but certainly filled in.

Computing on rings was terribly cool. Equally cool and almost unheralded, however, was JavaSpaces—the "man behind the curtain," the Mirror World framework that allowed all those compute transactions to easily and seamlessly occur.

Since that event, spaces computing has slowly emerged in the Java platform. Jini network technology has found some application beyond the early (mistakenly) device-specific marketing spin it suffered.

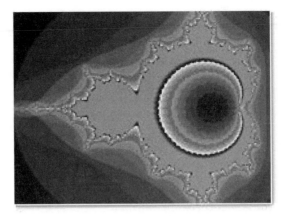

Figure 3.4  JavaRing/JavaSpaces problem, JavaOne 1998

### Commercial Potential

Some purveyors of spaces computing frameworks beyond Gelernter's work and JavaSpaces have recently begun to emerge. GigaSpaces, an Israeli software venture, announced a commercially hardened JavaSpaces in 2001 that promises a vital framework for solving myriad NDC problems to-day.[11] Complementary to, if not competitive with, other approaches like Web Services, spaces computing may yet capture a critical mass thanks to its simplicity, an attribute which may become more dear in an increasingly complex NDC world.

## Peer-to-Peer Computing

All the assumptions and institutions that brought us here are being fun-damentally challenged by the work we do in computer science. The net-work metaphor is laden with both promise and foreboding, depending on the context of deployment and the justification of purpose. The very idea of intellectual property and its inherent value (as codified by existing laws and protections) is disrupted in an era in which all information of all kinds can easily be duplicated at near zero costs and transmitted at light speed to any number of receivers.

Napster served as an early warning system insofar as the institutional cognitive dissonance endemic in NDC can harbor.[12] Even as it pioneered the vast potential that can be gleaned in Internet-wide peer-to-peer (p2p) deployment, it gave p2p a bad name. By utilizing simple, "organic" networking concepts, Napster illustrated both the potential and the unease p2p engenders.

The concepts behind p2p are relatively simple and amazingly effective. One way to understand how p2p works is to view it from the perspective of the node that may need to engage a p2p network.

To begin, the uninitiated node must have some knowledge of at least one peer. The joining of a node to a network has traditionally been a function of hands-on system administration; even with advances like Dynamic Host Configuration Protocol (DHCP), an administrator must be involved at some juncture at least to ensure that any new node has a view of a DHCP server.[13] In most p2p implementations, the address of another peer is required information.

If a node can locate and communicate with a peer node, it is possible that the peer node may have further addresses, as well as descriptions of services that might be available from other nodes. So the newly initiated peer can then discover the existence of other peer nodes and realize the ability to communicate with them simply by knowing of the first peer node. The ability to discover other peers is exponentially derived from knowing the location of the first peer node, and a cascading series of discoveries is thus enabled.

This method of "learning" does not depend on access to a central repository of knowledge about the network. As the World Wide Web grows in scope and degree of information distribution, it may very well be that the more organic approaches to NDC software architecture, like p2p, will be the only ones that can adequately navigate the complex relationships that are emerging.

# Collaborative Computing

> The main idea is to regard a program as a communication to human
> beings rather than as a set of instructions to a computer.
> —Donald E. Knuth

It is the collaborative computing fitscape of NDC that produces most implementations of *groupware,* a concept that implies groups of people working together on shared projects. Types of groupware include collaborative drawing and writing tools, frameworks for scientific collaboration, shared applications, video communications tools, Web-based conferencing, work-flow and workflow management tools, the emerging field of knowledge management, and even email. Since groupware, by definition, involves groups of human being, it might follow that academic disciplines with more of a humanities focus might find a haven in research in this area, and such is the case.

Humans beings have the disturbing habit of being human. Our best efforts to systematically impose rational ontologies on human activities fall short, even as we find the tried-and-true scientific method occasionally lacking when it comes to understanding a reality that is inherently subjective, complex, and squishy. Most endeavors to date, for example, in the vein of artificial intelligence, have led to dead ends. Perhaps we are coming to realize that technologies serve us better when we strive to foster human intelligence, rather than replace it. Some collaborative computing research seems to reflect such postcyborg sensibilities, at least in the area of knowledge management (KM).

What is KM? Alas, there is no universal definition. It's probably most useful to think of KM in the broadest context. From a collaborative computing perspective, KM is the process through which organizations generate value from their intellectual and knowledge-based assets—humans. "Best practices" approaches fall within the KM sphere. Much in the way of persistent conversation (like email and instant messaging), if mined properly, has the potential to provide knowledge value to the firm. But there are no solid rules when it comes to KM, except perhaps for one: people are key.

There is no knowledge without human beings. Technology, for example, is not knowledge. It is knowledge incarnate and perhaps a means for collating knowledge. But it's the taxonomy-defying masses that constitute the "mine" from whence knowledge must be extracted. As such, NDC developers who focus on collaborative computing would be well served to learn as much about human beings as possible—through literature, history, religion, economics, biology, sociology and psychology—since it is only through cross-disciplinary activities that the most valuable resource any company may boast can be fully exploited.

Collaborative computing would also be a fruitful pursuit for scientists eager to share data. Biotech researchers, for example, are well aware of the potential of technologies like XML, which, when properly extended, can facilitate collaborative efforts specific to research disciplines. The Interoperable Informatics Infrastructure Consortium,[14] an ad hoc organization whose stated mission is to facilitate and enable data exchange and knowledge management across the entire life science community, is just one example of a discipline-specific instantiation of collaborative computing, which itself is utilizing technologies for other collaborative computing efforts (as embodied by the W3C).

The broad NDC spectrum of collaborative computing is cross-disciplinary by nature; it is likely through R&D efforts in this broad category that humanizing influences will be felt by computer science at large.

# Dependable Systems

Fault-tolerant DC was an active research field during the last two decades of the 20th century and continues to be in the current era. Once the domain of mainframe systems, dependability in NDC systems is a natural result of global competitive pressures. *Dependability* in any system can be defined as the ability of the system to ensure that it (and the services it may deliver) can be relied upon within certain measurable parameters, the definition of which depends on the context of deployment. Generic concepts such as reliability, availability, scalability (RAS), and security define dependable NDC systems characteristics. Measures such as mean time between failures (MTBF) traditionally evaluate the reliability for such systems.

As global dependence on NDC continues to increase, the probability of crises rooted in network and system failures also increases. While the consequences of these failures are often petty inconvenience (my pager stopped working), the probability that key application failure could give rise to large economic perturbations or even loss of life also increases. As more NDC applications become the norm, failures too become more distributed. Dependable systems must engender trust from many perspectives if NDC is to continue enriching human activities without introducing equally large measures of risk.

Dependable NDC systems require dependable hardware, which is beyond the scope of this book. A bigger part of the equation, however, is NDC software. A brief discussion of software dependability is germane at this juncture.

Below are two examples of many fault-tolerant software approaches that are applicable to NDC application development—techniques which, when used with other well-engineered development processes and components, will serve to provide more dependable NDC systems software going forward.

## Checkpoint-Restart Technique

While discussions of dependable NDC software date back to the earliest experiences with networked computing,[15] a growing body of research in this category parallels the growth of the Internet over the same period. An excellent summary of the state of software fault tolerance status relevant to this era was published in 2000 by Wilfredo Torres-Pomales from the NASA Langley Research Center in Hampton, Virginia.[16] Torres-Pomales cited a number of general approaches to software fault tolerance, many of which are applicable to NDC, including Single-Version Software Fault Tolerance techniques (that is, redundancy applied to a single version of a piece of software, designed to detect and recover from faults). The most common example of this approach cited by Torres-Pomales is the check-point-and-restart mechanism pictured in Figure 3.5.[17]

Most software faults (after development has been completed) are unanticipated and usually depend on state. Faults of this type often behave similarly to spurious hardware faults in that they may appear, do their damage, and then disappear leaving no vapor trail. In such cases, restarting the module is often the best strategy for successful completion of its task, one that has several advantages and is general enough to be used at multiple levels in an NDC system or environment. A restart can be dynamic or static, depending on context: a static restart brings the module to a predetermined state; a dynamic one may use dynamically created check-

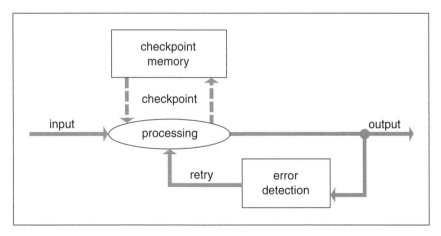

Figure 3.5  Single-version, checkpoint-restart technique

points at fixed intervals or at certain key points during execution. All this depends on error detection, of course, which also has several applicable techniques that can be used.

## Recovery-Blocks Technique

Multiversion software fault tolerance techniques are, as the name implies, based on the use of two or more variants of a piece of software (executed either in sequence or in parallel), the assumption being that components built differently (by different designers using different approaches, tools, and so on) will fail differently. So if one version fails with a given input, an alternative version should provide appropriate output.

One example Torres-Pomales cites is a "Recovery Blocks" technique, which shares some attributes with Byzantine agreements discussed later.[18] The Recovery-Blocks technique combines the basics of checkpoint and restart with multiple versions of a given component; if an error is detected during processing in one variant, a different version executes. As shown in Figure 3.6, a checkpoint is created before execution, and error detection in a given module can occur at various checkpoints along the way, rather than through an output-only test.

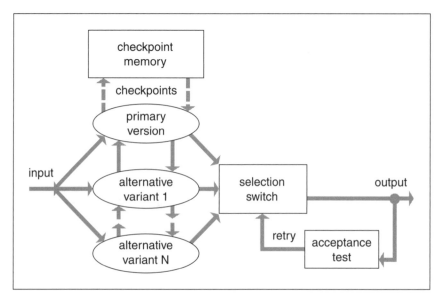

Figure 3.6 Recovery Blocks technique

Although most of the time the primary version will execute successfully, the Recovery-Blocks technique allows alternative variants to process in parallel (perhaps to lesser accuracy, depending on CPU resources available) in order to ensure overall performance if such are the requirements of the application.

# Security

Security, like every other fitscape of NDC, can hardly be discussed in isolation. But our sciences are narrow fields of study if measured progress is to be made. Security is based in mathematics but enabled by engineering. and in the context of NDC, any discussion of security is ripe with paradox. In more practical terms, security is mired in encryption, but encryption is not nearly enough to provide reasonable assurances for NDC. Information can be hidden by encryption methods, but encryption doesn't solve other, more basic, issues of trust, including data origin, access control, and privacy.

Juxtaposing engineering and pure mathematics is one way to examine NDC security. Another, more paradoxical, dichotomy is that of privacy versus data transparency, which would yield measurable availability characteristics if done well. The IETF has offered the following definition of security in RFC 2828, intended to define Internet needs:[19]

1. The measures taken to protect a system
2. The condition of a system that results from the establishment and maintenance of measures to protect the system
3. The condition of system resources being free from unauthorized access and from unauthorized or accidental change, destruction, or loss

Security is a proper subset of trust. Trust, however, implies not only security as defined by the IETF but also protections against conditions that are not a function of unauthorized access or even accidental damage. Trust implies a correctness of function, including communications, which might define fault-free computing.

Maintaining security within a single node is simple compared to security issues in NDC environments; most breaches of the security in solitary nodes are due to poor engineering, which can theoretically be addressed. Assuring security in NDC environments in which all hardware components are under the physical control of one owner is also relatively simple; many systems are designed to run well in such environments, a good example being Sun Microsystem's NFS, which supports secure sharing of data while also providing sufficient data transparency to users. Next in difficulty is the environment in which the endpoints are controlled by the owner but the networks are public; virtual private networks (VPNs) strive to solve NDC security matters in those cases.

Alas, most modern NDC applications cannot be as constrained as these models if they are to ultimately fulfill the promise of ubiquitous computing. Typically, users have their own nodes—perhaps many of them—connections between which are increasingly intermittent, utilizing the random communications fields that mobile and wireless computing make possible. Furthermore, intelligence is migrating to every conceivable niche; Moore's law implies not only more capable traditional systems but also much smaller technology applications, potentially as disposable as the envelope that delivered your last credit card bill. When processing capabilities are pervasive, no assumptions can be made with respect to their nature. Users will store secrets on computer devices as lacking as today's smartcards, which means NDC security requires radically innovative solutions going forward.

In the context of NDC, security weighs in at many levels. It can potentially be "baked in" at a fundamental protocol level, it can be layered in at higher protocol levels, it can be application specific or even network specific. Clearly, however, it cannot be ignored.

## Languages

How many spoken languages has our species uttered? Although some 6,000 remain today, despite the language pruning effects of global competitive pressures of the last century, some experts assert that all but 250 to 600 languages will become extinct by the end of the current century.[20] While it might be more efficient from an economic perspective if all humans spoke one and only one language, how immeasurable would the loss be?

Imagine our world today without the influence of Plato, Aristotle, or Archimedes. Imagine Western legal systems without Exodus or the New Testament. Though their languages are officially extinct, civilization today is ineffably indebted to the written words of ancestral giants, many of whose tongues would otherwise be silent in the modern world. Language conveys thought beyond the essence of message-passing. It provides the foundation for worldview, which cannot be expressed with words but rather between them. Alas, the loss of human language diversity is accelerating—a consequence of our shrinking planet.

Computer languages may be subject to Darwinian selection mechanisms, but once compiled, the binary code will run as long as a processor exists that can execute the target instruction set. In a metaphorical sense the language is still in use, although not "spoken." This too presents a problem for our collective well-being. While spoken languages, if not used by a large enough body of humans, disappear, computer languages can go on for years after the last line of code is compiled. As such, the maintenance of aging code can become problematic, especially when the larger fitscape rewards developers who may be fluent in whatever language happens to be popular at the moment.

An example of this exposure was the much-hyped Y2K problem, which never materalized because so many organizations made considerable effort to ensure that applications were Y2K-aware. But the lessons of COBOL (which is currently still in use, albeit not the language of choice for any number of new NDC development projects) and language paradigm persistence should be clear: the code we write today may last a lot longer than we anticipate. As such, our choice of language is as important as any other project choice we may make.

---

In the 1970s to 1990s, many computer programs were written that used only a two-character field to contain the year of any particular date to save memory and storage. This practice was based on the assumption that the data and the code written to manipulate that data would not survive past the turn of the century. Unfortunately, developers who made this assumption were wrong. When the calendar turned from 1999 to 2000, applications designed to use only two characters to represent the year were suddenly confused because not only was data storage involved in the shorthand but algorithms were as well. Previously sound code would suddenly break—or so the Y2K story went. But a cascading set of system crashes did not occur. Indeed, the calendar turned without much notice from the IT community. Perhaps due to the investments made by large organizations to correct the problem in advance or perhaps due to the overestimates of Y2K-injured code, the problem in retrospect appears to have been a nonproblem.

NDC efforts have brought computer languages into the forefront of research as well as coolness. For example, the Java programming language arguably bootstrapped a new generation of Internet applications. With the Java specification, the essence of C++ without the shortcomings was married with byte code and the promise of Write One, Run Anywhere, and new models for applications that would span the public networks could be imagined. The Java platform was a solid step in the direction of a network-aware platform. The fact that Microsoft's C# (pronounced "C sharp") platform is a close syntactic and runtime mirror of Java platform designs attests to the visionary appeal that brought Gosling's invention such dramatic acclaim.[21]

But just as nothing stands alone in the Network Age, nothing stands still. The Java platform has evolved considerably since "dancing Duke" first graced a Web page.[22] And since languages are the first line of expressive capability, it follows that computer languages in a general sense should continue to evolve.

As with all the other categories of NDC, language evolution represents its own complex fitscape. Containing layers within layers, a computer language ultimately relies on an underlying theory of computing in order to provide a usable tool set from which NDC developers can choose to implement algorithms of choice. Examples of language R&D that NDC developers should at least be cognizant of going forward include the following:

- ◆ **Java/C#**— Object oriented, virtual machine interpreted languages
  The Java platform started evolving from the moment it was announced. From its modest beginning came a standard version (J2SE), an enterprise-aware version (J2EE), a version targeting smaller and mobile devices (J2ME), a community process to enable standardization (the Java Community Process), and much more. The dream of Write Once, Run Anywhere, once a holy grail of computer labs worldwide, unfolded thanks to a C++ type of syntax, a virtual machine, baked-in security considerations, and the collective imaginations of millions of developers around the world. Java (and Microsoft's C#.NET) is one aspect of NDC languages that continues to evolve because of research and fitscape development pressures.

- ◆ **XML** (eXtensible Markup Language)—A language for high-level language creation

With XML came the ability to create HTML-like higher-level languages to serve specific needs. Portable data, supported by the portable behavior of the Java platform, proved a compelling vision. But XML provides only the basis for creation of metadata-centric approaches to data standardization. The hard part is the creation of domain-specific extensions; such efforts require communities of agreement, not unlike the JCP. An analogy would be a new spoken language; if I decided to invent a new language, it would provide no benefit to anyone unless others understood and spoke the same tongue. Now imagine that this new language must be created and agreed to by a committee of individuals who will ostensibly use it to compete with each other. That's the inherent problem XML faces.

- **The Fox Project**—A strongly typed intermediate language with proof-carrying code
  This language layer was pioneered by Carnegie-Mellon University. Funded by the Defense Advanced Research Projects Agency (DARPA) of the U.S. government, the Fox Project's goal is to develop language support for building safe, highly composable, reliable systems. For the goal to be reached, a return to the mathematical basis for programming languages is deemed to be a certain requirement. While the current emphasis has been on applications for ensemble composition in embedded systems, the Fox Project is a comprehensive program of research that is applying theoretical foundations of programming languages to development tools and techniques for systems in general. Interesting features of the Fox Project include the following:

  - Typed intermediate languages, which extend the benefits of type safety enjoyed by higher-level source languages to the intermediate and target languages of a compiler

  - Certifying compilers, which provide a foundation for trust-free code dissemination, by which code can be shared in an untrusted environment without sacrifice of safety

  - Proof-carrying code, a technique by which a host computer can automatically verify that code provided by an untrusted agent is safe to execute

- **π-calculus**—A theoretical computing model for mobile code
  Robin Milner of the University of Cambridge is one of the early advocates of this theoretical model. The π-calculus recognizes

that communication is a fundamental component of theoretical computing models, which differ from other models of communicating behavior primarily in their recognition and treatment of mobility: The movement of pieces of data inside a program is treated exactly the same as the transfer of a message (which can be an entire program) across the Internet. The $\pi$-calculus differs from other models in its capacity to simply classify behavioral equivalence among entities, as well as in its patterns of interactive behavior. It holds that previous theory (that is, classical automata theory), upon which most of today's parsers are built, does not appear to be correct when an automaton's actions consist of reactions between it and another automaton. In other words, a fundamental network-awareness needs to be part and parcel of the computational theories upon which our languages (and hence our systems) should be built.

Each of these NDC language developments represents a different layer of computer language implementation, just as each represents the evolving nature of languages in the current period.

These examples of language evolution in NDC have three things in common:

1. Research on all began in earnest in or after 1995 (year zero of the Network Age).

2. All introduce a heretofore absent network-awareness into computer languages.

3. All reexamine communication approaches between distributed computing nodes.

## Pervasive Computing

I don't want to carry my laptop around with me any longer. It doesn't matter that it's lighter or more powerful than the first boat-anchor DOS system I used to carry on flights in the late 1980s. It doesn't matter that the battery allows me to work several hours at a time. The fact is, I don't need the laptop; I need access to my data, an application interface that allows me to manage that data, and a connection to the Internet.

*Pervasive computing* is the idea that information should follow me and become available to me where and when I need it; securely, efficiently, completely, and timely. Very often the term "pervasive computing" is used synonymously with "ubiquitous computing," but there is a very real difference between computing and network resources that *can be available* anywhere and similar resources that *are present* everywhere. Hence, the different categories.

The pervasive computing category represents adoption patterns as much as it does enabling technologies. For the information that I require to be available where and when I need it, the work in many fields must culminate in fruitful solutions. In fact, we are beginning to realize the potential of pervasive computing, at least in western economies. For example, I was able to access my Sun-proprietary email account from anywhere in the world (given a reasonable Internet connection) since 1996, when I first used my Sun-issued DES Gold "enigma" card, which provided dynamic password access to a Sun employee portal designed specifically to enable mobile workplace interaction. My laptop also featured a virtual private network (VPN) capability that allowed an even finer granularity of access to proprietary information through the Sun wide area network (SWAN), as if I were sitting at a traditional workstation behind a traditional firewall.

Internet cafes began in 1995 with the advent of the browser (coincident with Netscape's initial public stock offering), when what had once been the domain of geeks (the Internet) became lodged in a general public zeitgeist. (This was due, I'm sure, to Netscape's dramatic capital market success; arguably, Netscape's coming-out party was the day the dotcom debacle began.) Despite the public misreading of the potential of the Internet during the late 1990s, the Internet continues to grow, Internet access continues to become more pervasive, and the era of pervasive computing continues to promise increasing productivity and material ephemeralization. The computer science challenges in this fitscape are almost entirely contained by other aspects of NDC, with technology adoption as the central issue.

# Cluster Concepts

NDC progress in the fitscape of cluster computing, as well as the use of cluster systems for scientific and commercial applications, involves participants (researchers, developers, and users) from academia, industry, laboratories, and commerce. Advances and trends in this area include but are not limited to the following:

- System modeling and architecture
- Hardware systems and networks
- Single-system images

- System software and tools
- Programming models, environments, and languages
- Algorithms and applications
- Performance modeling and evaluation
- Resource management and scheduling
- High availability
- Scalable clustered systems
- System management and administration

Strictly speaking, clustered systems have not been traditionally thought of as networked distributed systems. Although network datacom can be a key part of the design of any cluster, what we normally think of as networks (or the middleware typically found in an arbitrary network) has not been traditionally involved. This is, however, changing. Because of competitive pressures and the need to incorporate COTS technologies into more and more areas of technology, some clusters too are starting to utilize protocols traditionally found only in less synchronization-demanding applications, even as COTS-level operating system technologies are entering the fray. Beowulf systems, for example, are high-performance clusters constructed from commodity hardware running open source operating system infrastructures, connected by private internal networks running open network protocols.[23]

Key to the notion of clustered computing is the idea of a single-system image. A cluster is generally a group of nodes that are coupled in such a way as to present the image of a single node to an application that runs on or interacts with the cluster. Clusters are designed to either scale or fail over smoothly; when one subnode in the cluster fails, another is there to take its place, with the application (including its users) hardly noticing. Hybrid clusters, those with sufficient subnodes and intelligence to fail over and scale well, are also useful.

Early clusters were more or less proprietary systems; tightly coupled CPUs that shared a common bus for memory and storage to reasonably share data at very high speeds, not very different from multiple-CPU systems. Advances in datacom capabilities have made it possible for clusters to leave the shared-bus environment, existing now across buildings and even across campus. Indeed, a cross-town cluster is not unthinkable, depending on the quality and speed of the dedicated datacom connection.

While the constraints of light speed may make it difficult for computer engineers to build a global cluster today, dedicated fiber-optic capabilities may one day make such an arrangement imaginable. A global cluster using the public Internet for datacom, however, is not so easy to imagine, given the inherent indeterminacy of the network and the state of Internet protocols today, regardless of increasing bandwidth. But there may yet be clever approaches to overcoming even those intrinsic limits.

## Distributed Agents

An *agent* can be many things. The broadest accepted definition is that of an entity that acts on, or has the power or authority to act on, behalf of another. An agent can be thought of as a means by which something is accomplished or is caused.

In any agent-based model, a human being (or even a non-human agent) may delegate some authority to the agent, which may be "intelligent," mobile, or both. Given the false start that AI appears to have suffered, it may not be realistic to speak of intelligent agents in NDC. We can say, however, that an intelligent agent may be able to make rule-based inferences and conduct probabilistic decision analyses or learning on behalf of its client.

In the context of NDC, a *mobile agent* may move between nodes to accomplish assigned tasks; this vision is of particular interest to mobile users and mobile communications. Such a view naturally raises many questions with respect to security and trust-based models, not to mention assumptions regarding code viability on a given node. Recall Deutsch's Eight Fallacies; many of those fallacies must either be ignored or addressed by substantial work at an industrywide level if a standard agent-based model for NDC is to become reality. And given the presumed relationship between the concept of distributed agents and so many other fitscapes of NDC, it is difficult to imagine a scenario that proffers the ultimate achievment of ubiquitous computing (which I consider to be the teleological vector of NDC, if one exists) without such a standard framework.

Not all nodes must sing the same song—quite the contrary. But "agentness" must be well formalized if a semblance of the intelligence needed to traverse an arbitrary network is ever to be realized.

Within NDC, agents and the characteristics of distributed agents were first considered in the problem space of systems and network management. The standardization of distributed agents is now being explored in the context of the Semantic Web as well as the DARPA Agent Markup Language (DAML).

# Distributed Algorithms

> The notion of an algorithm is basic to all of computer programming,
> so we should begin with a careful analysis of this concept.
> —Donald Knuth

A distributed system is a collection of individual computing components that can communicate. This basic definition covers processing organizations ranging from a VLSI chip to the broadest set of cooperative ensembles that might one day be available as a result of resource convergence over the widest of global public networks. The heart and soul of all such systems is the abstraction expressed by the algorithm.

Algorithms are the step-by-step definitions of computational and communications flow. From a research perspective, algorithms are the research domain of theoretical computer science practitioners, as well as practical references for real-world application development. The study of algorithms has proven to be a successful endeavor in solitary computing node arrangements, providing a basis for understanding problems of practical importance as well as affording a framework for articulating intrinsic limitations (such as computability).

But NDC is inherently different from local computing. Indeed, Deutsch's Eight Fallacies would teach that not only are computing models never uniform across the network, but communication ambiguities also provide indeterminate failure attributes that cannot easily be masked. NDC introduces interesting complexity measures mired in time and space variables that are simply not visible to local computing models. And just as there are greater challenges from greater complexities, the plethora of approaches to NDC serves to further complicate the NDC fitscape, making real-world architectures even more difficult to manage.

Three main architectural models, generally differing in degree of synchrony and decoupling, are algorithmically identifiable in NDC today:

1. A synchronous message passing model. RPC-like models include RMI (Jini network technology), JAX-RPC, and earlier synchronous message passing systems.

2. An asynchronous message-passing model. Java Messaging Service (JMS), which provides a basis for Java platform implementations of Web Services, is representative of this approach.

3. An asynchronous shared-memory model. The more tightly coupled approaches to NDC like grid computing, cluster concepts, and spaces computing can all benefit from distributed computing algorithmic advances gleaned from this model.

Algorithmically, systems can be considered to be asynchronous if there is no fixed upper bound on how long it takes for a message to be delivered or for elapsed time of processing between steps. Email, for example, typically takes only a few seconds to arrive but may also take several days, depending on network temperament. As such, asynchronous models cannot, by definition, provide reliable temporal guarantees. On the other hand, the reliability (also understood as uncertainty reduction) of asynchronous models may be enhanced with other benefits like message persistency. Goff's axiom applies here.

In addition to matters of synchrony, network topology is also a domain of distributed algorithms; determining shapes and boundaries of dynamic networks to effectively navigate the growing rivers of datacom is a matter of much interest. The commercial popularity of the Internet has given rise to a substantial increase in research and development in distributed algorithms, as it has so many other aspects of NDC.

## Distributed Databases

Distributed databases are sets of databases that are stored on multiple nodes but appear to applications as a single database. Through this mechanism, an application may concurrently access and modify data in several databases on a network. Typically, each database in the meta-database is controlled by a local node but cooperates to maintain the consistency of the distributed database and to provide the application-level illusion that a single database is involved.

Database vendors have had interesting challenges to face for a number of years. Companies like Oracle, for example, have added important value to businesses over the past two decades by balancing mission-critical data demands against the often less-than-reliable COTS technologies that their customers are forced to deploy because of increasing competitive pressures.

The closer a database engine operation is to the hardware, the easier it is to provide reasonable assurances of data viability; by the same token, the closer the database engine operation is to the hardware, the less reliant it can and must be on interfaces provided by the host operating system. To easily play with COTS technologies, therefore, database vendors face a catch-22, which becomes even more acute as more NDC COTS technologies are enjoined by databases . . . yet another salute to the flag of paradox emblematic of the Network Age.

Because of inherent constraints in NDC, the meaningful data-integrity guarantees that database vendors must deliver become difficult beyond a tightly configured cluster. These challenges must be overcome if a truly distributed database is to go beyond the illusion of the metadatabase.

This is not to say that the larger, enterprisewide, geographically dispersed metadatabase is not tractable; Oracle offers an impressive array of products that today enable even the largest enterprise manager to glean up-to-date data from the globally distributed firm. The data itself, however, is maintained in many databases, but ideally, only one database. Realistically, as we imagine an age of ubiquitous computing, many databases will likely still need to be knitted together in some fashion. The NDC exploration areas of pervasive computing and distributed agents are both related to problems encountered when distributed databases are considered, as are dependable computing, peer-to-peer computing, security, and others.

## Distributed Filesystems

In regard to data access, the balancing of guarantees of data availability with security and efficient resource utilization is the product of the distributed filesystems fitscape of NDC. The first viable distributed filesystem was the Network File System (NFS) from Sun Microsystems. NFS enabled distributed storage, distributed media, cluster concepts, collaborative computing, and more. It was used on Sun's UNIX-based workstations exclusively at first (circa 1983) but became a standard file sharing mechanism for many operating systems with the public release of NFS 2.0 in 1985. NFS version 3 came along around 1994; major revisions are currently being implemented to allow better performance across the Internet, ultimately turning NFS into a true WAN filesystem.

NFS is not so much a filesystem as it is a collection of protocols that collectively give rise to a client-perspective distributed filesystem. Key to NFS is the concept of a remote file service that is managed by a remote server. Clients need not be aware of a file's location, but rather are given an interface similar to what a local filesystem might offer; the interface offers various file operations that the server is responsible for implementing. This approach can be viewed as a *remote access model,* as contrasted with an *upload/download model,* as shown in the Figure 3.7.[24]

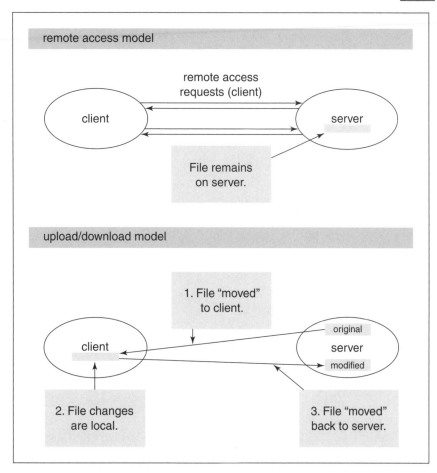

Figure 3.7  General distributed filesystem models

A rudimentary example of an upload/download model is an Internet FTP service when used by a client to obtain, modify, and store data on a remote server.

NFS is implemented on top of RPC. Filesystem interfaces have, for the most part, been abstracted from operating system interfaces to traditional local filesystems to transparently offer distributed filesystem capabilities. A virtual filesystem interface (VFS) has been a standard feature in UNIX and UNIX derivatives since the mid-1980s.

Basically, all requests for file access, whether they be remote or local, go through the operating system's VFS interface. This allows applications to treat all files uniformly, which is of great benefit to NDC application developers. Nevertheless, it is also important to remember the inherent local/remote differences; the ambiguities and uncertainties of remote computing must be considered at the interface level if uniform filesystems access is to be provided.

When it comes to distributed filesystems, two general approaches should be considered. Either multiple nodes access a filesystem managed by a single node, or the data in a filesystem is distributed across several nodes.

Other notable research in NDC distributed filesystems includes the Farsite work of Microsoft (discussed in the operating systems category below), which provides for replication of files, to increase data availability across arbitrary networks, and the Extensible File System, proffered in the early 90s from research at SunLabs, that explored a stacking filesystem, wherein one filesystem can be stacked on top of an existing one, thereby allowing the sharing of the same underlying data in a coherent manner.[25]

## Distributed Media

Distributed media (or multimedia) is one of those catch-all fitscapes of NDC research projects and emerging technologies. Products related to user-friendly multimedia creation, presentation, search, communication, and presentation within distributed environments come from this fitscape area.

Today's euphoria over the World Wide Web does not do justice to the true potential of the Internet. Given Moore's law and Gilder's law (which together give meaning to Metcalfe's law), it is inevitable that the Internet (or more likely Internet2) will support distributed interactivity based on processes that require increasingly larger amounts of data for visualization in real time. If there is a StarTrek-like holodeck in our future, distributed media will be one of the areas responsible for firing it up. Even without such ambitious dreams, this fitscape will enable a new generation of media-savvy users that are prepared for, and in fact demand, such developments.

Consider my 12 year-old niece Tyrell, who lives in an Idaho town so small that all grades in public school—K through 12—share physical facilities. Yet her school is not lacking in resources. One of the courses it offered last year was television production. Using low-cost production gear, made possible by rapid developments in digital media, her class studied hands-on processes and techniques that just a few years ago were limited to only the best-funded schools and professional production studios. Her entire class had the opportunity to leave behind the technology inhibitions and shortcomings that might have been all but inevitable for an earlier generation as geographically remote as hers. It's this catch-all NDC fitscape, facilitated and enabled by the economic implications of the Nth Law metatrends, that will be the enabler of the most prolific generation of computer scientists and users the world has seen. Telepresence will be as natural as cell phones to my niece and her peers, given their early exposure to distributed media, the tools that create it, and the networks that carry it.

## Distributed Storage

The Nth Laws also give rise to an exponentially growing amount of data itself. Vast pools of data require ever-increasing means of storage; Moore's law applies as well to storage capabilities as it does to CPU power. As such, the kinds of storage available today not only feature several orders of magnitude greater capability; they also ensure that legacy storage becomes increasingly outdated. Nonuniform tiers of storage very quickly emerge in any enterprise that has had IT dependencies for more than five years.

The distributed storage category of NDC takes into account the nonuniform tiers of storage available in the modern enterprise, which is itself a fitscape that continues to evolve. In general, the cost of storage is inversely related to the access speed of the storage medium in question. If this were not so, it would probably make sense to have hundreds of terabytes of RAM available for each node and dispense with other storage media altogether. Until an all-optical network and holographic memory systems replace the mountains of disk drives, magnetic tape readers, and removable storage devices currently in vogue, distributed storage will be preoccupied with the costs, access speeds, and reliability of persistent data.

The concept of the storage area network (SAN) was pioneered in the mid-90s, along with so many of the other areas of NDC, stemming, no doubt, from the more commercially uniform emergence of the network metaphor.

The acquisition of computer resources as well as the management and storage of data was an enterprise-centric concern before the 1980s. As such, capital budgets of organizations were impacted by all computer resources, that is, no IT decision was made without careful examination by managers of capital budgets for organizations. With the advent of the first IBM PC in 1981,[26] computer resource purchase decisions were no longer constrained by the more watchful eyes of capital budget managers. An item that can be expensed in a given year[27] can evade detection, making it much less visible from a corporate budget perspective.

As the PC started to become something "aspirational" in firms,[28] more and more PCs started showing up on desks without specific IT decisions to goad their purchase—flying below the capital budget radar, as it were. The dilemma that firms then had to face was that of corporate data access and backup. Since the PC operating environment quickly became dominated by Microsoft and since Microsoft chose not to bundle TCP/IP with their operating systems until 1995, a data-backup gap ensued that provided a serious problem for corporations that were becoming increasingly dependent upon data stored on compute islands not designed to be connected to the corporate IT infrastructure. The same problem also gave rise to opportunities for vendors to help solve the problem.

Proprietary networking protocols like Banyan Vines and those from Novell provided the basis for networked-PC data management in the era immediately preceding the Network Age. It is from those roots that companies like Veritas, Network Appliances, and EMC produced the basis for what is today evolving into sophisticated data management applications that span the multiple storage tiers and multiple network infrastructures that have grown from those islands of PCs. Storage consolidation is a vital to any firm that is concerned with total cost of ownership. The SAN approach features "full fabric SAN infrastructures," which are highly available and support large-scale consolidation, covering wide area networks, load balancing, and ease of management.

Modern firms require global data management strategies. The need for storage, access, security, and availability of data increases as the volume of data increases, which makes the distributed storage fitscape one of NDC's more interesting fitscapes in terms of increasing opportunity and investment.

# Grid Computing

The grid-computing fitscape aims to contribute to the development and advancement of technologies that enable standard, universal access to computing power and resources, all of which are used in a manner similar to electrical power. A computational grid is conceptually similar to an electric power grid. Grid computing envisions the coupling of geographically distributed resources to offer consistent, inexpensive, location-agnostic access to a wide variety of resources, thereby enabling the aggregation and sharing of such things as supercomputers, computer clusters, SANs, distributed databases, embedded networks, instruments, nodes on an arbitrary network, and, ultimately, people. Solutions for large-scale, CPU-bound, and data-intensive NDC applications are naturals for a grid-computing approach. Once specific to particular applications, grid computing for general-purpose commercial use was first made widely available by Sun Microsystems.

Sun Microsystems was the first large computer vendor to make grid computing available for general-purpose commercial use.* On July 24, 2000, Sun announced the acquisition of Gridware, Inc., a privately owned commercial vendor of advanced computing resource management software that originated in Regensburg, Germany. Gridware developed resource management software, which was used primarily in compute-intensive, technical computing environments, such as electronic design automation. Its products were deployed to optimize utilization of workstations, servers, and dedicated compute farms, an area of strategic interest to Sun.

Thanks to the acquisition, Sun released a general-purpose grid-computing production that allows any organization to reap the benefits of such an approach, for example, the following benefits:

♦ Specialized agents on each machine to identify and deliver the compute resources as needed

♦ A GUI and command-line interface for user job submission and control

♦ A queuing system to manage priorities and to assign jobs to available resources

*Gridware, www.sun.com/gridware/

Clear resource utilization benefits can be achieved with products like Gridware. If an organization can better aggregate the compute power of existing servers and desktop nodes, a highly scalable clusterlike resource (which can include thousands of processors) is the result. Many organizations have made heavy investments in compute resources; many of those nodes remain idle much of the time. Estimates of electricity consumed by Internet-connected nodes in the United States range from 2 percent to 8 percent,[29] which may not seem substantial, but any waste of processor capability is a waste of resources. The grid computing fitscape of NDC will help address better resource utilization in the aggregate. Interestingly, the Gridware product from Sun also reflects the trend toward ephemeralization with respect to software product cost; the basic engine is free.

## Massively Parallel Systems

In the early 1990s, parallel processing systems started to emerge from the shadow of the vector processing supercomputers which they would complement and arguably replace.[30] Parallel processing began with dozens of ordinary processors that could be connected in such a way as to allow simultaneous calculations of different units of data from some larger problem.

Thinking Machines Corporation was founded in 1983 with the intention of providing compute resources to support the always-nascent artificial intelligence field. Business concerns led TMC to adjust, ultimately becoming the market leader for massively parallel systems around 1990. TMC's Connection Machine 5 (CM-5) was the first large-scale, massively parallel system, which utilized a single-instruction stream multiple-data stream (SIMD) architecture, essential for parallel processing.[31] The CM-5 was an all-Sun Microsystems play, featuring a Sun 2000 SMP front-end compile server and a bevy of Sun workstations using SPARC microprocessors working under the Solaris operating environment.

TMC is no more. While a leader in massively parallel systems for a short time, its business model was evidently lacking. But the concepts and history of massively parallel systems echo into the Network Age, with grid computing, languages, and distributed algorithms all beneficiaries of early massively parallel systems (MPS).

Computing approaches like that of SETI@home are similar in many respects to MPS systems. The SETI (Search for Extra-Terrestrial Intelligence) project began in 1984 with a single mainframe system to analyze the data harvested from radio antennae around the world. The ability of one system, regardless of its power, to adequately analyze data across a wide range frequencies and a wide swath of pattern probabilities is very limited. But a project like SETI is easily victim to budget cuts during political cycles when such matters make for visible policy adjustments; no funds were available to buy the needed processing capabilities to adequately do the job. Enter SETI@home in 1995. With the growing deployment of home PCs, which consume electricity whether their CPUs are busy or not, the advent of the commercial Internet and the browser gave rise to a resource ripe for harvest. The SETI@home project capitalized on this opportunity. By distributing a free screen saver that was actually an application that performed CPU-intensive calculations on discrete units of data gathered from myriad antennae, the project utilized the capabilities of a indeterminately large number of otherwise wasted cycles in a worldwide NDC massively parallel system. Other efforts with similar needs will inevitably follow.

# Middleware

In the context of NDC, the middleware fitscape eases the task of designing, programming, and managing distributed applications by providing simple, consistent, integrated distributed programming environments. Middleware is essentially a distributed software layer, or "platform," which attempts to abstract complexities and even mask many of Deutsch's Eight Fallacies from developers.

## Platforms

Different middleware platforms support different programming models. One popular model is object-based middleware, in which applications are structured into (potentially distributed) objects that interact by location-transparent method invocation. Examples of this type of middleware are Common Object Request Broker Architecture (CORBA), from the Object Management Group, and Microsoft's Distributed COM (DCOM).[32] Both platforms offer an interface definition language (IDL) that abstracts the fact that objects can be implemented in a variety of suitable programming languages. Both also offer an object request broker, which is responsible for transparently directing method invocations to the appropriate target object, as well as a set of services including naming, time, transactions, and replication, which further enhance the distributed programming environment. A word of caution here, with reference to *A Note on Distributed Computing:* There are inherent differences between local and distributed objects that may not be so easy to ignore. While some work can be accomplished with models like DCOM and CORBA, other NDC applications designs may not so readily lend themselves to this type of approach. (Some of the limitations of DCOM and CORBA from a middleware perspective are discussed later.)

## Other Paradigms

Not all middleware is object based. At least two other popular paradigms exist, as well as many derivatives, which are the subject of research and investigation. Event-based middleware and message-oriented middleware are both in use today. Both employ a "single shot" communications approach rather than the request-reply approach found in object-based middleware. Event-based middleware is particularly suited to the construction of noncentralized NDC applications that must monitor and react to changes in their environment. Examples include process control and Internet information channels such as stock tracking, sports score tickers, and the like. Event-based middleware proponents claim this paradigm has potentially better scaling properties than object-based middleware for such applications, which may be a reasonable claim given the less communications-intensive approach. Message-oriented middleware, on the other hand, is biased toward applications in which messages need to be queued and persistently stored. Workflow and messaging applications are examples.

Interesting areas of investigation include charming approaches like "mChaRM: Reflective Middleware with a Global View of Communications," which is a multichannel reification model being pioneered by Walter Cazzola of the University of Genova.[33] In computer science, *reification* (from the Latin *re,* "thing," to regard or treat an abstraction as if it had concrete or material existence) refers to the action by which information is transferred (read or copied) from an internal mechanism of a system into the domain within which it may be utilized as a processing entity. *Reflection* is the action by which information is transferred from the domain of such a system to its internals. The Java Core Reflection API, for example, "provides a small, type-safe, and secure API that supports introspection about the classes and objects in the current Java virtual machine. If permitted by security policy, the API can be used to

◆ Construct new class instances and new arrays

◆ Access and modify fields of objects and classes

◆ Invoke methods on objects and classes

◆ Access and modify elements of arrays [34]

Walter Cazzola's mChaRM as shown in Figure 3.8 is a reflective model that allows the system to reify multipoint communications instead of objects. Each method invocation can be reified into a multichannel, which can perform metacomputations about it before real activation need occur. In this way, classic communication semantics can be enriched with new

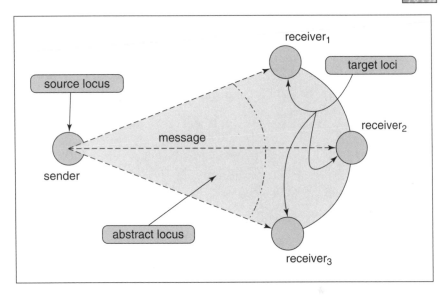

Figure 3.8  General distributed filesystem models: mChaRM, multi-channel reification model (dsonline.computer.org/middleware/articles/dsonline-mcharm.html)

behaviors and properties, and theoretically the flow of communications in an ensemble could be modeled before the ensemble is assembled, which could potentially be very powerful indeed.

Middleware has been responsible for much of the contention, confusion, investment, and progress of NDC. It is also key to the future if progress toward global ubiquitous computing is ever to be realized.

## Mobile and Wireless Computing

The mobile and wireless category of NDC is another broad field that encompasses technologies ranging from radio and television broadcasting to pagers, mobile phones, Bluetooth-enabled PDAs, and satellite communications. Even as the newest next-next-generation mobile phone hits the shelf, standards and protocols for that phone are being updated or even discarded. The fitscape is moving rapidly, as is the rapidly expanding wireless world that would serve wireless LANs.

### Standards and Protocols

One driver is the acceptance of the WiFi standard. With Microsoft vocally committed to the standard, and companies like Sun Microsystems actively engaged in disseminating products that enable developers to bring applications to the space, wireless local networking for computers and other devices is spreading rapidly in many cities around the world.

Most wireless communications discussions split technologies into two general types: local and wide area. In time, these discussions will segment even further, as shown in Figure 3.9, ultimately reflecting a broader IEEE 802 vision:

♦ Personal (wireless personal area network [WPAN]) local (within my clustered campus [LAN])

♦ Wide (across town—metropolitan area network [MAN])

♦ Very wide (across planet [WAN])

The problems, opportunities, transmission frequencies, and data rates shift as we traverse the various ranges of wireless datacom.

Radio frequency identification (RFID) is a wireless protocol sponsored by AIM, the global trade association for the Automatic Identification and Data Capture (AIDC) industry.[35] AIDC technology started tracking and access applications during the 1980s, providing for noncontact, low-bandwidth datacom. Effective in manufacturing and other hostile environments where barcode labels are not appropriate, RFID is established in a wide range of markets such as livestock identification and

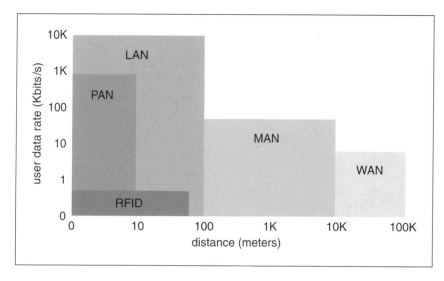

Figure 3.9  Taxonomy of wireless datacom (grouper.ieee.org/groups/802/)

automated vehicle identification systems. RFID is found in "smart labels," which feature thin programmable stick-ons with a very small microchip and antenna to transmit product information. Tracking moving objects is a key feature of RFID. Incorporating RFID solutions into myriad ad hoc personal services will be inexpensive and easy as wireless LAN/MAN solutions provide integratable information fields.

## Personal Devices

Personal devices in years to come will include a bevy of connectables, including Internet-enabled eye-glasses with retinal projection systems, which will be linked with voice-activated input devices or hand-sized keyboards (innovative keyboard layouts will be necessary, perhaps a Nintendo-style input device, complementing voice-activated input devices). Such devices will also link with the simple wireless devices common today, such as automobile remotes, garage door openers, 900 MHz cordless phones, and wireless 802.11 networks. All of these devices operate within a short distance, typically just a few meters. Intelligent, integratable wearables that can sense "information fields" that will traverse the range of wireless datacom capabilities will become standardized, very likely around these and other protocols like Bluetooth.

Wide-area wireless devices operate over a much greater area, although many are similar to the more local wireless devices, which then touch global land-based support networks. Most mobile phones fall into this category. Other wider-area (somewhere between LAN and WAN) providers, such as Wave Wireless,[36] are pioneering stationary, broadband-wireless solutions in 18+ GHz frequencies, using proprietary protocols. Solutions for remote broadband (short of satellite, which can be problematic if symmetric datacom services are required), these kinds of wireless solutions can provide point-to-point broad-band (11 Mbps and beyond) covering distances up to 40 kilometers.

## Applications

But there's much more to wireless and mobile computing than datacom protocols and frequencies. Indeed, the preceding discussion might have been better suited to the network protocols category in any event. Application requirements are clearly different for mobile devices than for other general areas of NDC, so discussion of wireless and mobile platforms is also germane. Take the Java platform, for example.

The Java platform leads in wireless with the Java 2 Platform Micro Edition (J2ME), specifically designed for small or mobile devices. J2ME technology addresses a large number of intelligent consumer devices, ranging from pagers to set-top boxes. To address wireless and mobile needs, J2ME requires the mobile information device profile (MIDP), a set of Java APIs which when combined with the connected limited device configuration (CLDC) provides a complete J2ME application runtime environment. Targeting all types of mobile information devices, which generally have memory restrictions as well as tiny user displays and limited battery life, the MIDP/CLDC specifications address issues such as user interface, persistence storage, networking, and application model. J2ME through MIDP/CLDC provides a standard runtime environment that allows new applications and services to be dynamically deployed on the growing array of small, mobile devices, effectively enabling such devices to become intermittent nodes on the Internet.

### Even As I Write . . .

The wireless fitscape is evolving at an incredible rate. The mobile and wireless category of NDC will have changed substantially by the time the ink is dry on these pages. Developments here also affect and are affected by a number of other fitscapes in the broad scope of NDC.

# Network Protocols

Network protocols define the sets of rules governing communication between nodes on a network. Timing, format, sequencing, error control, routing, reliability, and security are all considerations that network protocols either have or will encompass. To cope with burgeoning network complexities, protocols are broken down into steps or layers, each with its own set of rules for operation and data organization. Each layer, in essence, is its own protocol.

Modern datacom is founded on the principles of Shannon's information theory, which consists of a set of elegant mathematical models for describing stochastic processes and ergodic systems made up of such processes. These models give rise to a probabilistic approach to data encoding and transmission characteristics. With Shannon, the ability to encode and effectively transmit binary codes in an environment that is always prone to noise (transmission errors) is made tractable. The stack approach to datacom is enabled at the lowest level by Shannon. The physical transmission of bits, which are transcribed and framed at the Data Link layer (OSI 7-layer model), relies almost completely on Shannon's information theory. Modern data transmission protocol inventions like DSL, 802.11, Bluetooth, are all founded on Shannon's work.[37]

There are a lot of datacom protocols. Novell offered a proprietary stack called internetworking packet exchange/sequenced packet exchange (IPX/SPX) for use with their NetWare operating system, one of the early players in the PC-networking space. Another is NetBIOS (network basic input/output system) from IBM, a now-standard interface that permits PC applications to communicate directly with other PCs at the transport layer. Which brings us to Transmission Control Protocol/Internet Protocol (TCP/IP), the standard that enables the internet. Loosely based on the ISO OSI 7-layer model,[38] TCP/IP provides basic networking capabilities for computing nodes that provide and consume Internet resources.

Myriad protocols building on top of TCP/IP give rise to other interesting applications. The now-indispensable browser relies on HyperText Transfer Protocol (HTTP), which operates above the transport layer, as do File Transfer Protocol (FTP), Simple Mail Transfer Protocol (SMTP), and Simple Network Management Protocol (SNMP). With the advent of Web Services, additional network protocols are being considered to enable a new generation of networked applications. Baked-in security and reliability, for example, are both required at the protocol level if the Web Services vision is to be realized. Indeed, additional protocols that build on top of the transport layer are becoming quite common and are likely being utilized as competitive differentiators in a business sense as much as they are standardized communication frameworks in a more secular NDC sense.

In NDC, communications protocols are of utmost importance. Indeed, many of the topics covered later in this volume contain discussion of the protocols germane to them. Suffice it to state here that network protocols are as abundant and complex as are the broad categories of NDC itself—that is, evolutionary forces will likely trim this fitscape too, given sufficient time, consumption, and investment.

# Operating Systems

Operating systems have been around since ENIAC, the first modern computer system, and still provide the basis for software development and deployment. My first computer science love was the mysterious and enabling world of operating systems, where software must ultimately meet hardware. Operating systems are responsible for a variety of tasks for a given node, including the following:

- Managing and scheduling resources (CPU, disk, printer, memory, and so on)
- Scheduling tasks, and jobs
- Controlling I/O
- Handling error recovery
- Providing security
- Supplying a basis for user commands

With the proliferation of NDC, operating systems too are subject to change resulting from competitive pressures and network-derived innovations. Once, researchers were content with sensible implementations of a simple IPO model, connecting to the network only as an afterthought. But today, research in operating systems reflects the assumption that any node of interest will be connected to other nodes and share data and processing responsibilities with them. Given this worldview, operating system metamorphosis is inevitable. It should be noted that some operating system designers have long recognized connection to a network as a given. For example, the first system ever sold by Sun Microsystems came with a TCP/IP stack integrated into the system.

Several notable approaches recognize new opportunities for Internet-aware operating systems. One example is the Odyssey project at Carnegie-Mellon University being pioneered by Mahadev Satyanarayanan, a computer science professor who envisions application-aware operating systems, which can adapt as needed depending upon any number of context-dependent variables (e.g., available bandwidth, network load, battery power in a mobile device).[39]

Imagine you're in the back seat of a taxicab enjoying a full-motion color video conversation with your mother on the latest and greatest cell-phone cum Internet portal, via a high-bandwidth wireless MAN, when your cab stops at a light in the shadow of a tall building, temporarily degrading the signal. In this scenario, the operating system provided by the Odyssey vision notifies the (presumably smart) color video application that signal degradation has occurred; instead of the 2 Mbps stream you had so far enjoyed, you are temporarily restricted to 200 Kbps. The application adjusts from a 10 frame/sec color rendering to something more sustainable, perhaps 2 frame/sec black and white. But your conversation, complete with video, continues.

Another example of operating system research is Microsoft's Farsite (Federated, Available, and Reliable Storage for an Incompletely Trusted Environment) project, which promises a more distributed approach to data storage, fault tolerance, self-tuning, and serverless computing that resembles peer-to-peer sensibilities implemented at the operating system level.[40] Microsoft promises implementations as soon as 2006.

IBM, too, is advertising a self-healing, highly scalable approach they're calling "Blue Gene," which is principally founded on their emerging Autonomic Computing initiative, a program that would imbed operating systems with notions like "self-optimization," as well as self-healing (not unlike the autonomic nervous systems in living organisms).

In 1998, Sun Microsystems announced Jini network technology, which brought such notions as self-healing networks to the forefront of the computer industry. The fact that both Microsoft and IBM too now recognize that requirement is testament to the efficacy of that vision. NDC requires ever more "organic" approaches to software development and network deployment as the level of complexity increases. It is only natural that operating systems too begin to reflect that need.

## Real-Time and Embedded Systems

Just as the Internet has grown at a phenomenal rate since its inception, so too have processors that are not connected to an open network, per se, but that provide useful functionality nonetheless. All but the simplest of electrical devices feature an embedded processor today. Why? Because embedding intelligence in a device provides value to consumers. Televisions, coffee pots, telephones, microwave ovens, automobiles, traffic lights, home-climate systems, room air conditioners, CD players, radios, refrigerators, dishwashers, washers and dryers . . . there seems no end to the devices and products that include intelligent processors to meet emerging consumer expectations. And just as the Internet brings great value by connected computing nodes, embedded networks (EmNets) bring great value to real-time and embedded processors. Indeed, the coupling of EmNets and the Internet will provide interesting opportunities in myriad directions over the next few years.

EmNets, especially those with hard real-time requirements,[41] demand tighter specifications and particular sensibilities, typically not required in NDC development. But with the growing integration of real-time and embedded systems intended to leverage and share general-purpose platforms, all developers face design and architectural challenges in managing these newly shared resources. As embedded systems are applied to diverse and potentially adverse environments, appropriate protection of performance characteristics must be ensured. All this has led to increased need for design methodologies for system and application software, operating-system support mechanisms, and resource and application control techniques for these novel forms of embedded systems.

When NDC meets these newly emerging real-time and embedded systems, areas of interest can include such diverse topics as these:

- OS support for mixed response requirements
- Real-time applications in COTS operating systems (e.g., Linux)
- Real-time software components
- Novel kernel-level mechanisms
- Open architectures for resource control
- Embedded control applications
- Secure real-time systems
- Middleware support
- Java implementation and applications
- Power-aware resource management
- QoS-aware application design
- System modeling and analysis

As real-time and embedded networks are knitted together and emerge as services available from the World Wide Web, the sensibilities of each general category (for example, time-bound versus time-agnostic) will influence and impact the other. Further, NDC developers will increasingly become more time aware, even if hard real-time requirements do not immediately constrain network application development.

# Commentary

The end of this unordered list of NDC R&D fitscapes marks the beginning of the journey for software developers. There is no avoiding the complexities we've unleashed if we would move forward.

In a little over two decades, NDC R&D, coupled with the immutable laws of supply and demand and seasoned by an early 21st-century shock wave of realization that Moore's law really was an accurate, practical forecasting model rather than science fiction, has given rise to a interleaved group of fitscapes that is beginning to rival some of nature's own more interesting efforts. Not unlike the universe it would help us to understand, the sphere of computer science is enjoying an inflationary era, as the rate of innovation continues to accelerate, following its own exponential vector—somewhere between Moore and Gilder, applauded by Metcalfe.

In this era of ever-changing change, it may be wise to consider Stuart Kauffman's observation that the rate of innovation cannot exceed the ability of the fitscape to adequately test the novelty without risking systemic collapse. If we move too fast, we may experience spectacular collapse, the magnitude of which we cannot even grasp, let alone predict.

If any conclusions can be drawn from an overview of NDC and the relationships among its 24 fitscapes, they can be summarized as follows:

1. Complexity will continue to increase, absent radically different approaches.

2. Formal methods are enjoying a renaissance while standardization efforts both ignore and embrace formal methods.

3. Increasing global competition and COTS technologies will prune the complex undergrowth of NDC R&D options.

4. Technology adoption will continue to increase only if perceived value is obvious to the markets (and hence consumers) which that technology would serve.

5. No one individual, standardization effort, organization, or concern can adequately prestate NDC configuration space. Indeed, as Kauffman asserts, it is very likely impossible.

6. The kaleidoscope of NDC categories are all related; convergence among categories of NDC R&D is inevitable.

## Notes

1. dsonline.computer.org

2. The term *teleology,* from philosophy, denotes the study of ultimate aim or purpose in nature. With respect to technology, we can use the term to mean the ultimate aim of technology insofar as it can be discerned.

3. Arg!: a technical term from early email protocol; an emotive signifying frustration.

4. xml.coverpages.org/MS-GlobalXMLWebServicesArchitecture.html

5. Abraham H. Maslow, *Toward a Psychology of Being* (Princeton, NJ: van Nostrand, 1968).

6. Paul Watzlawick, Munchhausen's Pigtail or Psychotherapy and Reality (New York: Norton, 1990), p. 125.

7. Tim Berners-Lee, James Hendler, and Ora Lassila, "The Semantic Web," *Scientific American* (May 2001).

8. The basis for the U.S. government's suit against Microsoft.

9. David Gelernter, *Mirror Worlds* (New York: Oxford University Press, 1991).

10. Dallas Semiconductor.

11. www.gigaspaces.com

12. For a history of Napster, see Joseph Menn, *All the Rave: The Rise and Fall of Shawn Fanning's Napster* (New York: Crown Business, 2003).

13. Jini network technology provides an interesting alternative to this traditional constraint, which is useful to consider as the idea of self-healing becomes more widely held in networks as well as within nodes.

14. i3c.org

15. From "Brief Timeline of the Internet" (http://www.webopedia.com/quick_ref/timeline.asp) "October 1, 1969: Second node installed at Stanford Research Institute; connected to a SDS 940 computer. The first ARPANet message sent: 'lo.' Trying to spell log-in, but the system crashed!"

16. Wilfredo Torres-Pomales, "Software Fault Tolerance: A Tutorial," NASA/TM-2000-210615, citeseer.nj.nec.com/torres-pomales00software.html

17. Dhiraj K. Pradhan, *Fault-Tolerant Computer System Design* (Upper Saddle River, NJ: Prentice Hall, 1996).

18. Brian Randell and Jie Xu, "The Evolution of the Recovery Block Concept," in *Software Fault Tolerance,* Michael R. Lyu, ed. (New York: Wiley, 1995).

19. www.ietf.org/rfc/rfc2828.txt

20. Janet Raloff, "Languishing Languages: Cultures at Risk," Science News Online (February 25, 1995), http://www.sciencenews.org/sn_edpik/aa_1.htm

21. The Java platform (which includes language specification and run-time virtual machine specification—hence, the Java "platform"—was invented by James Gosling of Sun Microsystems and announced by Sun in 1995.

22. Duke, the Java mascot, emerged in the summer of 1992, when the Green Team—the pioneers at Sun who created the Java programming language—built a working demo of an interactive, hand-held home-entertainment device called the *7 ("Star 7"). The *7 featured Duke, an animated character who served as an agent for the user and who could interact with multiple objects on screen.

23. www.beowulf.org

24. Andrew S. Tanenbaum and Maarten van Steen, *Distributed Systems, Principles and Paradigms* (Upper Saddle River, NJ: Prentice Hall, 2002), p. 577.

25. research.sun.com/techrep/1993/smli_tr_93-18.pdf

26. The IBM PC wasn't the first personal computer, per se. But when IBM introduced the 5150 in August 1981, the PC era began in earnest.

27. Generally, tax laws treat capital purchases and expenses differently. Capital purchases are items that must be depreciated over time, whereas expenses are generally deductible from income in the same year as expenditure. Capital purchases usually have a higher minimum amount associated with the purchase, for example, "all items under $5000 can be expensed."

28. It can be argued that many PCs purchased during the 1980s were aspirational as opposed to functional. If I am a first-line manager, for example, and the manager in the cube next to mine has a PC, which is becoming something cool to have, then I too must have a PC.

29. usinfo.state.gov/topical/global/ecom/01020603.htm

30. Vector processors perform CPU-intensive calculations analogous to an assembly line. A central processor doles out the first unit of data, the second processor performs a calculation and hands the task to the next processor, and so on. Vector processing is well suited for

problems that feature well-organized, parallelizable datasets, like calculation of weather patterns. For years all supercomputing was synonymous with vector processors.

31. Multiple-instruction stream, multiple-data stream (MIMD) machines feature processors that function in an independent or asynchronous manner. SIMD architectures are more tightly coupled from a memory perspective and offer superior ability to manipulate vectors, offset by a disadvantageous approach to managing memory exchange.

32. www.omg.org, www.microsoft.com/com/tech/DCOM.asp

33. www.disi.unige.it/person/CazzolaW/, Walter Cazzola, Univ. of Genova, Italy, Dept. of Informatics and Computer Science.

34. Java Core Reflection API Specification, java.sun.com/products/jdk/1.1/docs/guide/reflection/spec/java-reflection.doc.html

35. www.aimglobal.org/technologies/rfid/

36. wavewireless.com

37. C. E. Shannon, "A mathematical theory of communication," *Bell System Technical Journal* 27 (July and October 1948): 379–423; 623–56.

38. www.webopedia.com/quick-ref/OSI.Layers.asp

39. www.2.cs.edu/~odyssey/

40. research.microsoft.com/farsite

41. Realtime applications can be classified as either hard or soft realtime. Hard realtime applications require a response to events within a predetermined amount of time for the application to function correctly. If a hard realtime application fails to meet specified deadlines, the application is considered to have failed. Soft realtime applications, however, do not necessarily fail if a deadline is missed. An example of a soft realtime application is an airline reservation system where temporal delays do not necessarily constitute failure, although a "reasonable" temporal component is implied.

# CHAPTER 4

# NDC Theory

Theories arise to explain practice, even as practice models existing theories. The paradoxical nature of NDC today lies in both the age-old disciplines of mathematics and logic and the phenomena as recent as the early commercial adoption of URLs. The more we learn, the more we realize how little we know.

NDC, as with all of computer science, is founded in theory. This chapter briefly explores some of the theories that are fundamental to computer science and identifies areas of theoretical computer science that are challenged by the explosion of interest in NDC occurring in the Network Age. Just as NDC forces reexamination of previously accepted concepts and reenergized cycles of discovery in virtually all aspects of science, the theories upon which NDC is founded are subject to revelations made manifest by the very same tools.

As with the scope of NDC practice and research, theoretical work in the NDC space is rather abundant and involves multiple complex relationships. To map theories across the 24 topical areas cited in chapter 3 would defeat the purpose of this book, which is to instead provide a more general overview of the evolution of NDC, including history, practice, and future directions. To this end, a more parsimonious view of NDC theories is appropriate.

The following areas of theoretical computer science are considered in this chapter:

◆ Foundations

◆ Theory versus practice

◆ The Halting Problem

◆ Message passing systems

◆ Byzantine failures and leader election

◆ Mutual exclusion

◆ Fault tolerance

◆ Synchrony, causality, and time

# Theoretical Foundations of NDC

Some of the theories that drive computer science are as old as Ancient Greece. For example, prime numbers (which provide the mathematical basis for modern encryption algorithms) were first articulated by Euclid circa 330 BC in a compendium of all known mathematics at the time, a 13-volume set called *Elements*. Euclid proved that if a prime number $p$ divides a product $mn$, then $p$ divides at least one of the two numbers, $m$ and $n$. He also proved that every natural number is either a prime or can be uniquely expressed as a product of primes, and that prime numbers constitute an infinitely large set, in an era in which such elegant mathematical proofs were as fresh as the culture giving rise to them.

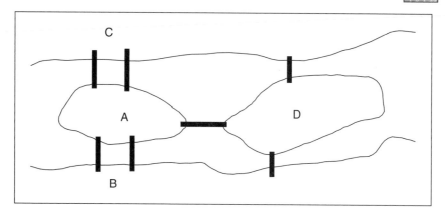

Figure 4.1  The Königsberg Bridges problem

Leonhard Euler, the great Swiss mathematician, contributed much to the beginnings of computer science in the 18th century, including an understanding of primitive network routing issues and early topology efforts arising from his solution to the classic Königsberg Bridges problem. The old Prussian city, located on the River Pregel, had two islands which were joined by a bridge. In addition, one of the islands had two bridges to each shore, and the other island had one bridge to each shore. This arrangement is shown in Figure 4.1.

The citizens of Königsberg had a habit of taking walks every Sunday. Paths would often take them over several of the bridges. The question of whether it was possible to take a walking tour of the town that traversed each of the seven bridges exactly once was studied by the townspeople until Euler proved that it could not be done.

Euler's great insight was the realization that the layout of the bridges and the islands was irrelevant to solving the problem. All that need be considered was the way in which the bridges connected the islands and the shores—in other words, how a network was formed between the shores, the islands, and the bridges. This network is shown in Figure 4.2.

Each island and each shore could be regarded as a single point. What mattered was the connections—not the length or shape of the connections, but which points were connected to other points. This geometry-agnostic observation is the essence of topology, as well as the basis for most networking algorithms. Euler's observation gave rise to the mathematical branch of topological study known as network theory, which provides the theoretical basis for many modern datacom applications.

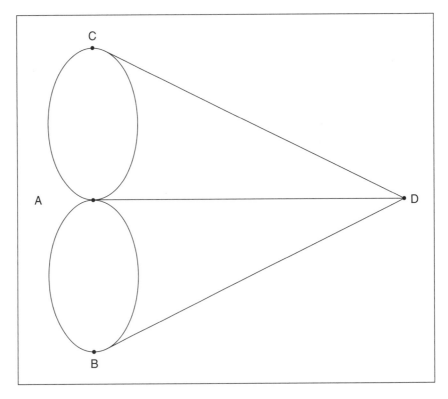

Figure 4.2 Euler's network observation

George Boole, a 19th-century mathematician, is also noteworthy as one of the giants upon whose shoulders computer science stands today. Offering insights responsible for propositional logic and truth tables (Boolean logic), Boole set the stage for Giuseppe Peano and Gottlob Frege, at the end of the 19th century, to articulate predicate logic, the arcane symbolic representation of logical propositions needed to express computational theories upon which modern compute models are built. NDC today is the beneficiary of these and many other pre-20th century mathematical innovations and discoveries.

Modern computing theory began with Alan Turing and the Turing Machine. The articulation of algorithms for sequential systems, à la the IPO model, has been very successful. Concepts like computability and NP-complete[1] have been well covered by theories that enable much in the way of modern computing devices. NDC research does the same thing for distributed systems. But as we've seen, local computing is fundamentally different in nature and scope than distributed computing. The essential differences between general computing theory and the body of theory on which NDC is based can generally be expressed by examining four broad theoretical NDC areas: algorithms, communications and persistence, models of computation, and synchrony.

Most compute problems specific to NDC theory attempt to address questions that arise when considering essential differences in these four areas. The intense ongoing research in NDC discussed in Chapter 3, compounded by the continuing convergence of more and newer networks, makes theoretical work even more important if these convergent networks are to be viable.

## Theory Versus Practice

Design and implementation are two different things. It is entirely possible to spend a lifetime studying and making meaningful contributions to theoretical computer science without having to even touch a computer keyboard, let alone connect to the World Wide Web. It is likewise possible to annually refresh real-world development skills as a sophisticated, highly paid, hands-on NDC developer without having to even learn, let alone master, the cryptic symbols of abstract thought that articulate modern theoretical computer science. As such, the gap between theory and practice is often misunderstood and even more often ignored. The sometimes arcane language of real-world software development may even seem unrelated to the more mathematical expressions of theoretical computer science.

But just as modern datacom would be impossible to imagine without the elegant theories expressed formally and mathematically by Claude E. Shannon (as discussed in Chapter 3), NDC developers owe a similar debt to the theoretical bases that provide algorithms, facilitate communications and data persistence, manage synchrony, and describe compute engines—the abstract components from which nodes and networks are made. Without the theories, the Internet and all it encompasses would be reduced to copper, silicon, and plastic.

The fact that theoretical computer science can so be easily ignored during the day-to-day meanderings of a typical NDC software development project is a testament to the success of the NDC providers who have implemented those theories. As Waldo et al. have observed,[2] there seem to be cyclical tendencies in the broader NDC fitscape that alternately mask and expose the fallacies Peter Deutsch has articulated. While it may never be possible for developers to mask all the fallacies all the time, the theoretical foundations of NDC often provide a basis for containing their own impact on NDC implementation, very often allowing day-to-day developers to ignore the fallacies.

Reducing the development complexity that the software architect must consider would make it easier to more quickly deliver value in a globally competitive environment, so simplifying assumptions at the interface level are highly desirable. Paradoxically, to offer simplifying assumptions, theory must be encouraged to focus on complexity. The edges of theoretical research (and therefore a likely set of future developments in computer science) seem to indicate not only a questioning of some of the classic theories upon which systems today are based but are also beginning to reflect a recognition of the science of complexity, which must be acknowledged if those theories are to evolve. In short, we still don't know what we don't know, but we are at least realizing that we may not confidently know what we once thought we knew.

## The Halting Problem

Arguably the first great paradox of computer science was articulated by Alan Turing.

Kurt Gödel, you may recall, popped the balloon of completeness, which was then eloquently held aloft (in the tradition of Euclid) by the labors of Bertrand Russell and Alfred North Whitehead in *Principia Mathematica,* in which they attempted to reduce mathematics to a few simple axioms. Within their system, assertions were either "provable" or "disprovable" (true or false). The idea was that a system that began with a few simple indisputable axioms could provide a mechanical means of deriving theorems upon which all mathematics could be derived.

In 1931, Gödel invalidated this approach completely. Not only did Gödel find a hole in Russell and Whitehead's work, he demonstrated that the goal itself was not achievable. Specifically, Gödel showed that for any formal axiomatic system, there is always a statement about natural numbers which is true but which cannot be proven in the system. In other words, mathematics will always be incomplete. The statement "This statement is false" represents the essence of Gödel's Incompleteness Theorem; neither true nor false, it transcends any system that would claim to reduce all statements to such a measure.

The Halting Problem, articulated by Turing in 1936, is related to Gödel's theorem. Suppose we have a computing device (a Turing machine) that will run any arbitrary program. Now suppose that one of the programs that we might run is one called WillHalt($P,i$), where $P$ is any program and $i$ is an input for the program P.

The WillHalt( ) program will return true if $P$ will not continue forever given input $i$, and return false if $P$ will loop forever given input $i$. So far so good. Now consider the following C program snippet:

```
void nP( char *i ){
      while( 1 ){
            if ( WillHalt( nP, i) )
                  continue;
            else
                  break;
      }
exit( );
}
```

In other words, if WillHalt( ) determines that the program nP( ) will halt, it will loop forever; otherwise it will exit. Clearly, this is unsolvable, as is the canonical example of Gödel's proof. Just as Gödel demonstrated that all logical systems of any complexity are, by definition, incomplete, so does the Halting Problem illustrate a similar limitation in computer science. One conclusion we can easily reach is that the initial assumption we made regarding the validity of function WillHalt(P,i) was in error; the function cannot exist.

The implications for programmers lead to other philosophical considerations akin to those faced by mathematicians, linguists, physicists, and biologists. *No closed system can be certain of what it knows about itself by relying upon what it knows about itself.* Indeed, along with bootstrapping many of the ideas that drive computer science today, Turing also defined the initial boundary conditions limiting what computer science may contextually accomplish. Understanding what is "unsolvable" or "undecidable" or "uncomputable" is a central requirement of theoretical computer science, as are evolving models that allow us to transcend the fundamental limits of previous models. NDC now represents challenges sufficient to force computer science to ultimately grow beyond the compute models defined by Turing and his contemporaries over a half century ago.

## Message Passing Systems

NDC, by its very nature, is a message passing system. Some would argue that a shared memory view should also be considered; but ultimately shared memory systems can be distilled into message passing models. Thus, message passing arguably provides the basis for all program communication as well as coordination.

In theoretical computer science, formal models for synchronous and asynchronous message passing systems are explored. Failures are often ignored in theory in order to define basic complexity measures and express abstract algorithms in pseudocode. Generally, messages are passed between nodes in bidirectional communication channels (which isn't always the case in practice). The patterns of connections between nodes define the topology of the network, which is itself discoverable by theoretical means.

*Asynchronous* models are those in which there is no fixed upper bound on the time it takes for a message to be delivered or how much time may elapse between consecutive steps of a processor. Email, for example, is asynchronous on the Internet. While an email message may sometimes take only a few seconds to be delivered, that same unit of email could take hours or even days to be received, depending on routing or processing uncertainties.

*Synchronous* systems, on the other hand, function in lock step. Each node in a synchronous model executes in a partitioned round based on messages just received. While convenient for algorithmic design, this model is generally not very practical in NDC, although the abiding value and utilization of remote procedure calls (RPC) may argue against such an assessment. An asynchronous algorithm will also work in a synchronous system; a synchronous system is a special case of an asynchronous one.

## Complexity

Complexity in computer science is as difficult to define and quantify as it is in any other field. The "science of complexity" is a potpourri of terms and disciplines that is still in its infancy and may very well remain there, given the unknowable nature of much of what seems to be implied. Despite valiant attempts, complexity measures remain entrenched in the speculative category of nature. In computer science, the original and still classic Kolmogrov measure,[3] which is (roughly) the shortest program capable of generating a given string, is algorithmically uncomputable, thus harking back to the Halting Problem, which is Gödel's theorem in disguise. In general, complexity measures either pick up where Kolmogrov complexity leaves off, involving some abstract compute model that may predict a pattern of interest, or they attempt to build on information theory and produce something like Shannon's entropy, which is computable in principle but difficult to calculate reliably in real systems. Still, measures of complexity are topically relevant in most theoretical computer science texts.

In message passing systems, two complexity measures of interest are the number of messages generated and the amount of time required by distributed algorithms. Best-case/worst-case analyses provide the basis for algorithmic assessment of both message complexity and time complexity measures.

## Topology

In NDC, message passing provides the theoretical basis for node communication in any arbitrary network, regardless of topology. A few simple examples regarding topology serve to illustrate this point. Consider the simple networks shown in Figure 4.3.

The ring network is a fairly straightforward graph. The spanning tree is a little less obvious, but not that difficult to understand. A tree is a connected, undirected graph without repeats or cycles; a spanning tree graph is one that contains all the vertices (nodes in a network) of the graph. There are two main types of spanning trees: the breadth-first search (BFS) and the depth-first search (DFS). Algorithmically, we'll examine a simple BFS spanning tree.

We'll start with a simple algorithm for broadcasting a single message which should work in either network. In the case of the ring network, the node *n0* has some message *M* that it wishes to share with all other nodes

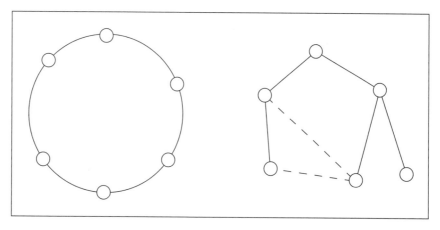

Figure 4.3  Ring network and spanning tree

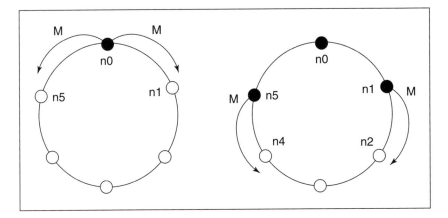

Figure 4.4 Ring network broadcast: Step 1 and Step 2

in the ring. Each node in the ring has exactly two neighbors, so in Step 1, *n0* sends the message to *n1* and *n5,* as shown in Figure 4.4.

In Step 2, nodes *n1* and *n5* share the message with nodes *n2* and *n4,* respectively. Algorithmically, we need to identify the relationship between nodes (through communication channels) as well as the states a given node may occupy with respect to the message—either a message has been received and processed or it has not.

Initially, *M* is sent from *n0* to all of its neighbors, which we know from the ring's topology to be exactly two, but which we will treat as a variable quantity for the sake of algorithmic flexibility. To that end, let's consider each neighbor to be a child, in the spanning tree sense.

```
Step 1:
1.  For each child, send M
2.  Terminate
Step 2:
1.  Upon receiving M from parent
2.  if M not previously received,
    send M to all children
3.  Terminate
```

The test in Step 2.2 ensures that the message will not continue to propagate around the ring once it has been received by all nodes. Note that by treating the message sender as a parent in the ring, we can apply the algorithm equally well to a BFS tree, as shown in Figure 4.5.

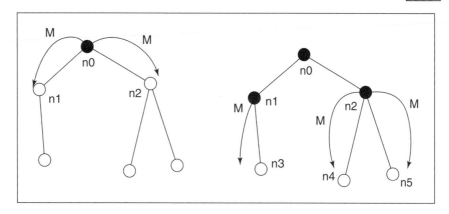

Figure 4.5  BFS spanning tree broadcast: Step 1 and Step 2

This simple example of a broadcasting algorithm may apply equally well to either a ring or a tree topology. Most distributed algorithms are not so flexible, however. Consider the reverse of a broadcast, for example: the convergecast. A broadcast requires one-way communication to all the nodes in a tree, from the root to the leaves. The complementary problem is one of collecting information from the leaves. The broadcast algorithm is initiated by the root, and the convergecast algorithm is initiated by the leaves. A leaf is distinguished by the absence of children in the tree; hence, the convergecast algorithm cannot be applicable to a ring topology.

## Constraints and Problems

NDC is defined to be a collection of individual computing nodes that communicate with each other. The activities of the nodes are coordinated and data otherwise shared by the passing of messages, as we've seen, either synchronously or asynchronously. The sharing of resources is the primary motivation for constructing NDC systems. Message passing is subject to the NDC constraints cited earlier, such as the lack of a central authority, indeterminacy, and so on. But the convergence of wireless and mobile computing and the Internet introduces entirely new sets of problems that have only recently begun to be considered in the theoretical computing domain.

The IEEE standard for LANs and MANs (802.1d) provides for the creation of spanning trees with the Spanning Tree Protocol (STP), essentially through a spanning tree algorithm that senses when a switch has

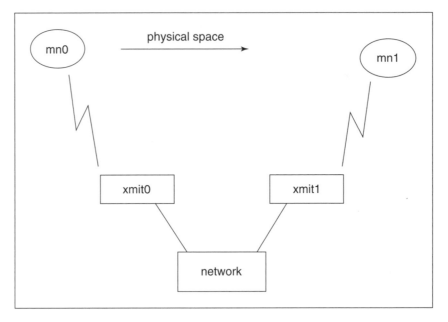

Figure 4.6 Two mobile nodes (*mn0* and *mn1*) network-connected by
transmitters (*xmit0* and *xmit1*)

more than one way to communicate with a node and then determines
which way is best, based on optimal path cost (a function of time). Most
modern LAN switches follow this standard. But with the advent of mobile
Internet appliances, the algorithmic optimization for path cost must cache
alternative paths in case the primary path becomes unavailable; this solution
may not be optimal. Consider the simple example shown in Figure 4.6.

In the example above, a network-connected mobile node (*mn0*) is
traveling through physical space, exchanging data with another mobile
node (*mn1*). The transmitters *xmit0* and *xmit1,* respectively, facilitate
network communication between these two nodes, effectively acting as
switches. Since these are wireless connections with limited areas of cover-
age, and *mn0* is traveling through physical space, at some point another
transmitter must facilitate network communication for the traveling node,
as shown in Figure 4.7.

As shown, on some event (the fading of a signal, for example), *mn0*
may be switched to another transmitter. There is a movement through
physical space as well as a movement through virtual space, but it is important not to confuse the two. The node itself moved through physical
space, but it was the linkage between the nodes that moved in virtual

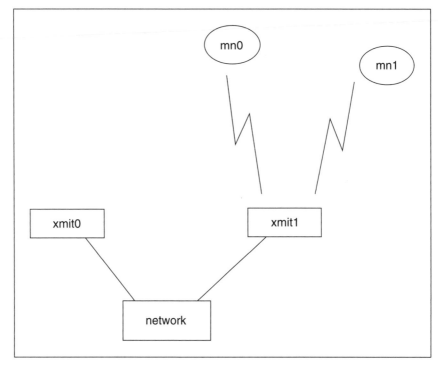

Figure 4.7  *mn0* and *mn1* both network-connected by *xmit1*

space; from a theoretical computing perspective, it is the virtual movement that is important. The mobile node needs to be switched to a new transmitter, and the switching needs a protocol to seamlessly facilitate this handover. The STP, which is the standard for switches, is not designed to optimize or even recognize this kind of network routing problem — something that mobile telephones in a cellular network accomplish routinely.

NDC, especially with the growth of mobile and wireless computing, requires a rethinking of many of the theoretical constructs that gave rise to the Internet in the first place. Message passing algorithms are the basis of that work.

## Byzantine Failures

An overconfident reliance on cleverness and deception arguably led to the ultimate failure of the Byzantine Empire — a matter for historians to consider. But in computer science, the term *Byzantine failures* has become synonymous with the deceptive aspect of that civilization. In NDC, a Byzantine failure is not one in which a given node has crashed, but rather one in which one or more nodes or communication channels may be lying. This is a problem distinct from a node crash and must be dealt with accordingly.

There are several classes of failure in NDC. Some failures are due to the inherent differences of NDC; others are endemic of computing in general. Recovering from failure is a large part of any program's essence, regardless of the execution environment. As much as 85 percent of the code running on traditional mainframe systems is devoted to failure detection and recovery. Failures can be generally categorized according to their severity, source, and effect as listed in Table 4.1.

Table 4.1    Classes of failures in NDC

| Failure Type | Source | Description |
|---|---|---|
| Stop | node | A node stops and does not restart. Other nodes may detect this state. |
| Crash | node | A node crashes and does not restart. Other nodes may not be able to detect this state. |
| Channel-omission | channel | A message sent never arrives. |
| Send-omission | node | A node completes a send but the message is not received. |
| Receive-omission | node | A message is received but the process on the node does not process it. |
| Byzantine | node or channel | A node/channel exhibits arbitrary behavior, including omissions, arbitrary messages, stops, or incorrect processing steps. |
| Clock | node | A node exceeds acceptable bounds on clock drift. |
| Node performance | node | A node exceeds processing-interval bounds. |
| Channel performance | channel | Message transmission exceeds bounds. |

In NDC, Byzantine failures are the most challenging type of failure. For example, a node may set inaccurate data values, or a process on a node may return the wrong value upon invocation. In addition to inaccurate or incomplete data, arbitrary failures can include sporadic message omissions or timing failures. Such failures are the most difficult to detect, making recovery from NDC Byzantine failures one of the better-explored areas of theoretical computer science.

The Byzantine Generals problem is a classic in theoretical computer science. In the problem, a group of army generals must agree to attack or retreat. One, the leader, is to issue the order to either attack or retreat. The others are to decide whether or not to attack or retreat; but all are aware that one or more of their peer generals may be "treacherous," which here means arbitrarily prone to failure. If the leader is treacherous, he will propose attack to one general and retreat to another. If one of the other generals is treacherous, he will tell one of his peers that the leader ordered an attack while telling another that a retreat had been ordered. The Byzantine Generals problem is related to but distinct from the problem of reaching consensus among nodes.

To reach a consensus, every node begins in an undecided state and proposes a single value drawn from a set R (i = 1, 2, 3, ... , N). The nodes communicate with each other, exchanging values. Assuming a reliable multicast operation, each node then sets a decision variable, based on the value from R that occurs in the highest frequency or a special value not from R if no majority exists. When it sets the decision variable, each node enters the decided state, in which it may no longer change the value of the decision variable. Again assuming a reliable multicast operation, agreement and integrity are guaranteed by the definition of a majority; every node receives the same set of proposed values and uses the same evaluation function.

In the Byzantine Generals problem, instead of each node proposing a value, the requirements are as follows:

- *Termination:* Each node eventually sets its own decision variable.

- *Agreement:* The decision value is correct if all nodes have the same value and are in the decided state.

- *Integrity:* If the leader is correct, then all nodes will have agreed to whatever the leader proposed.

This approach to consensus allows for arbitrary failure if more than three nodes are involved. In cases of three or less NDC nodes that send unsigned (not rigorously identifiable) messages, whether synchronous or asynchronous, there is no solution that guarantees to meet the conditions of the Byzantine Generals problem if one node is allowed to fail.[4]

In addition to Byzantine failures in which arbitrary failures can be introduced, the modern NDC developer must also be acutely aware of issues of security, which are orthogonally related to Byzantine problems.

## Leader Election

As with failure conditions, NDC raises computing issues that are not germane to local computing. Leader election is typical of such issues, especially in rings. Rings are a convenient network topology that facilitates message passing and often corresponds to physical instantiations of networks such as token rings. The election of a leader can simplify coordination and communication among nodes in a ring, making it easier to solve a number of problems, such as deadlock resolution and enhanced fault tolerance.

There are a number of algorithmic approaches to leader election. The problem is similar to consensus, in that eventually each node must also come to one of two conclusions: either it is the leader, or it is not and exactly one of its peer nodes is. One approach algorithmically solves the problem by satisfying the following conditions:

♦ *Terminal state:* A node is either elected or not-elected at the terminal state.

♦ *Correct execution:* Exactly one node is elected the leader; all remaining nodes are not-elected.

An anonymous ring system is one in which nodes in the ring do not have unique identifiers that can be used by an algorithm. In such a ring network, it has been demonstrated that there is no leader election algorithm that can give rise to an anonymous leader.[5] Therefore, unique identifiers must be available for dynamic leader election to occur.

One simple algorithm in a ring network in which unique identifiers, as shown in Figure 4.8, are available is for each node to send a message with its identifier to its left peer and then wait for messages from its right peer. When it receives messages, it checks the identifier in the message. If

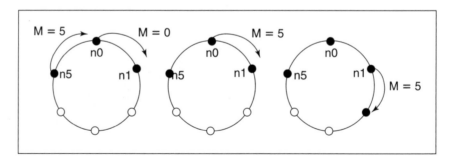

Figure 4.8 Leader election with unique identifiers

the identifier in the message is greater than its own, it forwards the message to its left; otherwise, it does not propagate the message. When a node ultimately receives a message with its own identifier, it can then declare itself the leader.

Ultimately, the node with the greatest unique value ($n5$ in Figure 4.8) will receive a message containing its own identifier, which will signify the end of the election process. Note that the number of messages passed in this example will be equal to $2n - 1$, which would hold true of any ring network in which the nodes are uniquely ordered as above, regardless of the number of nodes.

## Mutual Exclusion

Mutual exclusion is just as important to NDC as it is to the work of multitasking operating systems or any local computing task that requires multiple threads of execution. Protection of critical regions of code to ensure consistency and prevention of interference, as well as providing a means for coordination of activities, is the motivation for algorithmic approaches to NDC mutual exclusion. Given the nature of NDC, it is also a requirement that we rely only upon message passing for implementation of any mutual exclusion solution.

Several approaches to NDC mutual exclusion have been theoretically explored. Central server approaches, ring-based algorithms, approaches using multicast and logical clocks, and voting among peers have all demonstrated varying degrees of effectiveness and complexity in NDC environments.

The problem of NDC mutual exclusion involves allocation of an indivisible resource that cannot be concurrently shared between nodes. An example of such a resource might be a printer; if more than one node had simultaneous access to a printer, the output would not be of much use. The same is true of databases or shared storage devices; any resource that requires exclusive access by a node (or by a process within a node) for some finite measure of time to provide meaningful value is a candidate for NDC mutual exclusion. The following are essential requirements for NDC mutual exclusion:

- *Safety:* At most one node may execute in the critical region at a time.

- *Liveness:* Requests to enter the critical region must eventually succeed.

♦ *Ordering:* Requests to enter the critical region are processed in chronological order; entry is granted in the order in which requests are received.

The simplest approach to achieving NDC mutual exclusion is with a central server approach, as shown in Figure 4.9. To enter a critical region, a node sends a request message to the server registering interest in the protected resources, and waits for a reply. A token signifying permission to enter the critical region is implicit in the eventual reply from the server.

In this example, the node *n0* requests the resource, which is currently in use by the node *n1*. The node *n2* has already placed a request in the queue, which is managed by the central server. When *n1* finishes its work in the critical region, it releases the resource. The central server then passes the grant token to the node *n2* and updates the queue accordingly, making *n0* the next in the queue.

Although this approach is simple to implement, it has some distinct disadvantages. Even when no process is using the critical region, two messages (the request and the passing of the grant token) are required in order to use it, adding unnecessary delays. Even assuming an asynchronous message passing system, this requirement does not delay the requesting process, but it does add message overhead to the NDC system in general. Another disadvantage is the performance bottleneck that a central server always represents, not to mention the single-point-of-failure and scalability issues inherent in central server approaches.

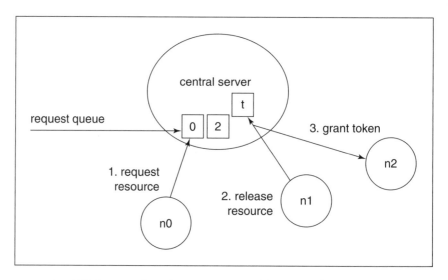

Figure 4.9 NDC mutual exclusion managed by central server

In 1981, Ricart and Agrawala published a distributed algorithm[6] that used multicasting and logical clocks to achieve mutual exclusion in an N-peer network. Nodes that require entry to a critical region send a multi-cast request message and enter the region only when all other peers have replied to the message. The conditions under which a node replies to a request are designed to meet the aforementioned requirements of safety, liveness, and ordering.

---

The "happened-before" (the relative time between two events occurring in a distributed system without a global clock) relationship is important when determining a partial ordering of events and in producing a logical clock for NDC. "Lamport Clocks" were formulated by Leslie Lamport, currently with Microsoft Research (see Lamport's home page: http://lamport.org).

In order to figure out the relative time between two events occurring in a distributed system without a global clock, the happened-before → relationship is defined as follows:

♦ On the same process, a → b if time of a < time of b (the time is given by the local clock).

♦ If a process sends a message to another process, then a → b if a is the send and b is the receive.

♦ For three events a, b, c, if a → b and b → c, then a → c.

The happened-before relationship is only useful in the partial ordering of events. It is not useful when considering concurrent events because a → b means that time(a) < time(b), but time(a) < time(b) does not mean that a → b.

---

As in the leader election problem, the nodes must bear unique numeric identifiers; also assumed are communication channels between all nodes. Each node must also keep a Lamport clock, sending messages that are of the form $(T, n_i)$, where T is the sender's timestamp and $n_i$ is the unique identifier.[7] Pseudocode for Ricart and Agrawala's algorithm is as follows:

```
On initialization
     state := RELEASED;
To enter critical region
     state := WANTED;
     Multicast request to all nodes (processes);
     T:= my timestamp;
```

```
        Wait until (number of replies received = (N - 1));
        state := HELD;
On receipt of a request (Tᵢ, nᵢ) at nⱼ (i ≠ j)
        if (state == HELD or (state == WANTED and
            (T, nⱼ) < (Tⱼ, nⱼ) ))
        then
                queue request from nᵢ without reply;
        else
                reply immediately to nᵢ;
        endif
To exit critical region
        state := RELEASED;
        reply to any queued requests;
```

Each node initializes its state, being outside the critical region (RELEASED). Wanting entry (WANTED) and being in the critical region (HELD) are variable states. If a node requests entry and the state of all other nodes is RELEASED, then all processes immediately reply to the request and the requesting node gains entry. If some node is in the HELD state, then that node will not reply until it has finished processing in the critical region; the requester cannot gain entry until the number of replies is equal to all other peers on the network (N − 1). If two or more nodes request the resource at the same time, the node with the lowest timestamp will be the first to collect N − 1 replies, granting entry. If two nodes have equal timestamps, evaluation of the unique node identifier will arbitrate queue ordering.

The advantages of this approach are complements to the disadvantages of the central server algorithm, albeit somewhat more complex to implement. In NDC, algorithmic approaches to mutual exclusion provide a basis for ensuring reliable resource utilization. Note, however, that neither approach made provisions for network failures, Byzantine or otherwise.

## Fault Tolerance

Recall that partial failure is one of the inherent differences between local and distributed computing. In a local computing environment, a failure is generally total, bringing down at least the application and perhaps the entire system. But in an NDC system, partial failure can occur when one component fails; such a failure may affect the correct operation of any number of other components while having no apparent affect on the operation of the rest of the system. One of the key differences in designing

NDC systems is a much greater need for software that can recover from faults and continue to operate in an acceptable manner when NDC components do inevitably fail.

Theoretical computer science has explored a number of techniques for ensuring reliability in NDC component software that is greater than that which the solitary node may itself require. Error-free software is impossible, however, at least for human designers and developers. Indeed, as Gödel and Turing have demonstrated, there are real limits to what can and cannot be computed with the models that are currently known.

Compounding matters in the NDC space, the explosive growth of networks and nodes and the convergence of wireless and mobile computing with the somewhat less intermittent Internet have given rise to a level of complexity that may yet prove an increasingly difficult challenge to reliability in software services. The provision of reliable software on the component level begs the question of reliability in composable ensembles in the wild, especially if dynamic, ad hoc software assemblies are to be envisioned. As highly desirable as innovation in software fault tolerance therefore may be, it may yet prove as elusive as the always-nascent artificial intelligence category of NDC today appears to be. But recovery from failures continues to be a growth area in the NDC theoretical computing noosphere.

## Transaction Processing

Within the context of fault-tolerant software, and related to the previous discussion of NDC mutual exclusion, is the realm of distributed transactions. Transaction processing systems, like mutual exclusion algorithms, protect critical NDC resources against simultaneous access by peer nodes. Distributed transaction systems are those that provide access to and modification of critical regions of data as though a single atomic operation were involved. (Atomic operations are either fully completed or not completed at all; as in physics, something that cannot be divided.)

Transaction processing comes from needs of businesses and is similar to business transaction. A business transaction may have a discussion and negotiation phase, during which both parties (sometimes more than two parties) determine the viability of the transaction from their own perspective and based on its specifics, which may involve, for example, delivery of some number of physical items to a certain location on a certain date at a certain price. Once the specifics of the transaction are deemed to be mutually agreeable, a contract formalizing the transaction is signed, committing all parties to the terms. Up to the point of contract signature, the parties are free to walk away from the deal and return to the state they were in before the beginning of negotiations. Once the contract is signed, however, the parties are legally bound. Transaction processing (TP) in computer science is conceptually similar.

**Transaction Properties** Transactions in computer science have specific properties that are common to all TP systems, distributed or not, as follows:

♦ *Atomic:* The operation is indivisible from an external perspective.

♦ *Consistent:* The transaction does not violate system invariants.

♦ *Isolated:* The transaction does not interfere with other concurrent transactions.

♦ *Durable:* Once committed, the transaction is permanent.

Commonly referred to as the ACID properties, these must be exhibited in TP systems of all types, including NDC TP systems. As with mutual exclusion, NDC TP systems must rely only upon message passing algorithmic approaches in order to effectively implement the ACID properties.

**Transaction Types** Transactions of the simplest type are called flat transactions, but NDC systems often require other approaches. Consider, for example, the booking of a flight that requires several airlines.

On a recent trip to a Sun developer event held in Yokohama, Japan, I flew from Reno to San Francisco and then caught a trans-Pacific flight to Tokyo. The first two legs were booked on United Airlines. Several days after the Yokohama event, I needed to travel to Shanghai, China. Since United Airlines doesn't serve the Tokyo-to-Shanghai route, I was forced to book with Japan Airlines, which doesn't have a code-sharing arrangement with United. From Shanghai I was able to book a United flight back to San Francisco and then home to Reno. My travel agent needed to book the flights as one transaction, even though two separate business transactions were required.

Conceptually, computer science knows this example as a nested transaction. Nested transactions are important in NDC because they provide a convenient means of distributing transactions across multiple nodes. A nested transaction is an assembly of a number of subtransactions; a top-level transaction may fork children that run concurrently on different nodes, to improve performance or simplify programming. That each child may also fork other nested subtransactions gives rise to problematic considerations. Since ACID properties must not be sacrificed at the top-level transaction and since it is also necessary for subtransactions, which can be nested to arbitrary depth, to make commitments before completion of the higher-level subtransaction, considerable work is involved in ensuring that all rollback data is preserved and utilized in the event the top-level transaction aborts.

Another type of transaction that is similar to but subtly different from nested transactions is the distributed transaction. Whereas a nested transaction is one in which the transaction is logically decomposed into subtransactions, a distributed transaction is logically flat but operates on distributed data. The main issue with distributed transactions is the need for separate distributed algorithms to handle data locking and commit sequences until the entire transaction is complete, which leads back to the discussion of fault-tolerant software.

## Measures of Dependability

In Chapter 3, the RAS measures of dependability were briefly discussed. In addition to those considerations, in fault tolerance in NDC software, we can add an "S," another "S," and an "M."

- The first S if for Safety, which refers to instances of systems that temporarily fail to function correctly but are still immune to catastrophic failures. Examples of systems that exhibit this need are those that control resources in the intensive care units of hospitals or the air traffic control systems at major airports. Such systems cannot fail without disastrous consequences.

- Security is another attribute of NDC fault tolerant systems, especially in light of events stemming from the September 11, 2001, attacks.

- M for Maintainability is an old measurable from the mainframe era. It refers to how easily a failed system can be repaired.

Faults are classified as transient, intermittent, or permanent. Transient or spurious faults occur once and then go away; the software in question executes successfully thereafter. Intermittent faults occur, then disappear, then reoccur, most often in an unpredictable manner. Permanent faults are those that remain until a faulty component is replaced. All faults need to be considered if fault-tolerant NDC systems can be trusted.

## Data and Component Replication

In addition to Byzantine failure recovery algorithms and Recovery Block techniques (discussed in Chapter 3), one of the main tradeoffs in fault-tolerant systems is that of data and component replication. In any NDC environment, given sufficient data, hardware, and communication channel replication, high degrees of RASSSM can be achieved; but throwing more hardware or replicated software at a problem is generally not the most cost-effective solution. Accordingly, theoretical computer science will continue to examine complex approaches to ensuring higher measures of NDC fault tolerance, while at the same time reducing the amount of resources (and complexity) required for implementations.

# Causality, Synchrony, and Time

## Event Coordination

Causality determination and clock synchronization are of critical importance to NDC as it goes forward.

Causality speaks to the order of events in time. In NDC, the lack of a central authority has historically extended to the time domain; the synchronization of clocks on a network can be problematic. But coordination of events in time is important in NDC for several reasons. Consider the TP discussion above; accurate measurement of time across nodes is vital to ensuring the ACID properties of a transaction. In fact, the essence of a contract is time; events occur at a specific, agreed-upon time, otherwise, there is no transaction. Timestamps are therefore vital to many distributed algorithms. Ricart and Agrawala's algorithm for mutual exclusion, for example, assumes that nodes on the network have some semblance of agreement with respect to time, to effectively arbitrate use of network resources.

Because causality between events is fundamental to NDC, and especially in light of the growth of asynchronous communications, some kind of clock synchronization across arbitrary networks must be achieved. Einstein demonstrated that the flow of time is relative to the observer and that even the relative order of events can be reversed on an observer basis, provided there is no physical causality between the two events.[8]

## Time Synchrony

Since the beginning of NDC, problems of clock drift and clock skew have plagued developers. Clock drift is the tendency of clocks to diverge over

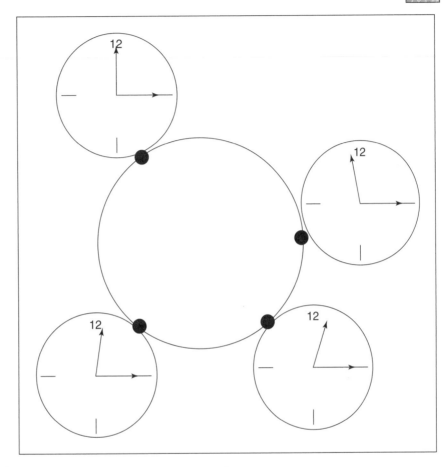

Figure 4.10  Clock skew on a network

time. No clock is perfect; the crystal-based oscillators that provide clocks for modern computer systems typically vary about $10^{-6}$ seconds/second, which means a one-second drift for every million seconds, which is a little over eleven days. Over the course of a year, that's over half a minute, which is unacceptable to most applications that rely on timestamps for accurate data processing. Clock drift gives rise to clock skew, as shown in Figure 4.10, which is the difference between the readings of clocks on a network.

In the past few years, some progress has been made in NDC clock synchronization, with new hardware and software mechanisms that allow systems to synchronize to within a few milliseconds of UTC (Coordinated Universal Time, synonymous with Greenwich Mean Time or GMT). New algorithms that use this emerging capability are starting to appear.

Progress in NDC time synchronization can be described by the steps that have occurred over time since the early days of the Internet, circa 1969:

**1. Synchronization of physical clocks.** This is the most straightforward approach. If I have a clock and you have a clock, we might simply agree to set our clocks to the same time. This approach, called internal synchronization, works well if all we are concerned with is our own two clocks and not any outside time source. As long as we understand the time implications of the messages passing between us, a periodic exchange of time data might keep us reasonably in synchronization with each other. But this does not prevent clock drift; our drift will be coordinated, but drift we inevitably will. External synchronization implies that we obtain our notion of correct time from some other system. So the two of us might defer to that external source to prevent drift and follow a similar procedure for ensuring synchronization. Clearly, however, on an arbitrary network with far more than two systems, transmission time uncertainties along with asynchronous message passing make physical clock synchronization difficult to implement and limited in effectiveness.

**2. Probabilistic synchronization.** In 1989, Flaviu Cristian published a paper entitled "Probabilistic Clock Synchronization" in which he suggested the use of a time server.[9] The server, which gets correct time information from a trusted UTC source (such as a broadcast signal), then dispatches this information to devices upon request. Since transmission times are often quite short, Cristian described the algorithm for time resolution at the client as *probabilistic*—synchronization is achieved only if the observed round-trip message latency between the server and the client is sufficiently short compared with the required accuracy. The inherent problems with the Cristian algorithm are those that any central-server approach must harbor: a single point of failure, server bottlenecks, and so on.

**3. Fault-tolerant averaging.** A variant of the Cristian algorithm is called the Berkeley algorithm.[10] Instead of a time server, one node on the network acts as a master while other nodes act as slaves. The master periodically polls each of the slaves for their notion of the correct time and observes the round-trip transmission times as well, giving it the ability to estimate the local time at each node. The master then takes a fault-tolerant average of all clocks (faulty clocks or those clocks outside a specified range are not considered in the average), and only the incremental difference in each local clock is transmitted (for example, "set your clock forward 3 milliseconds"). This approach eliminates the need for a fixed time server because any node can act as master, using a leader election approach.

**4. Network Time Protocol (NTP).** Although the Cristian and Berkeley algorithms are applicable in LANs, they cannot scale to the entire Internet. NTP was introduced in 1995 to allow nodes across the Internet to synchronize to UTC by several approaches, depending on local network characteristics. Multicast mode for high-speed LANs is supported, as is a procedure call mode similar to Cristian's algorithm. A symmetric mode intended for use by time servers within LANs is also supported. For all modes, messages are delivered unreliably by standard UDP Internet transport protocol.

Each approach achieves a progressively finer granularity of time synchronization over an arbitrary network while reducing resource consumption (either messaging or processing) on the network.

While significant progress has occurred since the early days of the Internet, it is likely that other interesting approaches to matters of time will bear investigation in theoretical computer science, especially given the growth of asynchronous message passing systems.

## Commentary

Theoretical computer science has given rise to a bevy of insights which today form the underpinnings of the World Wide Web and the nodes which provide its personality. In this chapter, we've touched on only a very few of the concepts and algorithms yielded to date. The complexities we must face as networks continue to converge will inevitably increase, making it certain that we will revisit and rely upon rigorous theoretical work. Indeed, much of what we have implemented to date, based on existing theoretical insight, is now somewhat brittle and even questionable, as mobile, intermittently connected devices marry real-time EmNets to a World Wide Web in search of tractable ontologies. While the connection between theory and practice may sometimes seem strained, each relies on the other if progress is to be made.

### Notes

1.  Nondeterministic polynomial. Informally, a computing problem is said to be NP-complete if answers can be verified quickly and a

quick algorithm to solve the problem can be used to quickly solve all other NP problems.

2. Samuel C. Kendall, Jim Waldo, Ann Woolrath, and Geoff Wyant, "A Note on Distributed Computing," Sun Microsystems Research Report TR-94-29 (1994) (http://research.sun.com/techrep/1994/abstract-29.html).

3. Ming Li and Paul Vitanyi, *An Introduction to Kolmogorov Complexity and Its Applications* (New York: Springer Verlag, 1997).

4. George Coulouris, Jean Dollimore, and Tim Kindberg, *Distributed Systems Concepts and Designs* (Essex, UK: Addison-Wesley, 2001).

5. Hagit Attiya and Jennifer Welch, *Distributed Computing* (New York: McGraw-Hill, 2000).

6. G. Ricart and A. K. Agrawala, "An optimal algorithm for mutual exclusion in computer networks," *Comms. ACM* 24.1 (1981), pp. 9–17.

7. Note that while a single node may host multiple processes, each of which may request a shared resource, identifiers can easily be extended to identify a unique process within a unique node.

8. A mind experiment involving a black hole, a ray gun, and three planets in space might even put physical causality in the realm of relativistic observations; but that discussion is beyond the scope of this volume.

9. F. Cristian, "Probabilistic Clock Synchronization," *Distributed Computing,* vol. 3, no. 3 (1989), pp. 146–58.

10. R. Gusella and S. Zatti, "The accuracy of clock synchronization achieved by TEMPO in Berkeley UNIX 4.3BSD," *IEEE Transactions Software Engineering* 15 (1989), pp. 847–53.

# NDC Protocols

# CHAPTER 5

The advent of NDC made communication protocols the essential underpinning of computing models. As all computing models, regardless of theoretical equivalence, must recognize and adjust to the implications and realities of communication, communication protocols must form part of the basis for any computing model.

Datacom protocols are the essence of the Internet. Understanding datacom at a rudimentary level should be as important to NDC developers as any language, development environment, or deployment platform consideration.

## Conceptual Background

The Church-Turing thesis states that all computing models, known or unknown, are *effectively equivalent*. What this means is that no matter which theoretical computing model you may choose, it will give rise to equivalent results that meet certain criteria, namely (where *M* is a method or procedure):[1]

1. *M* is set out in terms of a finite number of exact instructions with each instruction expressed by means of a finite number of symbols;
2. *M* will, if carried out without error, always produce the desired results in a finite number of steps;
3. *M* can (in principle) be carried out by a human being unaided by any mechanical device save paper and pencil;
4. *M* demands no insight or ingenuity on the part of the human being in question.

Turing formally approached computability from the perspective of the Turing machine, claiming that whenever there is an effective method for obtaining values from a mathematical function, that function can be computed with a Turing machine. The Church-Turing thesis extends the metaphor, asserting that any model for computation, the use of which is effective or mechanical with respect to a method as delineated above, is equivalent to any other computational model. This remains, in fact, a thesis—more than pure conjecture but less than a rigorously proven theorem. While the implications for NDC may not be immediately obvious, they are nonetheless real.

Given Kauffman's observations with respect to innovation and fitscapes, the inevitability of innovation in computing models should be assumed, despite the Church-Turing thesis. This means that Deutsch's Eighth Fallacy (the network is homogeneous) is itself subject to innovative pressures; the network will paradoxically become more heterogeneous over time rather than less so, despite good intentions, standardization efforts, and market-domination strategies to the contrary. That does not say the heterogeneity will not be expressed in new and different fashion; indeed, over time a "sedimentation" occurs from a functional perspective, as what was once a differentiator becomes the must-have-to-compete item of tomorrow, which includes computing interfaces and document structures. From a theoretical perspective, whether it be a finite-state machine, a pushdown automata, a standard Turing machine, or a Swarms computing model, the Church-Turing thesis pretty well guarantees that new networked arrays of various compute devices will continue to emerge as new problem spaces become available for innovation. The importance of interoperability, which is founded on communication protocols that must therefore be standardized, cannot be understated.

NDC interoperability, which includes protocol as well as data and document format issues, is covered later in this book. Network protocols, which serve as the communication underpinnings for interoperability, are important to understand, from both a theoretical and an implementation perspective. The history of Internet protocols is an interesting study as well.

# A Brief History: From ARPANET to the Modern Internet

The U.S. government's Advanced Research Projects Agency (ARPA) commissioned the ARPANET project in 1968, during the heyday of the Cold War. ARPA itself was formed after the 1957 launch of Sputnik, the first human-made satellite to orbit the earth. Sputnik was a creation of the now-defunct Soviet Union, and since the United States was highly reactive to Soviet developments at the time, the competitive pressures between the two nations gave rise to considerable research in many areas, including computer science. The objectives of the original ARPANET were to assist U.S. institutions in gaining experience in interconnecting computers and to improve computer science research productivity through a better sharing of resources and ideas. Military needs were also reflected in the original plans, as were scientific considerations.

From the beginning of ARPA to the first implementation of the ARPANET, considerable debate on a variety of issues, technical as well as political and organizational, delayed the ultimate awarding of the first contract to actually build such a network. At length, academic institutions were selected on the basis of either their network support capabilities or other unique resources that could be mustered. Technical capabilities were also a consideration since the development of protocols that would allow communications between a variety of types of computers was deemed a necessity for the ARPANET. The first four sites selected met the needs of that aboriginal network:

♦   Stanford Research Institute (SRI)
♦   University of California at Los Angeles (UCLA)
♦   University of California at Santa Barbara (UCSB)
♦   University of Utah (UTAH)

The original communication protocol called for an interface message processor (IMP) to be located at each site. The thinking at the time was that facilitation of communication between a wide variety of computer systems could be managed by one communication system, requiring deployment of a standard communication processor to handle the interface to the ARPANET. Thus, each site would have to write only one interface to one standard IMP. The beginnings of communication standards for the Internet were embodied in that early system, which utilized a modified Honeywell DDP-516 computer, a refrigerator-sized unit with a massive 12 KB of memory, one of the most powerful minicomputers on the market at the time. IMP-1 was delivered to UCLA two weeks before Labor Day in 1969. A few weeks later, SRI had its own IMP installed and was ready to test the first connection of the ARPANET. Using telephone lines for network communication, an undergraduate student at UCLA name Charlie Klein began a coordinated login process. The first successful message, "LO" was followed by another first: the network crashed before the G could be successfully transmitted.

From those inauspicious beginnings, the ARPANET slowly grew. Once two IMPs existed, the pioneers had to implement a working communication protocol. The initial set of host protocols included a remote login for interactive use (telnet) and a way to copy files between remote hosts (File Transfer Protocol), ancestors of similar capabilities that are still widely used every day on the Internet.

An asymmetric, client-server communication protocol was all that was initially available. Over the next few months, a symmetric host-host protocol was defined. An abstract implementation of the protocol became known as NCP (from the host-run network control program that had to be hacked into each operating system in machine-specific assembler language). That, along with telnet and FTP, seemed to be enough for a while. A seven-layer gestalt had yet to emerge in the collective consciousness of computer science.

Over the following decade, the expansion of hosts on the ARPANET was slow but steady. By 1981, 213 hosts exchanged data, with a new host added approximately every 20 days. In 1982, when TCP/IP became the communications protocol of choice for connected hosts, the term "Internet" was used for the first time, and the modern packet-switching network was truly born. That same year, coincident with the invention of TCP/IP, came the formation of a small private company called Sun Microsystems, whose first product featured a built-in TCP/IP communications stack. Since then, every product sold by Sun has been Internet-ready (no other company can make that claim for as long or for as many systems as can Sun). Sun's IPO came several years later, but the die had been cast.

From a governance perspective, the growth of the Internet has been a case study in cooperative anarchy. In 1979, the Internet Control and Configuration Board (ICCB) was formed, chartered with oversight functions of design and deployment of protocols within the connected Internet. In 1983, the ICCB was rechristened the Internet Activities Board (IAB), with an original charter similar to that of the ICCB. The IAB evolved into a de facto standards organization that effectively ratified Internet standards.

In 1986, the IAB morphed again to provide an oversight function for a number of subsidiary groups. Two primary groups emerged: the Internet Research Task Force (IRTF) to supervise research activities related to TCP/IP Internet architecture, and the IETF (the Internet Engineering Task Force) to concentrate on short- to medium-term engineering issues related to the Internet. Both are still in existence. The IETF today still serves as the global clearing-house for RFCs (request for comment), which were inherited from the aboriginal ARPANET project. RFCs are the means by which de facto Internet standards are adopted. IRTF and IETF are made up of engineers, enthusiasts, and representatives from like-minded organizations, representing virtually all global cultures today. The IETF and its supervisory body, the Internet Engineering Steering Group (IESG); the IRTF and its supervisory body, the Internet Research Steering Group (IRSG); and the IAB all operate under the auspices of the Internet Society (ISOC). The ISOC is an international nonprofit, nongovernmental, professional membership organization that focuses on Internet standards, public policy, education, and training.

By 1984, when William Gibson coined the term "cyberspace," the number of Internet hosts exceeded 1,000. Three years later, it was 10,000. On November 1, 1988, when a malicious program called the "Morris Internet Worm" (which took advantage of a design flaw in the sendmail daemon, which was easily patched) caused widespread havoc, there were approximately 60,000 Internet hosts. In 1995, the year the Network Age began, the Internet grew from roughly 4.8 to 9.5 million hosts, and URLs started appearing on television commercials. Email addresses, once the exclusive domain of computer scientists, programmers, and geeks, became more important than zip or area codes for upwardly mobile aspirational achievers, led primarily by the commercial sensibility of an under-30 generation and whisperings of dotcom riches to come. Since then, we have all learned a lot about irrational exuberance, but the Internet, despite pitfalls, is still growing.

---

Robert Morris Jr. was a graduate student in computer science at Cornell when as an experiment he released (from MIT, to mask its Cornell origin) a self-replicating, self-propagating program called a *worm* and allowed it to run free on the Internet. Morris was surprised when he realized that the worm was replicating and reinfecting machines a lot faster than he had anticipated. Nodes at locations all around the United States either crashed or became trapped in a swap-scheduler catatonia. Universities, military sites, and medical research facilities were affected, with recovery costs ranging from $200 to over $50,000 per installation. Morris was convicted of violating the computer Fraud and Abuse Act [Title 18] and received a sentence of three years of probation, 400 hours of community service, a fine of $10,050, as well as the costs of his supervision; his appeal was rejected.

---

As I write this, there are maybe 150,000,000 host systems on the Internet. An Internet host is one with a registered IP address; my systems at home, for example, all share one IP address that we multiplex through our home router. My wife and I have at least six and sometimes seven systems connected by one IP address most of the time, so the number of nodes on the Internet is considerably higher than the number of hosts would indicate, given the growing popularity of home LANs. Estimates for the number of Internet users worldwide today range from 550 to 650 million, or roughly 10 percent of all living human beings. From the perspective of Metcalfe's law, that may not be enough; given the events of September 11, 2001, it may be too many. The network metaphor works both ways, for good and for evil, another paradox in an age so riddled with paradox. But capitalism, if it is to be viable, must foster growth, which requires innovation, which demands increasing productivity and ephermalization. As such, the great potential of the Internet and NDC is as yet unrealized.

## Back at the Stack: OSI 7

Any honest examination of NDC today would not be complete without reference to existing datacom structures, for example, the stack. TCP/IP, which provided the datacom genesis of the Internet, was introduced in 1982. That same year, the International Standards Organization (ISO) published the Open Systems Interconnect (OSI) 7-layer conceptual model of data communications. The OSI 7 model wasn't adopted as a standard until 1984, so the implementation of TCP/IP predates the OSI 7 model by a few years. The OSI 7 model was designed for use with mainframes, identifying protocols necessary for those systems to communicate with devices such as modems and terminals. Although the OSI 7 model isn't directly reflected in reality as a wildly successful implementation such as TCP/IP, understanding the concepts behind OSI 7 helps put both TCP/IP and current NDC protocol research and development into better perspective.

The ISO OSI 7-layer model provides the means whereby we can meaningfully discuss the nature of datacom and how it can be conceptually approached. In the OSI 7 model, communication functions are partitioned into seven layers as shown in Figure 5.1.

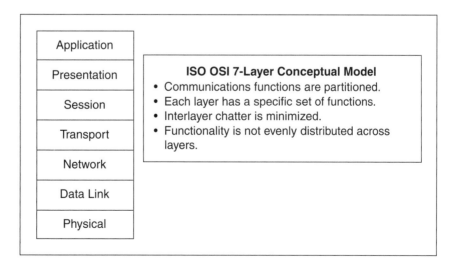

Figure 5.1 ISO OSI 7-layer conceptual model

Each layer has a specific set of functions; there is a minimization of inter-layer chatter; functionality is not evenly distributed across the layers. The rationale for taking this approach was to allow layers of technology to move forward without breaking everything else. For example, as new means of physically connecting nodes are engineered, it would be a shame to have to toss out all investments in software simply to accommodate that new means. Were it not for a conceptual datacom model like the OSI 7 stack, going from twisted pair to coax to optics to wireless would mean that everything that relies on datacom would have to be designed anew; all NDC applications would have to be rewritten. While that, in and of itself, may not necessarily be a bad thing, given the considerable investments made and anticipated in NDC, a monolithic approach was considered un-thinkable by the standards body.

In the OSI 7 model, each layer provides services to the next higher layer, including primitives and associated data. Each layer therefore relies on the next lower layer. The OSI 7 stack identifies seven distinct layers for the facilitation of datacom, as shown in Figure 5.2.

At the bottom, the Physical layer represents physical circuits and transmission of bits. Here, electrons or photons or the chirping songs of modems are simply transmitted. An understanding receiver is implied. At the Data Link layer, error detection and correction, something in the way of flow control, and the task of assembling bits into something we would call "frames" or discrete "packets" of bits occurs. The Network layer, too, contributes to flow control; it's a complex layer that facilitates the routing and transfer of data across a network, the topology of which can change in an instant.

The Transport layer provides for a logical connection—a virtual cir-cuit. This layer can either wait and ensure reliable transfer of data, or it can proceed without doing so; transmission speed is always a tradeoff with re-liability, and the Transport layer negotiates that deal.

The Session layer is where the user virtual circuit is established. The session begins, the session ends; there is work that must be done to con-struct and deconstruct the virtual circuit.

The next layer up is the Presentation layer, at which data transforma-tion can occur. A change from big-endian to little-endian, for example, can be handled at this conceptual layer.

And finally, the Application layer; the place where user programs would conceptually play. The circuit is complete at this layer; input is as expected in a format that requires no massaging or error correction, free-

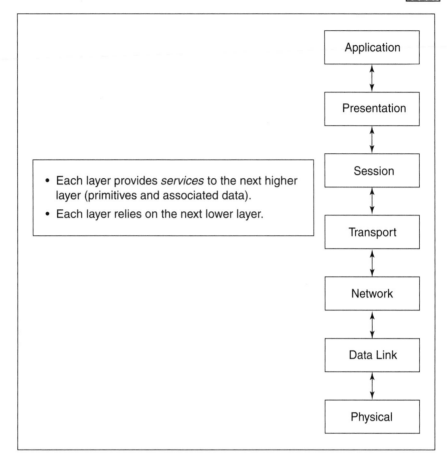

Figure 5.2  ISO OSI 7-layer separation

ing NDC applications to work without concern for routing, transmission errors, or packet assembly.

Part of the conceptual model is the idea of peer layer interaction—that one peer layer talks to another peer layer, but peer boundaries are not crossed. For example, the Transport layer on node A would not speak directly with the Data Link layer on node B. Layered functions must exist on both nodes for such a model to be valid. Peer layers communicate according to a set of rules, or protocols, that control data and dictate its format, coordination, and timing. Flow control is also implied.

Direct communication takes place only at the Physical layer; all other layers are indirect. If we were to look at node A and node B over an ar-

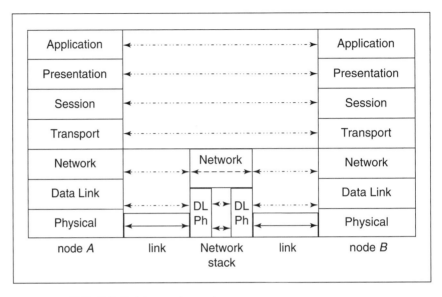

Figure 5.3 ISO OSI 7: Network stack

bitary network, there could be an indeterminate number of nodes in between that also host a Network stack, as shown in Figure 5.3. Note that the Network stack is also a node that presumably hosts software that complies with the same conceptual model; note also that in order to function as a routing node, all that node must do is ascend that stack to the Network layer in order to facilitate the further transmission of data.

Effectively, end-to-end communication is facilitated from the Transport layer up in the OSI 7 conceptual model. OSI 7 provides a means whereby we can reasonably consider evolution of datacom going forward, but implementations of that model are another matter. In the OSI 7 model, user data, data transfer, and links between host and network are clearly delineated. In the TCP/IP reality of the world, that delineation is not so clear.

# TCP/IP

The structure of TCP/IP can be visualized as shown in Figure 5.4.

The user exchange of data is bounded by Application, Presentation, and Session, the three top layers of the conceptual stack. The bottom three handle the network-dependent exchange of data. The Transport layer, the

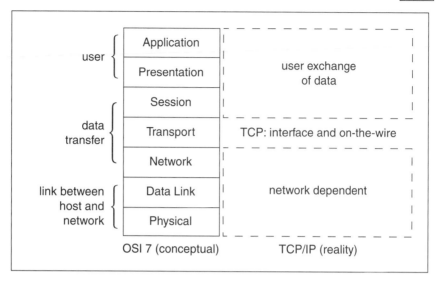

Figure 5.4  TCP/IP structure

layer that evenly divides the conceptual stack, is interesting to explore, given the implementation of TCP/IP and the reality of the world. At that layer we find the transmission control protocol (TCP), which is made of two parts: the interface (such as a socket) and the "on the wire" protocol (that which is actually delivered and managed by vendors).

In the Internet protocol suite (whence TCP and UDP are derived), the responsibilities of the top three conceptual layers—Application, Presentation, and Session—are assumed by programs that operate on those levels. As shown in Figure 5.5, this means that programs that operate on those layers must take responsibility for the tasks that have conceptually been assigned to those layers.

At the Transport layer, both TCP and UDP operate (along with other protocol options, discussed in later chapters); Transport is where the virtual circuit is made. Think of it as the warehouse for a shipping company. Packages arrive, packages leave; the responsibility of the warehouse is to ensure that "repackaging" takes place. All items from one truck from one location are unloaded and marked for a particular location and then repacked into another truck. The warehouse supervisor and the processes he oversees are analogous to the Transport layer. Packages that require signed receipts for delivery are akin to TCP; those requiring no signature

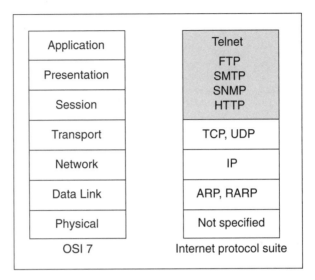

Figure 5.5  Internet protocol suite

and no assurance of error-free delivery, like bulk snail mail, are more analogous to UDP (User Datagram Protocol).

This brief discussion of the OSI 7-layer conceptual model and the TCP/IP implementation will serve as a basis for protocol discussions throughout the remaining chapters. Much of NDC is now defined and shaped by datacom protocols; indeed, the emergence of Web Services, Jini network technology, the JXTA Project, wireless and mobile computing, and much more is very much a story of protocol evolution.

# Email

Once the Internet hit its first plateau of critical mass, it started to dawn on people that it might be nice if the Internet could do something useful beyond swapping interesting research data. Two of the earliest protocols to open the Internet for use outside of strictly technical applications were RFCs 0821 (Simple Mail Transfer Protocol: SMTP) and 0822 (Standard for the format of ARPA Internet text messages). Both were introduced in August 1982 and both have since been made obsolete by subsequent definitions, but they paved the way for the beginnings of email, an application that remains one of the most useful, and widely used, application on the Internet. Reflecting the sensibilities of its name, the first SMTP protocol was simple. It focused on doing one thing really well—sending 7-bit plain text messages across the Internet Protocol Suite Network Layer protocol, called IP (Internet Protocol), between client and server. Since then, SMTP has evolved to accommodate modern messaging requirements.

In recent years, the evolution of SMTP has accelerated, reflecting the broadening use of the Internet. Extended SMTP (ESMTP) and Multi-purpose Internet Mail Extension (MIME) are two major advances that have enabled more interesting instances of spam in the modern age. ESMTP allows vendors to extend SMTP in order to manage broader classes of messages. MIME established rules for the labeling and transmission of data types beyond plain text within messages; MIME tells mail systems how to process parts of the message body so recipients see (theoretically) exactly what the sender intended. (Hence, the more interesting spam.) MIME also serves as one approach for the transmission of streaming data (audio or video).

Once email was established on the nascent Internet, some companies began to see the potential. Sun Microsystems was one of a handful of pioneers. Other early adopters (those companies that would later provide TCP/IP ports) included Digital Equipment Corporation (DEC, later acquired by Compaq), Apollo Systems (later acquired by Hewlett-Packard), Sperry-Univac (merged with Burroughs to form Unisys), IBM, Bull, Nixdorf (later acquired by Siemens), ICL (later acquired by Fujitsu) and a host of early UNIX players, most of whose names are now lost to the fickle memory of history. Along with email, phase I of Internet adoption technologies also included FTP, gopher (an indexed, early step toward HTML to facilitate searching), and news groups.

The first release of the Mosaic browser, the precursor of Netscape, wouldn't come until 1993. So Internet adoption phase I, from 1982 to 1993, was pretty well limited to academic institutions, geeks, computer scientists, programmers, and other computer enthusiasts. And yet by early 1989, in the wake of the Morris Worm, the critical need for one of the earliest agent-based (and therefore visionary) NDC application models found its fulfillment in the Simple Network Management Protocol (SNMP). There were finally enough nodes, LANs, and WANs, to merit investment in systems and network management tools and infrastructures.

At this juncture, early adopters could be classified as "commercial" in every sense of the word and had learned that resource management, which estimates claimed to have cost $15.5 million (arguably because of the Morris Worm), was simply too costly to ignore any longer; the Internet had reached a commercial level of respectability if only due to maintenance costs, not to mention national strategic value from the perspective of the U.S. government. Paradoxically, we may have Robert Morris to thank for that early wake-up call. In the following months, Internet management software was born. Note that a standard protocol was the basis for the evolution.

## Systems and Network Management Before Protocols

What specifically is management software? While some applications might have an obvious management function, such as the ability to react to and recover from a fault on an arbitrary network node, other applications might not. As local programming is intrinsically different from NDC, applications behave differently with respect to Deutsch's Eight Fallacies—some may be network aware, others may not, depending on the network-awareness of the NDC developer and the tools used during development. Any node may be host to a mixed bag of applications from a network-awareness perspective.

Based on traditional approaches, and, consequently, the capabilities expressed by existing or legacy infrastructures, the high-level functional areas for system and network management historically have been the following.

- ◆ Configuration management: inventory, configuration, and provisioning
- ◆ Fault management: reactive and proactive network fault management
- ◆ Performance management: number of packets dropped, timeouts, collisions, CRC errors
- ◆ Security management: not traditionally covered by SNMP-based applications
- ◆ Accounting management: cost management and charge-back assessment
- ◆ Asset management: equipment, facility, and administration personnel statistics
- ◆ Planning management: trend analysis to help justify a network upgrade or bandwidth increase

Management applications built since the adoption of TCP/IP tended to address network challenges in one or more of these areas. Noticeably absent from this functional list is the general area of storage management.

The need for the management of data itself came during a later phase of Internet adoption, after the PC's stealth invasion of the corporate desktop, which began in earnest in the early 1990s.

Sun Microsystems was one of the pioneers in software management; the SunNet Manager (SNM), first shipped by Sun in the late 1980s, was one of the first market entries in the wake of the Morris Worm. SNM provided a cost-effective, extensible product that could expand to meet the needs of businesses in the early 1990s, when the networking of smaller systems emerged from strategic goal to commercial health. In November 1997, Sun announced that no further development work would be funded for SNM, though echoes of it still remain in various instantiations, perhaps even now a cash cow too lucrative to slaughter.

Novell, a pioneer in networking itself, was also one of the early entrants in the management space, although its focus on a more proprietary network protocol (SPX/IPX) instead of TCP/IP proved to be an evolutionary dead end. That, and having the unfortunate karma of having its technology targeted by Microsoft, left Novell decimated, compared to their once enviable position in early PC LANs.

Today, a number of players exist in the management space, most of whom have provided point-to-point solutions within proprietary frameworks (although the advent of Web Services investments has once again changed the landscape). Computer Associates, IBM (Tivoli), Hewlett-Packard (Open View), and BMC represented the bulk of the big business players when it came to enterprise-scale management framework packages during the late 90s and early 00s. Other providers included Platinum, Cisco, Microsoft, and, of course, Sun Microsystems with its Enterprise Manager products.

The point-to-point approach gets a little dicey in a heterogeneous environment. Consider the network in Figure 5.6. Each node in the network—each network appliance, whether it be an end-user system, a server, an array of storage devices, a printer, a wireless Internet appliance, or a network enabler, such as a hub or a router—requires some form of management during its service cycle. Each appliance, coming from a different vendor, has its own interface. As such, point-to-point players in the management space must provide a solution for each possible connection within the network. Just as a network's value increases exponentially with the number of nodes, so do the management headaches. Web Services will make matters either better or worse, depending on the evolution of the management fitscape in the wake of emerging NDC innovation pressures.

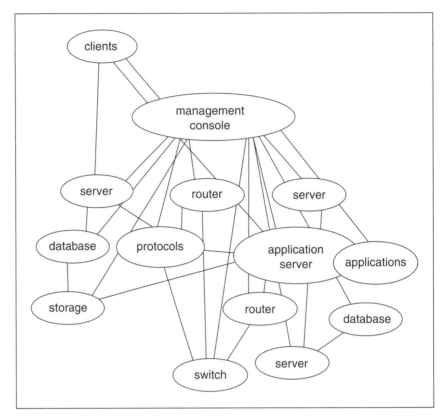

Figure 5.6 Point-to-point systems and network management

At this juncture, several players in the management fitscape are scrambling to plug a hole in the Web Services story: the promise of composable components exposes something of a transaction-assurance nightmare if examined in the cold light of day. Given this problem, one healthy first step toward ensuring a viable yet interoperable NDC infrastructure that can actually evolve beyond an N-tier application model is a systems and network management infrastructure that is Web Services aware.

## SNMP and UDP

The systems and network management fitscape is not without standards. As alluded to earlier, SNMP was the first from the IETF to emerge to facilitate some management activities.

The odd story of SNMP's ascendancy didn't begin with the Morris Worm. Internet standards take a bit longer to mature than the the the few months that elapsed between November 1988 and and February 1989, when the first two SNMP RFCs were accepted. The genesis of SNMP was earlier, in the second half of the 1980s, when the task force concluded that, simply due to its size, the rapidly growing Internet could no longer be managed on an ad hoc basis, and decided to use OSI's Common Management Information Protocol (CMIP). The Open Systems Interconnect Reference Model (whence OSI 7 hails), had been proposed in 1974 by ISO (the International Organization for Standardization) to address problems in networking that arise when proprietary approaches prevail. To fit CMIP into the TCP/IP-based Internet, a number of minor changes were needed; the modified protocol was called CMOT (Common Management Over TCP/IP). But despite the apparent good fit, the development of OSI management took quite some time.

Because the IETF didn't want to just sit and wait for results, it decided to further develop the already existing Simple Gateway Monitoring Protocol (SGMP), which was defined in 1987 by an RFC to manage the ever-expanding router network on the Internet, and use that modified protocol, which would become SNMP, as a stopgap solution. SGMP was quite short-lived dealing only with router management. But it did provide a basis for a broader management protocol, and thus SNMP traces its roots to SGMP. As a short-term solution, SNMP seemed to do the trick.

The task force intended to eventually replace SNMP with a structural solution based on OSI's CMIP. But the IETF was surprised, to say the least. Standards can become established in many ways, market adoption among them (even without monopoly at the helm); SNMP was the right solution at the right time, and adopters emerged in droves. Within a few years, SNMP demonstrated that it could satisfy the protocol demands of many managed applications and thus dealt with the majority of devices linked to the Internet at that time. As a result, today's producers of many datacom devices still incorporate SNMP by default. In short, the protocol has become one of the most important standards for network management. The unexpected success of SNMP was complete in 1992, when the IETF dropped its original plan of replacing SNMP with CMOT. Given the subsequent slow acceptance of the CIM (the Common Information Model from the OMG) it now seems unlikely that OSI will ever be used for network management.

SNMP uses UDP as the transport mechanism for SNMP messages, as diagrammed in Figure 5.7.

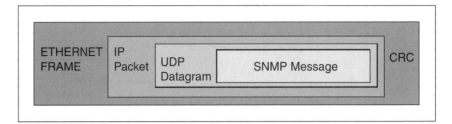

Figure 5.7 Transport mechanism for SNMP messages

In the TCP/IP suite, UDP allows application programs to send a datagram to other application programs on a remote machine. Basically, UDP is an unreliable transport service; delivery and duplicate detection are not guaranteed, as with TCP. UDP uses IP to transport a message between the machines, as do TCP and a lot of other Transport layer protocols. It is connectionless and does not use acknowledgments, establish flow control, or control the order of arrival. As a consequence, UDP messages sometimes get lost. But the tradeoff at the Transport layer is reliability versus cost (overhead); thus, the least intrusive choice for a management protocol is UDP as the transport mechanism. There are clear implications to NDC developers who play at the Transport layer: SNMP messages, like any others that utilize UDP, can be lost.

Clearly, the designers of SNMP could have elected to use TCP rather than UDP if data loss were a serious enough problem for management applications. But management issues are generally not that time critical. If an agent raises an alarm and does not hear back from a known manager in an arbitrary amount of time, it can simply raise another alarm. By the same token, if a manager polls an agent and does not hear back, another effort to poll the agent can easily be made without significant impact on either the manager or the agent, depending upon the nature of the relationship and the resources involved. For most management issues that rely on SNMP, UDP does the job and has the least overall impact.

SNMP succeeded thanks to a simple set of attractive features:

♦ It can be used to manage (almost) every node linked to the Internet.

♦ Implementation costs are minimal.

♦ By defining new managed objects, it easily extended its management capabilities.

In addition, SNMP is fairly robust. Despite the occasional lost datagram, management applications using SNMP proved effective in solving early network growth problems as the modern Internet-dependent enterprise evolved. Even in the event of a partial failure of the network, well-programmed management frameworks can often continue functioning.

And yet, even with a standard like SNMP, the basic problems of managing a heterogeneous network environment remain. Granted, every vendor on the network can agree to communicate via TCP/IP and to use SNMP when it comes to exposed management interfaces. But fundamentally, without common agreement on exposed managed-object properties, gnarly point-to-point solutions will naturally evolve, just as they have over the past decade. As mentioned earlier, the recent upswing in Web Services investment compounds matters further, perhaps creating opportunities for profitable problem solving.

## Early Network Agents

Protocols form the basis for any meaningful evolution of the Internet. Systems and network management frameworks and applications are just an early example of the relationship between protocols, problems, and profitable opportunities. That same pioneering approach to an application framework gave rise to what was arguably the first Internet agent-based model as well.

Agents, as discussed in Chapter 3, are separate entities that act on behalf of other entities. Early systems and network management implementations, of necessity, pioneered approaches to NDC agents. Consider the problems inherent simply in backing up, or making copies of, documents that are distributed over a local heterogeneous environment; once critical documents leave the domain of the central server, the need for an agent technology arises.

From the perspective of a backup server or that central place in which an organization wants to maintain timely copies of critical documents, it is necessary to dispatch an agent to act for each node on behalf of the server. Those agents need to accomplish much in the way of information collection, analysis, distillation, and state determination, and report that information back to the central server. The agents are subsequently responsible for scheduling and supervising the transfer of only the appropriate documents across the network for central server backup. Inherent questions include the following:

1. Which documents (or portions of documents) are candidates for backup?

2. If all documents are always candidates for backup, what is the cost in network overhead, and can all nodes take this approach to ensure adequate backup?

3. What is the local node environment (which by definition will be different than that of the central server) with respect to filesystems, data and time representation, file access characteristics (including permissions and namespace rules), and available resources?

4. What translation mechanisms are needed to preserve document integrity during and after backup?

5. What are the document restore implications?

6. How often are backups warranted? When should they be scheduled? Are means of backup scheduling available on the node in question, or must scheduling be the domain of the backup server?

7. How are backups initiated? In what format are documents transmitted? What actions are taken when backups fail?

Questions like these must be answered in any design of an NDC application that would offer backup services in an arbitrary heterogeneous LAN, which is just one example of the kinds of services to be considered in the systems and network management space. And this is assuming that proper protocols (such as TCP/IP and SNMP) are already in place. A generalized approach to agent technology was not part or parcel of the SNMP work, nor was it intended to be. Systems and network management frameworks therefore needed to create agent mechanisms in order to effectively provide services—and they did. But those frameworks are very much like the point-to-point example given above. Each agent was specifically crafted for the species of node to which it would be applied.

Early management frameworks were constrained to some workable subset of node types in the modern LAN. For example, if I'm a framework vendor, I may provide an agent to manage a SPARC/Solaris 2.7 or greater system, but not one for any earlier version, despite the fact that some nodes running earlier versions may remain on some networks. Once a node is devoted to a given task, which it does well, why disturb it? The adage "If it ain't broke, don't fix it" applies fully to NDC application provisioning. As such, the vast number of node configurations on the Internet tends to exceed even the most ambitious point-to-point type solutions.

Generalized agent frameworks, while imaginable with the Java platform and promised by the Semantic Web, remain the stuff of Internet fiction. Systems and network management implementations have had to solve some small part of the problem in order to provide services of sufficient value to carve out a profitable market niche. But in the end, pioneers only mark rough trails that others may one day pave.

# Later Players at the OSI 7 Transport Layer

In the context of systems and network management, there is much more to say in the way of implementations and protocols. Discussions of the CIM and relationships with SNMP implementations have not been included. From the perspective of network protocols, the SNMP segue serves to illustrate an important point regarding protocols, problems, and profits.

The point was made earlier that the Transport layer of the OSI 7 conceptual model was one of considerable interest (SNMP plays at the TCP/IP Application layer, which in TCP/IP covers all three of the top OSI 7 layers, or the user data area). Much work is done or not done at the Transport layer, depending on application needs. It's interesting to note that the only standard datacom layer that is specifically cited in Deutsch's fallacies is the Transport layer (transport cost is zero). Like the shipping warehouse described earlier, or a hub in the hub-and-spoke configuration of a modern airline, the Transport layer eliminates the need for point-to-point networks, which must be avoided if the Internet is to be viable. But as Deutsch has asserted, this flexibility does not come without cost.

IP plays at the Network layer. IP is a connectionless protocol featuring some type-of-service options (such as IPv6 over IPv4), but much of the action—and therefore cost—occurs at the Transport level. One 8-bit field in the IP header contains the Transport layer encapsulated protocol assigned to that given packet. TCP is protocol number 6 from the IP perspective; UDP is Transport protocol 17. An 8-bit field can specify up to 256 different protocols, so there is plenty of room for others at Transport.

A number of other protocols beyond TCP and UDEP have been standardized over the years, many of which are available in the Internet Protocol Suite. Many purposes would be served at Transport, including options like Transport Multiplexing (TMux, protocol 18), Host Monitoring Protocol (HMP, protocol 20) and Multicast Transport Protocol (MTP, protocol 92).

The following protocols are currently assigned an IP Protocol number and can therefore play at the OSI 7 Transport layer:

| | |
|---|---|
| AH | IP Authentication Header |
| AX25 | Internet Protocol Encapsulation of AX25 Frames |
| CBT | Core Based Trees |
| EGP | Exterior Gateway Protocol |
| ESP | Encapsulating Security Payload |
| GGP | Gateway to Gateway Protocol |
| GRE | Generic Routing Encapsulation |
| HMP | Host Monitoring Protocol |
| ICMP | Internet Control Message Protocol |
| ICMPv6 | Internet Control Message Protocol for IPv6 |
| IDPR | Inter-Domain Policy Routing Protocol |
| IFMP | Ipsilon Flow Management Protocol |
| IGMP | Internet Group Management Protocol |
| IP | IP Encapsulation (useful for Wireless/Mobile hosts) |
| IPPCP | IP Payload Compression Protocol |
| IRTP | Internet Reliable Transaction Protocol |
| MEP | Minimal Encapsulation Protocol |
| MOSPF | Multicast Open Shortest Path First |
| MTP | Multicast Transport Protocol |
| NARP | NBMA Address Resolution Protocol |
| NETBLT | Network Block Transfer |
| NVP | Network Voice Protocol |
| OSPF | Open Shortest Path First Routing Protocol |
| PGM | Pragmatic General Multicast |
| PIM | Protocol Independent Multicast |
| PTP | Performance Transparency Protocol |
| RDP | Reliable Data Protocol |
| RSVP | Resource ReSerVation Protocol |
| SCTP | Stream Control Transmission Protocol |
| SDRP | Source Demand Routing Protocol |
| SKIP | Simple Key management for Internet Protocol |
| ST | Internet Stream Protocol |
| TCP | Transmission Control Protocol |
| TMux | Transport Multiplexing Protocol |
| UDP | User Datagram Protocol |
| VMTP | Versatile Message Transaction Protocol |
| VRRP | Virtual Router Redundancy Protocol |

Each Transport layer protocol features attributes germane to solving certain specific NDC application tasks, providing a rationalized basis for growth of Internet usefulness and scope. But our examination of Transport layer needs is far from complete. Indeed, many current NDC standardization efforts are reexamining Tranport layer needs and costs, as the network metaphor extends further and further toward the edges of innovation. We'll come back to Transport issues and potential with comparisons of competing NDC frameworks, as Transport assumptions and needs must be meaningfully addressed by real implementations.

## Note

1.  plato.stanford.edu/entries/church-turing/

# CHAPTER 6

# NDC Messaging

Once communication protocols are established, conversations can commence. The basic assumption of communication is that both a sender and a receiver exist and agree to an extent on protocol, proper grammar and syntax, and processing capability. The essential ingredient of communication, however, is the message itself. Without the message, there can be no semantic agreement; with the message, understanding can begin.

Internet protocols provide the basis for NDC applications communication, as we saw in Chapter 5. But it takes more than protocols to facilitate the meaningful sharing of information. While protocols give some form to datacom capabilities, it is the purpose of communication that ultimately gives shape to the design of semantics and the desire for conversation.

Within a competitive, ceaselessly innovative fitscape, the nature of conversations and the semantic milieu in which they are conveyed may be in a state of constant flux. Some general communication models seem to be long-lived, however, and may therefore be universal, at least insofar as NDC is concerned. Some, too, transcend the protocols upon which they are built, giving credence to the original design principles and motivations behind the OSI 7-layer conceptual model.

What is the purpose of software? Beyond the broadest and most general sense, this question must be answered for each case, despite the risk of intellectual marginalization. Software does indeed have a purpose, though that purpose is served only through market or design requirements specific to the individual projects.

Although a larger software teleology may escape our view, we know that software is a player within various fitscapes—economically, socially, and technically—and must obey any common rule set governing these dynamic positive feedback systems, to the extent that such rules can be discerned. If we can say that software evolves, it must be constrained by the forces inherent in the system in which it evolves.

If we view the three metatrends—Moore's, Metcalfe's, and Gilders's laws—as forces that shape the software fitscape and are made manifest in specific terms, we might also speculate that any larger teleological vector for NDC software is directed by these three laws. Opportunities explored through NDC innovation can be considered as a function of the interaction of these three forces.

## The Essence of Communication

In essence, the NDC fitscape has given rise to several forms of messaging that are based on standardized protocols that are universally applicable in application development. Communication, which represents not only the transmission of information but the receipt and ultimate understanding of it as well, can be viewed in a manner akin to the OSI 7 conceptual model, as shown in Figure 6.1.

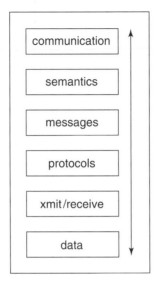

Figure 6.1  Conceptualizing communications

The point above cannot be overemphasized: *communication represents both transmission and receipt (and understanding) of information.* This may seem obvious, but the point needs be made precisely, if only because the theories of information upon which we rely for modern datacom—which tend not to include transmitter and receiver in the same equation—are descriptive of an approach that could be classified as a "transmission model" for communication. Shannon's information theory gives rise to a conduit metaphor for communication: the *source* translates thoughts into words and sends the words to a *receiver,* which then translates them into thoughts.

The notion of *transmission* and *receipt,* and the underlying metaphor of placing an object in a container and sending it through a conduit of sorts, may be misleading, however. Even after a message is sent, I presumably still have it; the receiver, who removes the object from the container, has in fact received a copy. This model also raises a question it was never intended to address: how does the object get into the container, and get out? More precisely, how do we put meaning into words, and how does someone else extract that same meaning from those words?

This semantic puzzle is as inherent in node-to-node communication as in head-to-head communication. By design, a transmission model does not deal with meaning, but communication represents receipt and understanding of information as well as transmission. Ironically, Shannon's

*The Mathematical Theory of Communication*[1] therefore leaves the question of *communication* itself out of the equations, even while the ability to transmit messages is essentially enabled—another paradox of the Network Age.

Shannon's brilliant work provided the means to quantify and facilitate data communication in real-world environments that regularly include noise, signal decay, and erroneous attributes, a foundation upon which higher-level protocols could be built. Given these protocols and the necessary message transmission capabilities, patterns of messaging grew, eventually giving rise to something in the way of genuine communication. Several winners in the messaging fitscape bear examination—patterns of messaging that are useful, common, and universal.

## Message Passing

From the genesis of the ARPANET through the modern Internet and wireless, mobile nodes, the one common thread has been message passing. Even during the dramatic growth of the Internet since the mid-1990s , the single most popular slice of the programming pie has been the essential passing of messages. The very notion of interoperability, the battle cry of Web Services models, is based on the simple concept of putting the object in a container so as to make it a message. That, in fact, is the essence of Web Services model: converting human-readable Web pages into messages. Once data is objectified and transformed into messages, the successful transmission of those messages to one or more receivers (which may also include routing at or above the OSI 7 transport layer) can be undertaken.

Message passing is the basis for all data transfer, which includes RPC as well as executable objects. Once a node decides to access or share data that is not in memory but physically within reach (that is, outside a high-speed bus or proprietary data link mechanism), a message must be passed. While there are many interesting and useful variations, that simple concept is the fundamental constituent of NDC. (Formalization of message passing has been one of the key enablers of parallel processing systems as well, though not necessarily those tied to NDC communication protocols.)

It should be clear that the approach provided by Shannon's simple model is not as robust or useful as those that drive datacom today. Indeed, as we've seen in the discussions of protocols, there is much in the way of error correction, stochastic analysis, and protocol-laden work that takes place on behalf of the message, with more to come as new Internet standards emerge. But message passing will remain NDC's essence, our anchor in a sea of NDC change.

The passing of NDC messages can take many forms. Just as the type of data that is transmitted is germane to the operation, so is the form of transfer. Broadcasting a message, for example, is a much different implementation than a one-to-one transfer. And timing naturally affects the nature of messages. A complex set of implementations arises from the simple transmission model, based on three general message considerations:

♦ Data transformation

♦ Synchrony

♦ Routing

These three considerations tend to differentiate the various flavors of message passing patterns that are commonly used today.

## Shared Memory Versus Cooked Messages

In general, NDC messages are used in one of two ways, as shown in Figure 6.2: a node sees either a shared memory, the access semantics for which are not significantly different from those used for local memory, or various "cookings"—manipulations and transformations—of the messages themselves; which become the means of creating a shared memory. Within each of these general patterns are further specializations with respect to the message considerations listed above.

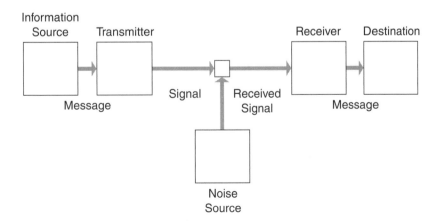

Figure 6.2 Message patterns

The reification of messages at each point along the way is essential, from a conceptual perspective, as a function of the cooking points at which message transformation operations occur. In general terms, the flow of messages over time is not bound to a specific or solitary operation or ordering at any of the potential cooking points. Nor is there any specific limit on cooking-point operations. As such, data-type classification or transformation, for example, can theoretically take place at a number of stops along the way, even in a synchronous message passing environment. The same can be said of potential routing operations.

Recall that the Transport level can provide a number of protocol-level options, including levels of message reliability, nonrepudiation, trustworthiness, and security. Operations can be glued atomically and often can be executed asynchronously, that is, if causality is not implied or required, two similar operations can transform an arbitrary message at two completely different stops along the message conduit. The exercise of such choices is both the art of NDC programming and the bane of framework providers who would sugar Deutsch's Fallacies with interface candy.

## Data Transformation

Paradoxically, XML is the culture in which we now grow framework-independent data, and in which we can implement operations specific to frameworks dependent on document types. The concept of data-type transformation is probably more accurately described as document-type transformation; data-typing on a language level is orthogonally germane to the data transformation that occurs in message passing, and RPC alludes operationally to that relationship. But the transformation of data on a per-document basis is operationally essential to message passing on the Internet and the nodes that feed it. For example, the encryption and decryption of a message requires sophisticated data transformations that must occur in a reliable, trustworthy, ordered manner. That cooking will, by definition, occur at multiple points distributed over time and resources. Some of these transformations may be more reliable than others, and that in turn affects overall application performance.

Regardless of whether a distributed shared memory view is available, interoperable data may require transformation in order to facilitate processing within a given framework. Beyond encryption, other examples of document transformation include Java-to-XML processing, metadata wrappers and containers, and style sheet transformations with approaches like XSLT.

Custom document generators benefit many NDC projects. (The term *document* in the context of NDC may include various artifacts.) The wide variety of activities in any software development effort leads to the production of documents in many forms. Whether it be a source programming language file, the compiled version of the source, the control files that facilitate compilation, or the messages generated by the running program, the concept of document transformation is essential. From the perspective of developing code alone, document transformation allows a higher degree of automation. The benefits of this approach can include enhanced provisioning, model-driven programming, and a higher degree of consistency driven by systematic document generation enforced at key points.

With ongoing XML extension, standardization efforts, and the growing availability of tools supporting those standards, it has now become possible to generate multiple types of documents. For example, XML document-transformation technology has made it easier to develop custom code generators in application development projects. As such, the interoperability of platforms and frameworks is theoretically enhanced.

# Marshalling Data

Different types of computers handle data in different ways. One of the most common transformations of network data is from the representation used by the application into a form suitable for transmission over a network, and vice versa. Encoding/decoding data for transmission is sometimes called marshalling/unmarshalling. This terminology comes from the RPC world, in which the client node invokes a procedure with a set of arguments that must then be brought together and appropriately ordered (marshalled) to form a network message.

The big-endian and little-endian transformations—named for a tale from *Gulliver's Travels*, in which two communities were in conflict over which end of an egg to broach for effective consumption—are a good example of the kinds of data transformations that must occur if interoperability among heterogeneous networked nodes is to be possible. The Motorola 680x0 is an example of big-endian architecture, the Intel 80x86 an example of little-endian architecture; internal storage and processing of data is different on the two different architectures. Take, for example the hexidecimal integer value 0x12345678. The Motorola's big-endian architecture sends that value as 12.34.56.78., whereas the Intel's little-endian architecture sends it as 78.56.34.12. Both are "correct," depending on the assumptions made; as with the communities in Swift's novel, it is a religious matter and neither approach is sacred.

Another reason for marshalling is that application programs are written in different languages, and—even more insidious—there may be more than one compiler for a given language. Since compilers may have a fair amount of latitude in how structures are represented in memory, such as how much padding they put between fields, the simple transmission of a structure from one node to another requires marshalling; even if both nodes are of the same architectural family and the programs are written in the same language, the compiler on the destination node might align the structure's fields differently.

# Document Transformation

In addition to marshalling and unmarshalling, other forms of message transformation are required in NDC. To the extent that a message consists of an assembly of structured symbols, document transformation is synonymous with message transformation; the absolute structure of a message is arguably a proper subset of all possible document types, depending on document taxonomy. But it is safe to say that a message can enjoin transformation as can a document. As such, document-transformation technologies can be viewed as message filters as much as processing and storage options.

The instantiations of NDC messaging constitute an active, evolving fitscape. For example, from a Java perspective, relevant document-transformation/messaging technologies include those provided by the Java XML Pack from Sun among which are the following:

- ◆ Java API for XML Messaging enables NDC developers to send and receive XML messages based on SOAP 1.1 with attachments.

- ◆ Java API for XML Processing enables developers to process XML documents by providing support for the XML processing standards SAX, DOM, and XSLT.

- ◆ Java API for XML Registries provides a uniform and standard Java API for interacting with XML registries such as UDDI and ebXML Registry/Repository.

- ◆ Java API for XML-based RPC enables Java technology developers to build Web applications and Web Services incorporating XML-based remote procedure call (RPC) functionality according to the SOAP 1.1 specification.

♦ Java API for XML Binding will provide for Java-to-XML and XML-to-Java document transformations.

The Java XML Pack provides an essential bridge between portable behavior (as exemplified by Java objects) and portable data (as encoded by XML). This combination is essential for NDC interoperability going forward, and is one of the cornerstones of next generation NDC development, whether it be Web Services, the Semantic Web, or other organic approaches covered later in this book.

# Synchrony

As discussed in previous chapters, NDC message passing employs two basic forms of synchrony: synchronous and asynchronous. An asynchronous message-passing model has traditionally been applied to loosely coupled nodes, generally found in WANs, whereas a synchronous message passing model is more of an idealization in which some amount of timing information about the network is assumed to be known (such as the upper bounds of message delay). Strictly speaking, an asynchronous model is less realistic in modern NDC environments. Synchronous message passing has a long list of implementations and is somewhat easier from a programming standpoint, giving rise to less complexity. But asynchronous message passing may offer advantages that can make the extra implementation effort worthwhile.

## XML-RPC

The RPC mechanism, long the message passing modality of choice in NDC, serves as one of the simplest and best examples of synchronous message passing. With XML-RPC, the forerunner of SOAP, much in the way of NDC development can be facilitated with what has to be one of the simplest interface approaches currently available. XML-RPC is a specification and a set of implementations that allow software running on disparate operating systems on nodes running in various environments to make procedure calls over the Internet. Using HTTP for transport and XML for encoding, designers made XML-RPC as simple as possible while still allowing complex data structures to be packaged as synchronous messages.

An XML-RPC message is an HTTP-POST request; the body of the request is in XML. A procedure executes on the server; the value it returns is also encoded in XML. Procedure parameters can be a number of data types, including scalars, numbers, strings, and dates, and can also be complex record. List structures are also supported. An XML-RPC request might appear as follows: [2]

```
POST /RPC2 HTTP/1.0
User-Agent: Frontier/5.1.2 (WinNT)
Host: betty.userland.com
Content-Type: text/xml
Content-length: 181

<?xml version="1.0"?>
<methodCall>
 <methodName>examples.getStateName</methodName>
 <params>
  <param>
   <value><i4>41</i4></value>
   </param>
  </params>
 </methodCall>
```

The first five lines in the example are the header. The format of the URI in line 1 is not specified. (In the example, the URI is /RPC2, which tells the server to route the request to the RPC2 responder). The URI line might be empty (a single slash) if the server handles only XML-RPC calls. If the server handles a mix of incoming HTTP requests, the URI helps route the request to the program on the server node that handles XML-RPC requests. A User-Agent and Host must be specified; in the example, these are Frontier/5.1.2 and betty.userland.com. The Content-Type is text/xml. The Content-Length must be specified and must be correct.

The balance of the XML-RPC message is the payload, which is encoded in XML and consists of a single <methodCall> structure. The <methodCall> must contain a <methodName> subitem, which is a string containing the name of the method to be called. The string may only contain identifier characters, upper- and lower-case A–Z, the numeric characters, 0–9, underscore, dot, colon, and slash.

It's entirely up to the server to decide how to interpret the characters in a methodName. For example, the methodName could be the name of a file containing an executable script, the name of a cell in a database table, or the path to a file contained within a hierarchy of folders and files. If the procedure call has parameters, the <methodCall> must contain a <params> subitem. The <params> subitem can contain any number of <param> entries, each of which has a <value>. A <value> can be scalars. Types are indicated by nesting the value inside one of a set of tags, which includes the <i4> tag, which indicates a four-byte, signed integral value.

The response format is just as simple. An example of a response to an XML-RPC request follows:

```
HTTP/1.1 200 OK
Connection: close
Content-Length: 158
Content-Type: text/xml
Date: Fri, 17 Jul 1998 19:55:08 GMT
Server: UserLand Frontier/5.1.2-WinNT

<?xml version="1.0"?>
<methodResponse>
 <params>
  <param>
   <value><string>South Dakota</string></value>
   </param>
  </params>
 </methodResponse>
```

Unless a lower-level error occurs, the response header will always return 200 OK. The Content-Type is text/xml. Content-Length must be present and correct.

The body of the response is a single XML structure, a <method Response>, which can contain a single <params>, which contains a single <param>, which contains a single <value>. The <methodResponse> could also contain a <fault>, which contains a <value>, which is a <struct> containing two elements: one named <faultCode> (an <int>) and one named <faultString> (a <string>). A <methodResponse> cannot contain both a <fault> and a <params>.

XML-RPC is a simple, extensible technology that provides for synchronous message passing in a heterogenous networked environement. Note that marshalling and unmarshalling for XML-RPC are assumed to occur as a function of transmission and receipt of messages.

## Java API for XML Messaging (JAXM)

From the simplicity of XML-RPC, NDC messaging runs the gamut to the complextities of problems addressed by interfaces like JAXM. JAXM messages also use XML, conforming to the SOAP 1.1 and SOAP with Attachments specifications, which prescribe the format for messages and also specify some things that are required, optional, or not allowed. With the JAXM API, developers can create XML messages that conform to the SOAP specifications by making Java API calls.

An XML document has a hierarchical structure with elements, subelements, sub-subelements, and so on. Many JAXM classes and interfaces represent XML elements in a SOAP message and have the word "element" or "SOAP" or both in their names.[3] There are two main types of SOAP messages: those that have attachments and those that do not. The *parts* of the SOAP message are referred to as just that.

A SOAP message may include one or more attachment parts in addition to the SOAP part. The SOAP part may contain only XML content; if any of the content of a message is not in XML format, it must occur in an attachment part. If a SOAP message is intended to contain an image file, for example, the message must have an attachment part for it. Note than an attachment part can contain any kind of content, including data in XML format.

The following outline shows the high-level structure of a SOAP message that has two attachments, one containing plain text and one containing an image.

```
I. SOAP message
   A. SOAP part
      1. SOAP envelope
         a. SOAP header (optional)
         b. SOAP body
   B. Attachment part (content is plain text)
   C. Attachment part (content is an image file)
```

JAXM provides the AttachmentPart class to represent the attachment part of a SOAP message. A SOAPMessage object automatically has a SOAPPart object and its required subelements, but because Attachment Part objects are optional, they must be created and added accordingly.

So far, JAXM is just a tad more complex than XML-RPC. But one of the distinct features JAXM provides is asynchronous messaging opportunities, which brings messaging providers into the discussion. All JAXM messages are sent and received over a connection, which can go directly to a particular destination or to a messaging provider. A messaging provider is a service that handles the transmission and routing of messages and provides features not available to direct connectors to the ultimate destination; the service works behind the scenes to keep track of messages and see that they are sent to the proper destination or destinations.

One of the most frequently touted benefits of using a messaging provider is that an application need not be aware of it. NDC developers can write applications that conform to the JAXM APIs, and the right things happen. For example, when a message is sent by a call to the ProviderConnection.send method, the messaging provider receives the message and works with other parts of the communication infrastructure to perform various tasks, depending on what the message's header contains and how the messaging provider itself has been implemented. The result is that the message arrives at its final destination without the NDC application being aware of any of the details involved in accomplishing the delivery.

JAXM also enables programmers to plug in additional protocols that are built on top of SOAP. A JAXM provider implementation is not required to implement features beyond those required by SOAP 1.1 and SOAP with Attachments, but it is free to incorporate other standard protocols, called profiles, that are implemented on top of SOAP. The ebXML Transport, Routing, and Packaging V1.0 — Message Service Specification, (ebXML TR&P), for example, defines levels of service that are not included in the two SOAP specifications. A messaging provider that is implemented to include ebXML capabilities on top of SOAP capabilities is said to support an ebXML profile. A messaging provider may support multiple profiles, but an application can use only one at a time and must have a prior agreement with each of the parties to whom it sends messages about what profile is being used.

A messaging provider works continuously. A JAXM client may make a connection with its provider, send one or more messages, and then close the connection; the provider stores each message and then sends it, perhaps resending a failed transmission until it is successfully delivered or until the threshold for the number of resends is reached. The provider also stays in a waiting state, ready to receive any messages that are intended for the client, and it stores them for forwarding when the client connects again. In addition, the provider generates error messages as needed and maintains a log in which messages and their related error messages are stored.

## Advantages of the Messaging Provider Approach

Clearly, the messaging provider approach gives rise to an asynchronous message-passing model in NDC environments. When a messaging provider is used, a message can be sent to one or more intermediate destinations before going to the final recipient; the delay in passing the message can be indeterminate. These intermediate destinations, called *actors*, are specified in the message's SOAPHeader object. Assume, for example, that a message is an incoming Purchase Order. The header might route the message to the order input desk, the order confirmation desk, the shipping desk, and the billing department. Each of these destinations is an actor that will take the appropriate action, remove the header information relevant to it, and send the message to the next actor. The default actor is the final destination, so if no actors are specified, the message is routed to the final recipient. If intermediate actors are specified, time considerations may be implicit—for example, a service-level agreement for input of an order may be implicit for the business in question—but the asynchronous nature of the message is a given.

As we have seen, asynchronous messaging is inherently more complex than synchronous messaging. With synchronous messaging, an atomic success/failure model is implied: either the message was transmitted successfully or it was not, and that information is known immediately upon completion of the exercise. Not so with an asynchronous messaging model. But the asynchronous model also provides opportunities for document transformation that are not available with the synchronous approach.

The message provider approach also creates the opportunity for greater reliability in message passing, depending on the characteristics of the nodes involved. If, for example, an intermittently connected mobile node is the originator of a given message, a message provider approach would be much more reliable than XML-RPC.

# Routing

Routing is one of the most interesting aspects of NDC messaging. Recall from the OSI 7-layer conceptual model that routing is the job of the Network layer. Navigating the dynamic pathways of the modern Internet is still functionally addressed in the lower datacom protocols of OSI 7. Beyond the network layer, routing is what is also meant in the context of message passing.

In the specific case of ebXML TR&P, routing functions beyond those offered by TCP/IP are provided by the ebXML framework (Electronic Business using eXtensible Markup Language), is sponsored by the United Nations (UN/CEFACT) and OASIS, is a modular suite of specifications designed to enable global enterprises of any size in any country to conduct business over the Internet.[4] OASIS is an international, not-for-profit consortium that designs and develops industry standards specifications for interoperability based on XML.[5] Routing at the network protocol layer provides the bedrock for message passing by identifying pathways wherein two (or more) nodes can be connected by a virtual circuit. The routing articulated by ebXML TR&P, which layers well above the OSI 7 Network layer, provides a more application-level flavor of routing, designed for more sophisticated NDC applications.

Consider a "Publish and Subscribe" class of applications. OSI 7 Network layer protocols do not generally provide a means wherein messages may be distributed to members of a list of parties, nor is anonymity necessarily an optional mechanism. By extending the routing metaphor above the OSI 7 stack, ebXML TR&P describes a means for message routing that is extensible for such purposes. Based on interoperability sensibilities and existing in tandem with legacy routing technologies, ebXML provides a more application-oriented set of interfaces that allow developers to implement Publish-and-Subscribe applications.

The earlier example of simple message passing with XML-RPC requires less intellectual investment on the part of the developer than does ebXML. But implementing something like Publish and Subscribe using XMP-RPC would be considerably more difficult because the developer would be required to not only provide a dynamic attachment capability à la SOAP but to implement something in the way of asynchronous message passing capabilities as well. (Publish and Subscribe, by definition, requires more than a simple RPC mechanism in order to function.) At its core, ebXML is based on XMP-RPC, as is SOAP, but using only unextended XML-RPC as the basis for NDC programming would be a limiting choice, depending on the type of application being developed. It's the classic "pay me now or pay me later" question; avoiding the initial cost of learning ebXML, for example, in favor of the less challenging option of XML-RPC, may result in a faster prototype, but will likely result in a longer and more difficult development cycle. Goff's axiom applies here— it all depends on the context.

# Broadcast and Multicast

Most often we think of messages as having one sender and one receiver. The bulk of messages do not fall into that category, however, if we include broadcast communication. In the past two decades the number of broadcasters has increased a hundredfold, if cable television (and satellite) options are any measure. While not NDC communications per se, these digital signals nevertheless betray a clear indication of the growth and penetration of NDC-capable technologies and also serve as an example of message transmission: one sender, multiple receivers.

In NDC, broadcast and multicast can provide flexible one-to-many transmission options. Strictly speaking, three types of transmission options are available on the Internet:

- ◆ Unicast: typical one-to-one
- ◆ Broadcast: global one-to-many (passed on by the router)
- ◆ Multicast: local one-to-many (stops at the router)

Think of broadcast as one amplified voice that everyone in the world hears, whereas multicast is more like a private party, where only those sitting at a particular table hear what is said. Broadcast NDC systems present many unique challenges for network management. These systems generally have both high bandwidth requirements (up to 20 Mbps per channel) and stringent QoS requirements for reliable, guaranteed delivery; some transmissions can be worth millions of dollars an hour. Some proprietary (that is, nonstandard) solutions exist in this space, but generally speaking, a standardized, reliable broadcast mechanism does not yet exist on the Internet.

TCP/IP based multicast has been utilized by some standard application frameworks such as Jini network technology and, to some extent, Project JXTA. For the most part, however, the standards communities have yet to meaningfully address the general problem of broadcast on the Internet.

## Summary

One useful perspective on any arbitrary network can be gained by examining the nature of its message passing and the opportunities for message transformations, or cooking points, it provides. The Web Services approach to NDC applications is, at its heart, a set of message passing specifications. To the extent that messages are marshalled and serialized, document transformation technologies can also be viewed as message transformation entities.

A transmission model serves as the presumptive mechanism for NDC message passing, implying both a sender and a receiver who share some semblance of shared processing capability. NDC message passing can be very simple or very complex, depending on the needs of the application and the preference of the developer. Regardless of the developer's messaging choice, a standardized, reliable broadcast specification is not currently available for implementation.

## Notes

1. C. E. Shannon, *The Mathematical Theory of Communication* (Urbana: University of Illinois Press, 1948).
2. Source: www.xmlrpc.com, the home page for the XML-RPC community.
3. An element is also referred to as a *node,* not to be confused with an NDC node.
4. See www.ebxml.org for more information.
5. See www.oasis-open.org for more information.

CHAPTER 7

# NDC Datacom: Wireless and Integration

The advent of mobile nodes gives rise to the promise of pervasive computing—the general availability of processing capability and network-connection potential. But the integration of wireless, mobile devices with an Internet grounded in copper and sheathed in glass cannot occur until we address significant software challenges.

Do you own a cell phone? How about an 802.11-enabled PDA? My Google Internet search found well over a million page references matching "free cell phone." Most mobile phone providers now offer some version of the "free cell phone" deal, in exchange for their relatively low-cost monthly service offerings. In the late 1980s, cellular telephone sales signed up the first million subscribers worldwide, with unit prices in the hundreds and even thousands of dollars—and the analog minutes were pricey.

Mobile phones are tiny, cheap, and prevalent today. What was once dear is now a cheap commodity, thanks to digital physical layer protocols like time division multiple access (TDMA), which first appeared as the basis for Europe's Global System for Mobile communication (GSM) in the late 1980s. An aspirational economic symbol by the late 1980s, the development and early commercial success of cellular phones required nearly 40 years to reach the million subscriber mark, roughly 15 years ago. Since then, mobile processing capacity has steadily increased even as costs and power requirements have decreased—the result of a fitscape-driven virtual cycle, typical of ephemeralization, enabled by software.

Novel approaches to mobile datacom based on Shannon's information theory have also given rise to physical layer protocols that dramatically increase transmission capacity for wireless devices, enabling true mobile nodes from a network perspective. Indeed, today many developers write code for mobile telephones, using protocols and frameworks designed specifically to enable such development, a practice that would have been impossible for the vast majority just a few years ago. But we are only beginning to address the difficult problems inherent in a network that now features an additional dimension of change. Integration of mobile nodes into the still-evolving fabric of the Internet is not without challenges.

## Analog Era

Fundamentally, a cell phone is a radio telephone. The Italian inventor Guglielmo Marconi is credited with having discovered "radio" with the advent of wireless telegraphy in 1896. Of course, invention is almost always the consequence of many previous discoveries and inquiries; in Marconi's case, he stood on the shoulders of giants like Faraday, Maxwell, Hertz, and Tesla. But his contribution opened the door to wireless transmission of analog signals, which enabled the heyday of world radio in the early 20th century. So why didn't we have radio telephones many years ago? The answer lies in the ephemeralizing nature of software, digital computers, and the tiny, powerful microprocessors that drive them. Microprocessors ferret through complicated operations with high reliability. Before the microprocessor, cell phones were simply not possible.

The barrier for early radio telephones was limited bandwidth; available frequencies (that is, channels) were often consumed by well-to-do individuals with radio telephones in their automobiles. Users often initiated a number of calls, starting very early in the morning, to guarantee channel availability when needed later in the day.

To be useful, a radio telephone has to work throughout an entire metropolitan area, supporting a large population of users. The scarcity of channels, exacerbated by frequency-reservation usage patterns as described above, could be solved by creating many smaller regions (which we now call *cells*) independently using the same frequencies. (That is, two callers in two different cells could use the same frequency without conflict.) Since a smaller area would likely host a smaller number of users, the available frequencies could be stretched. But what about movement from one cell to another? In principle, this problem could be solved by providing automatic switchovers from one cell to another, but such automatic switches turned out to be very complicated to implement. Then the digital era brought inexpensive microprocessors capable of performing the complex job of managing the switchover without losing the mobile call, and the modern cell phone was born.

## Digital Era

At first, speech conveyed through modern cell phones was still analog, with digital systems responsible only for the switchover. This type of mobile phone is still known as an analog phone. A true all-digital cell phone represents speech too as a series of bits, processed by its embedded digital intelligence. In addition, a cell phone that digitizes speech improves sound quality, eliminates line static, and increases battery life by nearly an order of magnitude.

---

In an analog communication system, an electrical current that is proportional to the quantity being transmitted is generated—essentially, an analog of the observed wave. In a digital system, the quantity being transmitted is encoded and expressed as a series of bits.

---

The migration of speech into the digital realm is more complicated than simply making the switchover process digital. The true all-digital cell phone had to wait for Moore's law to make microprocessors smaller and

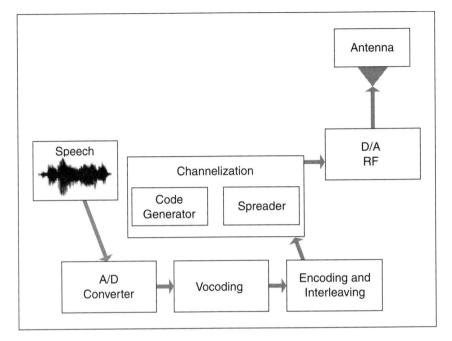

Figure 7.1 CDMA signal processing

more powerful, thereby make computing itself mobile. The first true all-digital system was the TDMA-based European GSM system introduced in the late 1980s. TDMA, which uses time slicing as the means to multiplex transmissions over shared frequencies, helped solve the multiple-user problems faced by early radio phones. TDMA all-digital systems became available in the United States in the early 1990s.

CDMA (code division multiple access) all-digital systems,[1] which slice frequencies by unique embedded codes to increase channel potential even more than TDMA, emerged commercially around 1995. Figure 7.1 illustrates the five signal processing steps in generating a transmission-ready CDMA signal.

1. Analog-to-digital conversion
2. Voice compression, or vocoding
3. Encoding and interleaving
4. Signal channelization
5. Digital-to-analog radio frequency (RF) conversion

The use of codes is a key part of this process. Encoding implies processing, which requires software. Clearly, a significant amount of processing needs to occur on both ends of the transmission pipeline for this scheme to work. Following its 1995 introduction, CDMA rapidly became one of the world's fastest-growing wireless technologies. In 1999, the International Telecommunications Union selected CDMA as the industry standard for new "third generation" (3G) wireless systems. Many wireless carriers are now building or upgrading to 3G CDMA networks to provide more capacity for voice traffic, along with high-speed datacom capabilities and services. Over 100 million consumers worldwide rely on CDMA for voice services, and an increasing number are leading the charge in using Internet data derived from a mobile phone.

The 1990s witnessed the transformation of mobile radio telephones from aspirational toys of the wealthy to all-digital commodity items that are now freely given away, a rapid transition fueled by Moore's law, the ephemeralizing nature of software by the network metaphor, and protocol breakthroughs like TDMA and CDMA. The fitscape in which mobile telephones play has given rise to something even more interesting, however: the basis for a wireless, mobile, application-driven network which, when married with the still evolving but grounded Internet, yields enormous potential for a profound paradigm shift in NDC. Before proceeding to that discussion, a few words regarding a few other wireless protocols are in order.

## Wi-Fi and Wi-Fi5 (802.11b and 802.11a)

In technical terms, the IEEE 802.11b standard is the family of specifications created by the Institute of Electrical and Electronics Engineers (IEEE) for wireless, Ethernet-based local area networks in the 2.4 gigahertz bandwidth space. The balance of English speakers will think of Wi-Fi as a means whereby our computers and other smart devices connect to each other and to the Internet, at very high speed, without wiring or significant costs. As the adoption history of many digital technologies (including the cell phone) teaches, the cost factor is significant if Wi-Fi is to spread.

For the record, there are several flavors of specification within the IEEE 802.11 family. The specification for 802.11a, or Wi-Fi5, is for wireless communication over a 5 GHz band. Plain Wi-Fi, or 802.11b, is for wireless communication over the 2.4 GHz band. All other derivatives, from "c" to "i," target performance, functionality, or security improvements in "a" and "b."

Fundamentally, 802.11a and 802.11b each define a different physical layer. Wi-Fi radios transmit at 2.4 GHz and send data at up to 11 Mbps, using direct sequence spread spectrum modulation. Wi-Fi5 radios transmit at 5 GHz and send data at up to 54 Mbps, using orthogonal frequency division multiplexing (OFDM). Conceptually similar to CDMA, OFDM is a method of digital modulation in which a signal is split into several narrowband channels at different frequencies. The difference lies in the way in which the signals are modulated and demodulated. Interference minimization is given priority, reducing crosstalk among the channels and symbols that constitute the data stream. Less importance is placed on perfecting individual channels.

Why use Wi-Fi instead of Wi-Fi5? Consider the differences:

♦ **WiFi (802.11b)**—Range requirements are significant. For larger facilities, such as a shopping mall or warehouse, 802.11b provides the least costly solution because fewer access points are needed. Many vendors already provide low-cost Wi-Fi solutions for devices, so cost may be a factor; the density of digital population is also a factor. If relatively few end users need to roam throughout the entire facility, 802.11b will likely meet performance requirements, unless these are very stringent.

♦ **WiFi5 (802.11a)**—Choose 802.11a if there is a need to support higher-end applications, possibly including video, voice, and transmission of large files, for which 802.11b probably won't suffice. Also, it is useful to note that significant RF interference may be present around the 2.4 GHz band. The growing adoption of 2.4 GHz phones and Bluetooth devices could crowd the radio spectrum within the facility in question and significantly decrease the performance of Wi-Fi wireless LANs. The use of 802.11a, which operates around the 5 GHz band, will avoid this interference. If end users are densely populated (as in computer labs, airports, and convention centers), competition for the same access point can be alleviated by 802.11a's greater total throughput capability.

## Bluetooth

Bluetooth is a royalty-free specification. Unlike many other wireless standards, the Bluetooth specification includes both OSI 7 link layer and application layer definitions for developers and supports data, voice, and content-centric applications. Radios that comply with the Bluetooth specification also operate in the unlicensed, 2.4 GHz radio spectrum.

Bluetooth devices use a spread-spectrum, full-duplex, frequency-hopping signal, which hops at up to 1600 hops/sec among 79 frequencies at 1 MHz intervals to ensure some degree of interference immunity. Up to seven simultaneous connections can be established and maintained with Bluetooth; for a personal area network (PAN) solution, multiple device support is mandatory. And PAN is indeed the intent of Bluetooth. Hence, Bluetooth and 802.11b should complement each other nicely, even though they compete for frequencies in the 2.4 GHz range. From a market perspective, a marriage of these two pioneering technologies will suffice. Note that other solutions may be required if the success of a Wi-Fi/Bluetooth combination starts to crowd available frequencies within the geographical constraints of 802.11b.

# Optics, Wireless, and Network Integration

Moore's law has received most of the attention in, and most of the credit, for the evolution of the modern global techno-economic fitscape. The productivity gains in knowledge-based economies that we have witnessed over nearly a decade are often correlated with the utilization of IT. But capital expenditures go far beyond the cost of personal computers; communication among people is just as key to harvesting the potential of Web dynamics; Gilder's law must therefore be given credit as well. Just as important as increased processing and storage capabilities at lower cost is increased bandwidth access at lower costs. Gilder's law describes the multiplication of synapses to the nodal neurons of this global shared brain.

George Gilder, prolific author and technology age pundit, observed that the total bandwidth of communication systems triples every twelve months. This law became a zeitgeist component with the publication of his book *Telecosm* in 2000,[2] coincident with the beginning of the steep decline of the NASDAQ that the next 18 months would witness. While the epiphany that shook the dotcom world also impacted the global telecommunications industry, the growth of global communications capacity remains an important factor if we would predict the shape of any future Internet.

## Fiber Optics

Fiber optics is a big part of the global telecom capacity picture. With a theoretical limit of some 30 Tbs per strand,[3] the potential of fiber far outweighs even the most promising wireless option when it comes to capacity and robustness. But I don't yet have a direct fiber link to the Internet, and not many people do.

The problem is one of "dark fiber"—or actually one of money, which is most often the case in any technology adventure. It's far easier and relatively less expensive to lay the millions of miles of fiber-optic cable around the world than it is to light it; the equipment costs for encoding, switching, and boosting fiber-optic signals is three to four times that of the actual fiber deployment. As such, millions of miles of fiber-optic cables are dark, awaiting the day when light will grace their core, even as more miles of fiber-optic cables are buried every day.

Since capital investments are driven by corporate profits, which are driven by consumption and enabled by capital markets, the economic malaise of the early 21st century may seem to have stalled the adoption of fiber optics, especially insofar as commodity connections are concerned. But the world is not a static domain.

In North Carolina, for example, efforts to connect rural areas have resulted in a three-year plan that would guarantee home access to at least 128 Kbps and business access to at least 256 Kbps, based on a fiber-optic backbone extended to rural areas. In California, the City of Palo Alto went even further, with a fiber-to-the-home (FTTH) initiative in a trial phase[4] from November 2000 to August 2002. Imagine having access to the throughput potential available from a single ultra-high-speed optical fiber that connects your home, and all the information appliances you choose within it, to the Internet. In Palo Alto, the efficacy of that class of connection, at what is effectively a commodity level, is still being actively explored.

FTTH is a commodity access technology that uses an optical network architecture optimized for simple, economical delivery of telephony, packet data, and video to the home through a single bidirectional fiber-optic strand. The Marconi[5] multimedia FTTH system was chosen for the trial. The services provided on the system are POTS (Plain Old Telephone Service), high-speed Internet access (data), and broadcast video. All three services are combined and distributed from the City of Palo Alto's Utility Control Center and transmitted to residential customers over a fusion-spliced fiber-optic network. The resulting Outside Cable Plant contains no active components and as such is referred to as a passive optical network (PON).

Data throughput is always a function of the lowest denominator in an end-to-end communication path. In the case of FTTH, that includes the inside house wiring, PC equipment, upstream gateway(s), ISP, and Internet bandwidth. In-house load testing in the Palo Alto trial has shown consistent payload throughput ranging from 3.5 Mbps to bursts of 7 Mbps. Compared to home fractional T1 products (ours cost roughly $450 per month, delivering bursts of up to 1.1 Mbps), a fiber-optic option today would be very appealing, especially if the price were competitive with Internet access delivered by cable television.

Will all home communications needs be met by a 3.5 Mbps reliable connection? Probably not. If multiple-channel, high-definition video, Internet traffic, audio, and voice communication are to flow concurrently, with complete reliability, arguably much more throughput to the home will be needed. But fiber optics at least holds promise for that ultra-high-speed future.

In the context of wireless and network integration, fiber optics presents a viable option and an important consideration for the NDC developer. At the same time, it also presents a bit of a problem: what class of consumer do I design my application to address? What bandwidth assumptions can I make? Are bandwidth considerations even germane to application development? Or should bandwidth, along with security, homogeneity, transport cost, and so on, be lumped together in a box labelled "fallacies" and placed mindfully in the closet, hopefully to be ignored by yet another generation of distributed computing software?

## Wireless

A wide range of bandwidth options is the least of our worries. Deep within the design premise of the Internet is the notion of geographically fixed nodes (another fallacy?). Even as wireless physical access spaces emerge, the premise holds; wireless nodes roam a physical space constrained by the limits of the devices, frequencies, and protocols utilized, but always cognizant of and dependent on a receiver that acts as the Internet gateway, which in turn is geographically static. The promises of wireless appear at the edges, but the fixed core of the net leaves us with a novel set of design constraints and potential for innovations. The challenge is one of blending something that is fluid with something that is fixed.

Consider the protocols cited earlier: Wi-Fi, Wi-Fi5, and Bluetooth. We might imagine mobile nodes that implement these very specifications, serving users who are either in proximity to or ready to install the necessary LAN/MAN equipment for wireless application deployment. My Bluetooth PAN-devices, like my augmented reality goggles, soul-catcher storage unit, digital identification and security apparatus, and physio-

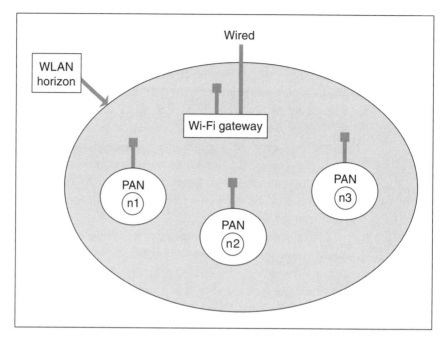

Figure 7.2  Wi-Fi and Bluetooth

stasis monitor share the seven available Bluetooth channels, transmitting and receiving through my wearable Wi-Fi-enabled system, which acts as my PAN gateway, as shown in Figure 7.2. The Wi-Fi-available building, enabled by one or more receivers, shares duty with the Wi-Fi5 connected campus units.

The Wireless LAN (WLAN) horizon for one building may overlap with another, providing interesting switching requirements that the wired Internet need not consider. The same is true if a seamless migration from Wi-Fi to Wi-Fi5 fields is part of our imaginary installation. If n2 decides to leave the WLAN in question and wander around the campus, problems arise, as shown in Figure 7.3.

As a node wanders through myriad fields, each of which represents a different entry point into an otherwise fixed network, the need for protocol hand-over should be obvious. On the other hand, it is not out of the question to consider engineering around the absence of a deep datacom infrastructure that is mobile-node aware. Clever edge implementations, which mask information field shifts from the user, may be viable. This is a choice that will eventually present itself.

Another wireless choice is a clever edge implementation that already masks information field shifts from the user to some extent, and that may

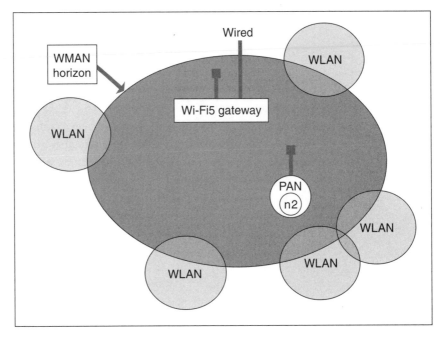

Figure 7.3  Wi-Fi, Wi-Fi5, and Bluetooth

soon be ready as a PAN gateway cum wearable digi-nexus. It's called a 3G mobile phone, and it may yet emerge as the hands-down winner in the Darwinian contest du jour. A Bluetooth chip in a CDMA phone could accomplish much the same thing as a PDA with Wi-Fi / Wi-Fi5 and would likely find a commodity outlet channel a lot faster, given the uptake of mobile phones worldwide. Would protocol hand-over be solved? Not quite yet. But from an application deployment perspective, mobile phones are increasingly interesting choice.

NDC developers enjoy a litany of issues and choices in this nascent Network Age. But as is the case with any reasonably complex fitscape, we haven't even begun to explore the possibilities.

## The π-Calculus and Protocol Hand-Over

Messages ride a medium, regardless of context. Whether the medium be RF, coherent light, IR, microwave, copper, or optical fiber, a message is always transmitted through a medium of some kind. Back when, when nodes on a network were tied down and geographically static, strategies for navigating the network could begin with these assumptions. But the deflection point born of the meeting of Moore's law and the wireless component of Gilder's law challenges those assumptions fundamentally and may represent a phase shift in NDC and the transformative software that drives it.

Recall the discussion of the Spanning Tree Protocol (STP) discussion in Chapter 4; some form of STP discovers and defines networks today. When a mobile node joins such a network, assumptions built into Internet datacom infrastructure, both software and hardware, are challenged; difficult problems arise, requiring a fundamental examination of previous assumptions. How do we effectively manage a network now made up of nodes that are not only intermittent but that also potentially manifest a constantly morphing network topology? The drawbacks of an STP in such an environment should be obvious. The answer may lie in the $\pi$-calculus, first discussed in Chapter 3.

Pioneered by a small group of theoretical computer scientists in the late 1980s,[6] the $\pi$-calculus is a theoretical tool designed to describe communicating systems in which it is possible to rigorously express processes that have changing structure. Where the component agents of a system are arbitrarily linked, communication between neighbors may carry information that changes that linkage. The calculus provides a means ". . . for analyzing properties of concurrent communicating process, which may grow and shrink and move about."[7]

The calculus gains simplicity over previous approaches by removing distinctions between variables and constants; communication links are identified by names, and computation is represented only as the communication of names across links.

From a process perspective, what does it mean to be "mobile"? Strictly speaking, computer science may harbor many interpretations of the term and many correspondingly contrasting solutions. A process may migrate from one node to the next, physically moving around the network; a process may migrate in a virtual space of linked processes; a link may move in a virtual space of linked processes. These are only three of the many possible definitions of a mobile process.

The calculus describes mobile processes from the perspective of their links; the location of a process in a virtual space of processes is determined by its links to other processes. Those within the communication horizon of the process in question are a function of the links that process may have; accordingly, the movement of a process can be represented by the movement of the links.

A complete description of the $\pi$-calculus, its nomenclature, and its rules, is beyond the scope of this book. For this discussion, it is enough to say that the introduction of wireless nodes into a network in which Metcalfe's law is to also prevail—that is, the maximization of possible node-to-node connections—requires a review of existing discovery and routing assumptions. The calculus offers hope in that regard.

# Summary

The wireless revolution represents a phase-shifting deflection point in NDC development. The baked-in topological assumptions of the Internet are fundamentally challenged by the advent of radio-frequency mobile phones, as well as the WLAN, WMAN, and PAN technologies that are today being gingerly explored by a generation of early adopters. Driven by rural connection needs and urban mobile possibilities, the convergence of ultra-high bandwidth via fiber optics with mobile broadband via Wi-Fi, et al., requires a rethinking of basic Internet premises. The resulting challenge and choices for NDC developers are legion.

## Notes

1.  CDMA was pioneered commercially by Qualcomm, Inc., of San Diego, CA: see www.qualcomm.com.

2.  George Gilder, *Telecosm* (New York: Free Press, September 2000).

3.  David D. Nolte, *Mind at Light Speed* (New York: Free Press, 2001). According to Nolte, an "all-optical network," which would provide optical switching as well as transmission, could theoretically maximize bandwidth to somewhere near 30 Tbs.

4.  www.cpau.com/fth/

5.  www.marconi.com

6.  See "A Calculus of Mobile Processes, Part I," by Robin Milner, Joachim Parrow, and David Walker, www.lfcs.informatics.ed.ac.ak/reports/89/ECS-LFCS-89-85/.

7.  Robin Milner, *Communicating and Mobile Systems: The pi-Calculus* (Cambridge, UK: Cambridge University Press, 1999), p. 3.

# CHAPTER 8

# Today's NDC
# Frameworks

The development of NDC applications is by definition a team sport, in which competing players theoretically agree to a set of rules. Standards arise from the realization that sound foundations, accepted and used by all agents within the fitscape, enable the competition to produce increasingly more valuable output. NDC frameworks provide an important layer of sediment in the common ground of interoperability shared by competing implementations, even as they attempt to solve the problems inherent in a constantly evolving milieu.

Bill Joy, one of the founders of Sun Microsystems, and until recently Chief Scientist for the firm, is credited with articulating Joy's law: Innovation occurs elsewhere. No matter who you are and regardless of your locale, financial well-being, intellectual property, or clarity of vision, innovation is going on all around you, out of your sight—innovation that affects the markets you serve and the work you do. Given the connected nature of a knowledge economy, any firm that denies the inevitability of innovation from outside is doomed to fail. For this reason, embracing standards and platforms based on standards is the only reasonable choice for developers, given at least rudimentary business constraints.

Since its inception, the Internet community has struggled to produce standards that can be leveraged to create applications that play well together in a common networked environment. With each layer of standardization, novel models of application design emerge, to either deliver value more effectively and efficiently than previous generations or to provide innovative business models, previously not possible, in lieu of heavy, proprietary investments. To the extent that players must adopt standards while competing, the business of standards itself is ripe with fitscape nuance. The "agree on standards, compete on implementation" approach, which oriented many early Internet collaboration efforts, is also subject to fitscape pressures as standards themselves become more significant to strategic business objectives. As such, the standards game has changed over the past decade, and it is useful to keep an eye on these changes as we examine NDC frameworks.

Recall our discussions of middleware in Chapter 1 and Chapter 3. Explored here are a few instantiations of what can reasonably be described as middleware, some history of the work that produced them, and some of their inherent drawbacks and promises. Comparing J2EE with the .NET framework from Microsoft is an inevitable segue to greener pastures, when organic frameworks begin to grow. But first, an examination of an earlier effort, which will provide a basis for comparison.

# CORBA

This story begins with CORBA, which is the acronym for Common Object Request Broker Architecture, from the Object Management Group (OMG). The OMG is an open industry consortium that keeps the flame for some specifications for interoperable enterprise applications. With about 800 members, including most large companies in the computer industry, the OMG is responsible for producing a number of NDC standards, including CORBA and the Universal Modeling Language (UML).

CORBA provides several useful facilities to NDC implementations, including its Interface Definition Language (IDL) specification. IDL allows developers to define interfaces to objects in a standard manner; IDL mappings bind the IDL definitions and types to languages such as C, C++, Smalltalk, and Java. As a result, CORBA provides a language transparency. Objects interact with one another through an Object Request Broker (ORB); using the language mappings, developers can create client-side "stubs" and server-side "skeletons" that their ORBs can understand and use in a cross-platform manner. As shown in Figure 8.1, stubs and skeletons serve as proxies for clients and servers, respectively. IDL defines interfaces quite strictly, so a given stub and a given skeleton should mesh fairly well, even if they are compiled into different languages or running on different ORBs from different vendors. Any CORBA-based program from one vendor should theoretically be able to interoperate with any CORBA-based program from any other vendor, transparent of operating system, programming language, or network—a powerful feature indeed.

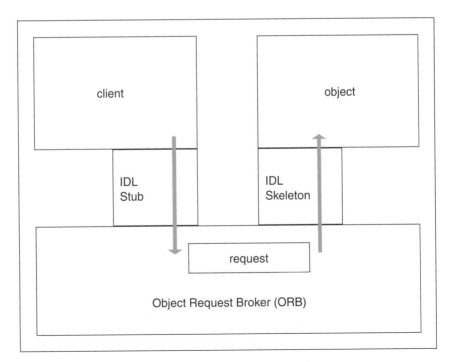

Figure 8.1  Client passes request through ORB to object

An IDL interface establishes a set of client-accessible operations, exceptions, and typed attributes (values). Each operation has a signature that defines its name, parameters, result, and exceptions. IDL is straightforwardly object oriented, as shown in this simple IDL interface describing the classic "Hello World" program:

```
module HelloWorldIDLExample
{
 interface HelloWorld
 {
  string sayHelloworld( );
  };
};
```

The separation of interface from implementation, enabled by OMG IDL, is the essence of CORBA, by which it enables interoperability with all the transparencies cited above. The interface to each object is defined very strictly by IDL. The instance of an object—its running code and its data—is hidden from the rest of the system (that is, encapsulated). Clients access objects only through their advertised interfaces, invoking only those operations which that instantiation of the object exposes through its IDL interface, with only those parameters (input and output) that are included in the invocation.

In CORBA, every object instance has its own unique object reference. Clients use these object references to direct their invocations, identifying to the ORB the exact instance to be invoked. The client acts as if it is invoking an operation on the object instance but is actually invoking it on the IDL stub. Passing through the stub on the client side, the invocation continues through the ORB and the skeleton to the object, where it is executed. CORBA uses Internet Inter-ORB Protocol (IIOP) for object communication.

To invoke any object instance, local or remote, a client first must obtain its object reference. Several easy approaches to do this have been explored by the OMG, constituting a finite set of services:

- ◆ Collection Service
- ◆ Concurrency Service
- ◆ Enhanced View of Time
- ◆ Event Service
- ◆ Externalization Service
- ◆ Naming Service

- Licensing Service
- Life-Cycle Service
- Notification Service
- Persistent Object Service
- Property Service
- Query Service
- Relationship Service
- Security Service
- Time Service
- Trading Object Service
- Transaction Service

To make the remote invocation, the client uses the same code that it used in the local invocation, substituting the object reference for the remote instance. From the perspective of the client code, the invocation is the same, whether or not the object is local. When the ORB examines an object reference and discovers that the target object is remote, it routes the invocation over the network to the remote object's ORB. In this way, CORBA— in the effort to achieve a modicum of interoperability—was one of the first NDC platforms to address Deutsch's Eighth Fallacy (The network is homogenous), even if others were effectively ignored.

All forms of RPC, including CORBA, require a fairly explicit detailing of the messages to be exchanged; functions must be specified tightly, and both sides must agree. RPC encourages developers to design protocols in which the messages have a reasonably specific meaning. In contrast, messages in XML have a general meaning, leaving it to the application to interpret what is meant.

Any RPC-oriented protocol encourages developers to think of a message as a distributed method call. But in every widely used programming language, with the exception of Java platform extensions (like JAXM) in which a messaging provider is employed, a method call is synchronous; applications wait for the result of a method call before continuing. This leads to an erroneous view of RPC interfaces; rather than reification of messages sent and their inherently asynchronous nature, this approach views a message as a normal class interface, which generally leads to unnecessary network chatter at the very least.

CORBA advocates solve this problem by making heavy use of threading, which has its own inherent problems, including impacted resource utilization, application robustness, code gnarl, and lack of platform portability, which may still be of some interest in an age that will witness the proliferation of extremely small, mobile datacom processing capabilities disappearing into everything, perhaps implanted beneath our living skin.

CORBA and, by association, RPC both tend to give rise to a degree of coupling that cannot be characterized as loose. Use of asynchronous messaging, which may seem programmatically more difficult, is also mandatory if the applications we write are to become as dynamic and mobile as the instruments that carry them. While a general-purpose messaging service could possibly be envisioned by the OMG, most of the services they help define seem to be forms of messaging in any event. RPCs seem to permeate CORBA.

The great thing about CORBA is that it is heterogeneous. The major flaw in CORBA is that it is heterogeneous! Its loyal adherents continue to use it for a subset of NDC applications. Arguably, CORBA became moot the day XML-RPC was envisioned. But echoes from previous generations of NDC thinking remain; new legacies to be embraced, new interfaces to spawn. So shall it be with CORBA. Still, as a tool for comparison, CORBA provides a fine base.

## SOAP and XML

Once XML-RPC was envisioned, SOAP wasn't far behind. The Simple Object Access Protocol, introduced by Microsoft, is not particularly simple, nor is it object-oriented. On first blush, SOAP may not seem like anything to get excited about; not actually new, it merely codified the existing practice of combining XML and HTTP to invoke methods in languages like the Java programming language. This practice was itself, to a certain extent, merely another way to do something that had been possible for some time with other approaches, such as CORBA IDL and IIOP.

If SOAP is significant, it is so because it represents a major step forward in the ability of applications (running on all types of devices) to utilize XML and the Internet as shown in Figure 8.2. To the extent that an XML-based Internet represents openness, extensibility, and true platform independence, SOAP can be viewed as an interoperability flag all concerns can salute.

Does XML provide all that? Despite all the investment in creating the underpinnings necessary to enable an XML-based Internet, many firms still rely on old-fashioned HTML, using tools that produce proprietary results offensive to at least one browser. Enabling business-to-business (b2b)

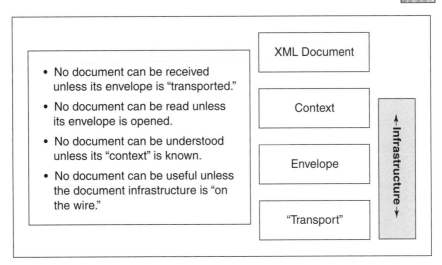

Figure 8.2  Web Services: SOAP with Attachments

with the productivity-enhancing network metaphor continues to lure bot-tom-line aficionados with the sweet promise of interoperability: if I don't like my current provider, I can just switch. Will interoperability too be-come competitively hygenic (i.e., expected value as with any commodity), more sediment forming the next newest layer of the Internet fitscape? Sed-imentation plays a steady role in the unfolding drama of NDC.

## J2EE: "Web Services" to "Services on Demand"

Recall the concept of sedimentation and consolidation from Chapter 1: things that were once differentiators become fundamental expectations. Software plays in a dynamic, positive feedback system, ripe with the fit-scape pressures, as the Zero Dollar Bill, which still drives software eco-nomics in the aggregate, further promotes sedimentation and consolida-tion toward an inevitable outcome; more and more functionality sinks to the standard platform layer. Microsoft, with the binding of its browser, multimedia interfaces and even digital identity to operating system inter-faces, is emblematic of this trend. Sedimentation and consolidation are also clear in the service stack of the J2EE platform, which envisions a layer including and beyond Web Services called "Services on Demand," as shown in Figure 8.3.

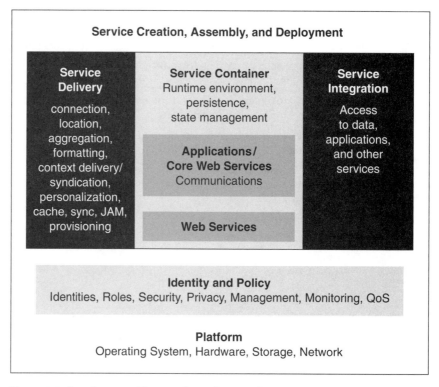

Figure 8.3  Services on Demand service stack

In a competitive sphere, that which was once a differentiator over time becomes a commodity. This is especially true with software. Propelled too by the open source software movement, the inevitability of functional consolidation within standard platforms is as apparent as it is disruptive to the fitscape from which those platforms arise. Sun Microsystems, as one of the top three major platform advocates, is not immune from these pressures; adaption in an oligopoly[1] of free offerings requires a vision based as much on Joy's law as on bottom-line issues. A win-win business model can side-step this apparent paradox, as long as the company, the partner, the vendor, and primarily the customer are satisfied.

The needs of all claimants, including NDC developers, are ostensibly met with the emergence of the J2EE platform. Sedimentation and consolidation are both addressed and even promoted, providing a strongly integrated NDC platform that appeals to a world of Sun customers. At the same time, the various sedimented layers in the platform, layers in which Sun competes with other vendors and partners, are based on published standards.

As the set of interfaces that enable interoperability continues to grow, seeded in XML and SOAP (which are putatively extensible), it follows that interoperability too is a candidate for sedimentation. In an oligopoly, interoperability should be a given. Witness the extent to which the airlines must cooperate in order to compete. Without an agreement on basic ground rules, your luggage would never arrive at all, much less when you do. Each airline would build and maintain its own airport; mechanics trained for one firm could never easily go to work for the next.

Interoperability at some level is an eventual given; despite concerns about small devices regarding XML bloat, that train has left the station. While XML, the message in this early Network Age, did nothing, in and of itself to guarantee interoperability, it was a good first step toward achieving it. SOAP was another step, as was XML-RPC, upon which SOAP is based. Java Message Service (JMS), found throughout the Sun Java System platform, is another good step.

Reliable delivery of a message has but one requirement: ensuring the successful transmission of the message from one node to another. XML-RPC can satisfy that requirement. But the inherently limiting synchronous primitive is overshadowed by JMS and platform technology that provides for reliable asynchronous messaging.

## Java Message Service

The JMS API specifies a common set of messaging concepts and facilities targeting Java programmers. The JMS provider implementation provides for a messaging service made of the following main components:

◆ One or more brokers. A broker provides delivery services on behalf of the messaging system. Supporting components may include connection services, message routing and delivery, persistence, security, and logging. A messaging service may use single or multiple broker configurations.

◆ Physical destinations. Delivery of a message is a two-phase process: first from a producing client to a physical destination maintained by a broker, then from that destination to one or more consuming clients.

Asynchronous messaging requires an intermediary of some kind; whether the service is running on my node or another is orthogonal to the discussion of reliable messaging. As such, the sedimentation and consolidation trend ensures that a messaging intermediary be present locally, on the network, and even offered as a service on the Internet. Indeed, email itself is nothing if not asynchronous messaging.

## Platform Technology

Platform services defined in the J2EE architecture for messaging service brokers include:

- ◆ Connection Services—Manage the physical connections between a broker and clients, providing transport for incoming and outgoing messages

- ◆ Message Router—Manages the routing and delivery of messages, which include JMS messages in addition to control messages used by the messaging system

- ◆ Persistence Manager—Manages the writing of data to persistent storage, ensuring reliable message delivery even in the event of system failures

- ◆ Security Manager—Provides authentication services for users requesting connections to a broker and authorization (access control) for authenticated sites

- ◆ Logger—Generates logs to file or console, enabling broker management

A multibroker messaging service allows clients to make connections among a number of distributed brokers. From a client perspective, each client connects to its individual home broker, sending and receiving all messages as if this broker were the only one in the cluster. But from a messaging service perspective, the home broker works in tandem with the others in the cluster to ensure delivery services to producers and consumers of messages.

While JMS is from the Java platform family of interfaces, XML is well represented in the J2EE platform mix, providing a bridge to high XML productivity for Java technology-trained developers. JMS is one of the Java XML Pack (described in Chapter 6), which together promise a baked-in interoperability framework that is also portable, a strong basis to which a growing number of developers are paying homage. "Services on Demand" stems from Sun's vision of the consolidation of business approaches to NDC, including the following:

- ◆ Local applications: Applications that run on dedicated workstations or PCs.

- Client-server applications: Applications that are split between presentation logic on a client and business logic on a server; N-tier applications are a derivative of the client-server model.

- Web applications: Applications that run over the Internet, such as stock trading, email, shopping and management information services, generally based on client browsers and standard protocols like HTML/HTTP.

- Web Services: Services that run over the Internet and can combine with other services to create more useful services; based on XML, this model provides loosely coupled integration (that is, interoperability) between applications, nodes, and platforms.

- Web clients: Applications written in the Java programming language and delivered through the Internet to Java technology-enabled devices such as PCs, cell phones, and PDAs.

Thus, the trend toward sedimentation and consolidation also gives rise to and enables the trend of decomposition and the drive to components (also discussed in Chapter 1), as standardized interfaces embrace all current flavors of NDC applications, including Web Services. In addition, complementary frameworks like Project JXTA and Jini networking technology, and other interesting and new NDC applications can also be envisioned. Embracing the mobile PAN by wirelessly aggregating augmented information fields, for example, can also easily allow interfacing with a dynamic system like JavaSpaces or a variant thereof. A JMS provider could be the glue.

## J2EE Versus .NET

In late April 2002, along with several of my cohorts, I represented Sun in a debate with evangelists from Microsoft sponsored by the Tulsa, Oklahoma, Java User Group (JUG). The event was hosted with style and aplomb. The industry-wide J2EE versus .NET debate has been deemed "the soap opera of the decade for geeks to watch,"[2] and the contest in Tulsa was indeed one short episode in that unfolding drama. But the event afforded some useful information.

Sun, IBM, and Microsoft now form a platform oligopoly. Nearly all NDC applications find themselves interoperating with systems from at least one of these three vendors. With its embrace of Linux and endorsement of the Java platform, IBM has brought the open source software community, kicking and screaming, solidly into the corporate fold. This does not mean that other platforms are not available or will not emerge as standards going forward; indeed, wireless technologies all but guarantee competition in the mobile space. And the open source software movement has its fanatics. But the Internet, which has been a great equalizer, has also served as a platform sieve, allowing natural commodity platforms to benefit from the connection of LANs around the world. With interoperability heralded as the new nirvana, a winnowing of platforms as commodity offerings should be expected. Will the field shrink further? Perhaps, but given levels of investment in all three platform philosophies, it is unlikely that one of the three will become marginalized any time soon.

To the extent that IBM and Sun both tout a UNIX derivative as platform operating system and the Java platform for NDC application development and deployment, the two firms can be viewed as direct competitors, which indeed they are in the systems marketplace. IBM has a much greater focus on services when it comes to site installations, compared to Sun; that is the J2EE platform offers a greater degree of consolidation; more bells and whistles are sedimented into the platform, as opposed to the site-service-intensive installations coming from IBM. These comparisons between Sun and IBM are germane to business decisions, but given their similar investment in UNIX and the Java platform, the more interesting comparison seems to be between Sun and Microsoft.

During the Tulsa debate with Microsoft, a number of similarities and differences between the two companies' offerings were cited. Fundamentally, Microsoft's .NET enables code that runs exclusively on Microsoft operating system platforms. To the extent to which Microsoft is the monopoly desktop platform, its penchant for proprietary software platforms should be expected to continue, leaving it somewhat hampered in a world that now honors interoperability first and foremost. Hence, Microsoft's embrace of vanilla Web Services and the three basic ingredients thereof: WSDL, UDDI, and SOAP, which are based on XML and are known collectively as WUS.

Sun, too, honors the WUS set of interfaces, to the extent that those interfaces are a starting place. Important functionality, which would more easily enable WUS interfaces to be useful in a global business environment, has been championed by the United Nations (through OASIS) in the ebXML extensions. The ebXML work has been a bone of contention in the standards world because the extensions offered compete with a proprietary product, called BizTalk, from Microsoft. But ebXML appears to have traction and should emerge as a viable alternative to a proprietary product that ignores fundamentals of interoperability in a business sense.

A brief comparison of J2EE and .NET illustrates many of the differences and similarities between the two.

## J2EE

The J2EE platform enables NDC developers to simplify complex problems with the development, deployment, and management of N-tier enterprise applications. J2EE is an industry standard, the culmination of a large industry initiative led by Sun Microsystems and the Java Community.[3]

Note that J2EE is truly a standard, not a product. A developer cannot download J2EE. Rather, the specifications that describe agreements between applications and the containers in which they run form the basis for the standard. As long as both sides honor the J2EE contracts, applications can be deployed in a variety of container environments from a number of vendors, as shown in Figure 8.4.

The goal of J2EE is to give customers a choice of vendor products and tools, recognizing the impact that Joy's law has on industry evolution. As shown in Figure 8.4, a J2EE application is hosted within a container, which in turn provides the level of service necessary for enterprise applications, such as transactions, security, messaging, and persistence.

The business layer performs business processing. In larger J2EE applications, business logic is built with Enterprise JavaBeans (EJB) components. The business layer connects to databases using Java Database Connectivity (JDBC) or SQL/J, or to existing systems using the Java Connector Architecture (JCA). Business partners connect with J2EE applications through Web Services technologies (including ebXML). A servlet, which is a request/response-oriented Java object, accepts these Web Services requests, using Java XML Pack technologies to perform the operations. Traditional clients, like applets, connect directly to the EJB layer through IIOP. Web browsers and wireless devices connect to JavaServer Pages (JSPs) which render user interfaces in HTML, XHTML, WML, or whatever ?ML may emerge. Note that J2EE is written in the Java programming language for Java technology developers.

## MS .NET

Microsoft's .NET platform[4] is a proprietary product suite that enables organizations to build Web Services. Note the important difference: .NET

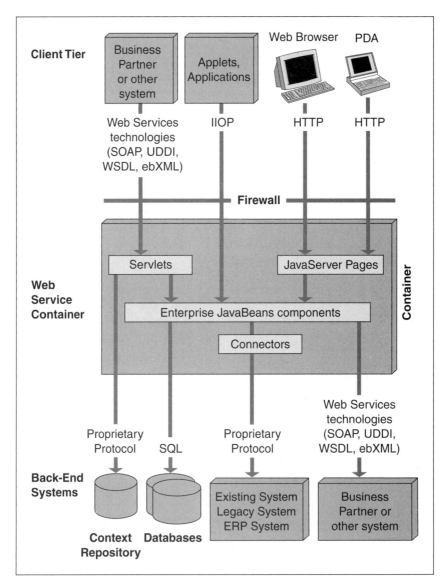

Figure 8.4 Delivering J2EE services

is a product strategy, whereas J2EE is a standard to which products are written.

The Microsoft .NET suite is, for the most part, a rewrite of Windows DNA (Microsoft's previous platform for developing enterprise applications), which includes many technologies produced by the Redmond giant. Incorporating Microsoft Transaction Server and COM+, Microsoft

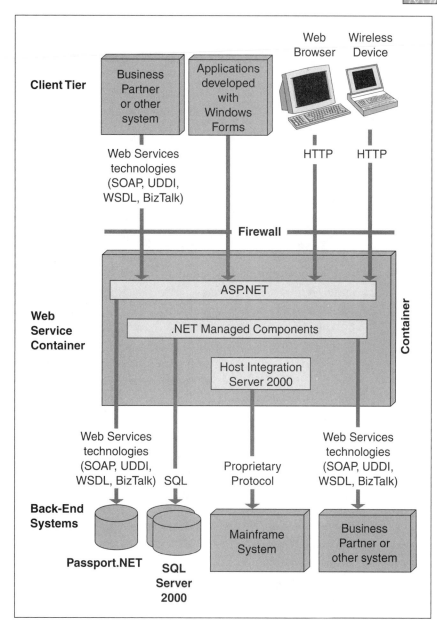

Figure 8.5  The .NET approach

Message Queue, and the Microsoft SQL Server database, .NET is a fine example of the sedimentation and consolidation trend (see Figure 8.5). The .NET Framework replaces those technologies while adding a Web Services layer and some improved language support.

All .NET applications are also hosted within a container, an arrangement that provides levels of service similar to those of J2EE. As shown in Figure 8.5, the business layer of the .NET application is built with .NET managed components, which provide business processing, and connects to databases with Active Data Objects (ADO.NET). Legacy system interfaces use services provided by Microsoft Host Integration Server 2000, which can also connect to business partners by using the WUS interfaces.

Key to the Microsoft story is a perceived value proposition leveraged by the ability of the .NET framework to interleave threads from diverse programming languages into a single component. For example, a .NET component can be written partially in VB.NET (the .NET version of Visual Basic) and C#, Microsoft's new object-oriented programming language, which is similar to the Java programming language in many respects.

To facilitate this magic, source code from any language is translated into Microsoft Intermediate Language (IL). This IL code, which is language-neutral and analogous to Java bytecode, is then interpreted and translated into a native executable, by a just-in-time (JIT) compilation on the target node. The .NET framework includes the common language runtime (CLR), which is analogous to the Java runtime environment (JRE) and is Microsoft's intermediary between .NET source code and the underlying operating system and hardware. All .NET code ultimately runs within the CLR.

This CLR provides many features, such as automatic garbage collection and exception handling, not available in earlier versions of Windows DNA but long a part of the Java platform. Cross-language inheritance is also included. But the promise of multiple programming languages is not nearly as inviting as might otherwise be anticipated.

Consider the IL, for example, which has some bothersome barriers to broach before it can boast. Any language that would integrate with the component runtime must define a subset or superset of itself that maps cleanly into and out of the IL runtime and must also define constructs that provide the component metadata that the IL requires. Once that work is done, then to-IL and from-IL compilers must be written to compile language structures into IL component bytecodes. Language-specific interfaces to existing IL components must also be written.

## The Multiple-Languages Debate

As part of the preparation for the Tulsa debate with Microsoft, the Sun team researched the issue of multiple programming languages and the claims being made. Based on published specifications, Sun can also boast of its efforts in this direction, which have produced well over 100 bridges from non-Java languages to the Java Virtual Machine (JVM), such as JPython, PERCobol, the Tcl/Java project, an Eiffel-to-JavaVM system, and several variants of LISP. Indeed, the number of possible programming languages that can target a JVM far surpasses the Microsoft set of languages. While Sun has taken no active part in the creation of programming languages (other than the Java programming language) that target the JVM, numerous languages have emerged worldwide. Yet these tools, with the possible exception of JPython, have not enjoyed a wide degree of adoption, despite the fact that they offer the means to write code for the Java platform in another programming language.

If multiple language support is so vital, why haven't alternative programming languages targeting the JVM enjoyed more popularity? It may be that there is really no reason to use another language, given the flexibility and ease of programming that the Java platform offers. It may also be that the approach envisioned by James Gosling, which included bytecode and a JVM, is executed most naturally with the language that was designed to best serve that vision. In any event, Microsoft's promise of multiple language support in .NET is somewhat dubious, given the IL barriers to entry for an arbitrary programming language. That, coupled with the proprietary extensions offered by Microsoft in the BizTalk/ebXML drama, means that the J2EE versus .NET debate does indeed offer entertaining possibilities.

## Conceptual Model for NDC Frameworks

At the end of the day, Web services are simply XML-based interfaces to application, node, and network services, each of them old soldiers wearing new uniforms. The following general approaches have enjoyed the widest industry acceptance, and each represents only one of the possible ways to deliver Web Services:

+ An NDC developer creates, assembles, and deploys a Web Service using the programming language, middleware, and platform of choice.

+ The developer defines the Web Service in WSDL, which is an XML document that describes the service to others.

+ The developer registers the service in a registry.

+ A prospective client finds the service by searching the registry.

+ The client application binds to the Web Service and invokes its operations by using SOAP, which presents interfaces in XML format for parameter and return-value representations over HTTP.

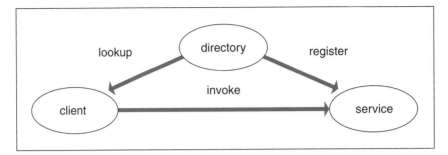

Figure 8.6 Client-Registry-Service conceptual model

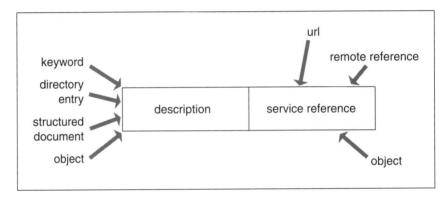

Figure 8.7 Directory-as-Registry conceptual model

The conceptual similarities with CORBA are numerous. As a matter of fact, almost all approaches to NDC frameworks utilize a basic conceptual model when it comes to the relationship between client, service, and service registration, as shown in Figure 8.6.

The same approach is conceptually valid whether we're discussing Web Services, CORBA, Jini network technology, and to some extent Project JXTA. That dynamic service invocation requires the client to discover services through an intermediary (the registry) is assumed in nearly all NDC existing frameworks that exist. The registry exposes attributes of a service very much like a directory in a conceptual sense; if we posit that a "directory" contains elements that certain attributes that can be wrapped in interoperable interfaces, the directory model is similar to that of a registry, as shown in Figure 8.7.

Note that very little in the way of dynamic assembly of components is overtly enabled by this simple approach. What happens "behind the curtain"—how the registry behaves, the underlying services that may be dynamically attached to a given service through its container to ensure a composable architecture—is left to the implementation and is therefore not standard. We say more about that later.

## Summary

NDC frameworks have similar characteristics that can be represented by a Client-Registry-Service conceptual model. Differences are expressed in terms of language bindings and wrappers. Some subtle differences in synchrony, document transformation, and routing, which form the basis for NDC messaging infrastructure, do have bearing. Meaningful interoperability between NDC frameworks thus goes well beyond a descriptive XML wrapper and may be less probable in reality than vendors admit. But the real differences are more aptly described in terms of business models. As with much in NDC, Goff's axiom applies.

### Notes

1. In economics, an oligopoly is a market condition in which sellers are so few that the actions of any one of them must materially affect price or have some other measurable impact on competitors.

2. Chad Vawter and Ed Roman, "J2EE vs. Microsoft.NET—A comparison of building XML-based web services," June 2001, www.theserverside.com/resources/article.jsp?l=J2EE-vs-DOTNET.

3. www.jcp.org

4. www.microsoft.com/net

# Tomorrow's NDC
# Framework Options

Emerging standard NDC frameworks, bearing many similarities in design and service level, enable a new generation of applications. The degree of interoperability provided by these frameworks both supports and limits the evolution of application development. As in any evolving fitscape, novelty is persistently explored; optional NDC frameworks providing interesting fitscape survival characteristics await discovery.

Vanilla Web Services (those represented by the WUS family of interfaces—WSDL, UDDI, and SOAP) provide an extensible NDC framework for application development. XML ostensibly provides a degree of baked-in interoperability. But without additional layers of definition, too much is left to vendor discretion, and interoperability is not ensured on the application level.

Microsoft has offered BizTalk, a product it markets as a solution to this problem, designed to address concerns specific to b2b transactions on platforms built on top of WUS. A community effort has produced ebXML, which also supports b2b by extending XML specifications over SOAP but which is not specific to any operating system platform. Such efforts in the b2b space are mirrored by similar efforts in application-specific fields such as biotechnology, which has seen several efforts to develop standard extensions in order to facilitate exchange of informatics data. Some of those efforts have been fruitful, while others have found insufficient traction with respect to community support and have since faded. This sort of disappointment points to Reed's law, another important force in the greater NDC fitscape.

In 1999, Dr. David P. Reed, an independent entrepreneur, advisor, and consultant, proffered "Reed's law,"[1] which speaks to community formation, potential value, and Metcalfe's law. The essence of his discovery is that while many kinds of value may be created within networks, there exist certain network structures that create value more quickly than others. Specifically, networks that support the construction of *communicating groups* create value that can scale exponentially with network size, which is much more rapidly than Metcalfe's law would suggest. Reed calls such networks group-forming networks (GFN).

Metcalfe's law is a mathematical truth: the number of possible links between nodes in a network is a function of the square of the nodes. From an economic perspective, it addresses potential value only. Reed's law not only clarifies another exponential of potential value—The number of non-trivial subsets that can be formed from a set of N members is $2N - N - 1$, which grows as $2N$)—but points to an NDC application strategy as well.

A GFN approach to applications, application development, developer communities, and business strategies seems plausible in the Network Age and is also very likely an evolutionary mechanism by which optional frameworks will emerge. Consider eBay.com, the definitive example of a GFN portal. Various instantiations of the *auction* fit well with GFN characteristics, which include such attributes as highly dynamic, scalable, structured, and purposeful. Given the increasing resource base available on the Internet, group formation will trump even peer transaction capabilities as the NDC fitscape evolves. And NDC frameworks that understand and promote group formation will be the means by which it occurs.

# The Renascence of Jini

To the extent that Jini network technology facilitates group formation and communication, Reed's GFN concepts can be realized in code. Over time, resources on the network increase exponentially. Moore's law spurs processor capabilities and storage capacities on the node level, at the same time decreasing the threshold for node deployment; tiny, embedded processors abound. Gilder's law ensures more and faster links among nodes of all kinds, with or without tether. The flow of research and development in the greater NDC fitscape constitutes a feedback system that itself is subject to and benefits from the results; phase shifts should be expected as autonomous agents innovate. And groups are the means by which this innovation occurs.

## Jini History and Design

Jini network technology is the mind child of Bill Joy, formerly Chief Scientist for Sun Microsystems. Joy, inspired by David Gelernter's *Mirror Worlds* (discussed in Chapter 3), based Jini on the Java programming language and Remote Method Invocation (RMI), the means whereby one Java Virtual Machine (JVM) exchanges marshalled data with another. The Jini approach was as innovative as it was misunderstood when it was announced in the summer of 1998. The initial announcement heralded Jini network technology as a competitor to Microsoft's then universal Plug and Play, targeting small devices that would connect to a network. The announcement alluded to services that could be built with Jini network technology, turning a laptop into a supercomputer. But there was a catch: there were then no tiny-device JVMs that supported RMI. Alas, a wild commercial uptake of Jini was not to be forthcoming . . . at least not then.

Mispositioning aside, the fundamentals of Jini network technology still allow developers to view resources on the network in a different way. A means whereby NDC application developers can meaningfully address network realities—the ever-present potential of a partial network failure and the lack of a central authority on the network—will always be of interest. Despite commercial challenges, the idea of a self-healing network, imaginable in the Jini environment, has given rise to a flurry of research into the more *organic* approaches to NDC frameworks, spurred by the Jini community.

A simple set of protocols provide the basis for Jini network technology:

♦ Discovery protocols: Three closely related discovery protocols are used by a device joining a network: one discovers one or more lookup services on a LAN, the second announces the presence of a lookup service on a local network, and the third establishes communications with a specific lookup service over a WAN.

♦ Join protocol: The join protocol makes use of the discovery protocols to provide a standard sequence of steps that services should perform when they are starting up and registering with a lookup service.

♦ Lookup server (LUS): Nodes that would participate in a distributed Jini network technology system (known as *djinn*) must first obtain references to one or more Jini lookup services, found on one or more LUSs. The discovery protocols govern acquisition of these references. Once the references have been obtained, a number of steps must be taken for entities to start communicating usefully with services in a djinn; these steps are described by the join protocol.

On its maiden voyage into a network, a Jini enabled device utilizes a UDP multicast announcment, a self-referential packet proclaiming its nature and needs. Communication between the device and the LUS is facilitated between JVMs by RMI.[2] Note the underlying assumption that the Java platform is ubiquitous. Any device that would join and consume from or provide a service in a Jini environment must be bound to the Java platform. Note the second assumption: an LUS is listening on the network, awaiting announcements from Jini enabled devices.

"Joining a network" is a state in which many components may find themselves in various deployed instantiations. Indeed, we can envision an LUS beginning from just such a state. Once a device successfully joins a Jini enabled network through an LUS, a unicast approach can be taken, as shown in Figure 9.1.

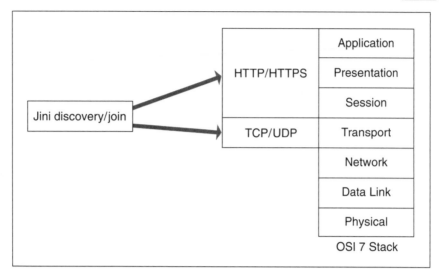

Figure 9.1  Jini at the OSI 7 stack

Another interesting aspect of RMI is its flexibility in playing on the OSI 7 stack, either through HTTP (which sits above TCP) or at the transport layer itself, through UDP, TCP, or other protocols. This dimension of flexibility is not natively present in either CORBA or Web Services.

## The Return of Jini

Between market mispositioning and the inevitable objection to the assumption of ubiquitous JVMs, it's no wonder a wild commercial uptake of Jini network technology was not forthcoming. The JVM assumption can be engineered around by proxies and the Jini Surrogate architecture, which identifies classes of non-JVM devices that can be specified from a communications perspective and therefore proxied. But even while the "Java everywhere" assumption fully addresses Deutsch's Eighth Fallacy (The network is homogenous), it may ignore other realities, Deutsch's and otherwise.

Even without commercial success, the Jini Community[3] has prospered. Thousands of developers from around the world have been active participants in an open community through the Sun Community Source License (SCSL) model. Like the Open Source model, SCSL creates a community of widely available software source code, but with two significant differences:

♦ Compatibility among deployed versions of the software is required and enforced through testing.

♦ Proprietary modifications and extensions, including performance improvements, are allowed.

A simple relationship emerges from the Jini protocols and the assumption of an LUS on the network. The essence of the relationship, as shown in Figure 9.2, should look familiar.

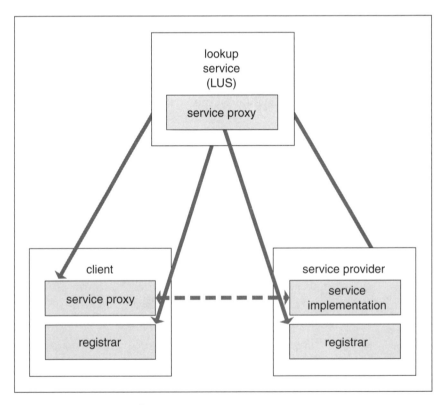

Figure 9.2  Jini protocols

Note the structural similarities with the Client-Registry-Service conceptual model; they tell us that the LUS should behave very much like a registry. An important and oft-cited difference between CORBA and Jini network technology is in the representation of objects: With CORBA, a string is used to identify object attributes, whereas on the LUS, objects are represented as extensible Java objects themselves.

In addition to the protocols, a Jini download includes a number of useful programming interfaces, which complete a GFN-capable framework:

♦ Distributed leasing: *Leases are* grants of a resource or service that are negotiated for a set period of time. Leases can be renewed, cancelled, or allowed to expire, and resources are allocated only so long as appropriate leases are renewed.

♦ Distributed events: An *event* is the reaction of an object to a state change in another object. On an arbitrary network, timely and reliable delivery of events cannot be guaranteed, according to Deutsch's First Fallacy (The network is reliable). Jini distributed events are based on an *observer* pattern for distributed systems.

♦ Distributed transactions: For atomic operations, Jini offers a minimal set of interfaces that specifies a two-phase commit protocol and that also provides for nested transactions.

Based on these protocols and programming interfaces, interesting services can be envisioned, exemplified by JavaSpaces, the aboriginal Gelernter-inspired Jini service. Given the recognition of network realities at the interface level, the spaces computing approach programmatically lends itself well to Reed's GFN concept. The leasing interfaces are most instrumental in that regard, providing a conceptual basis for transactions as well as a means to facilitate network self-healing; a framework for dynamic, arbitrary group formation is the result.

"Jini or something like Jini" became the evangelical mantra at Sun. Once the properties that can emerge on a network so configured became clear, a community of interest also emerged, one with sufficient traction to support, refine, extend, and employ the technology. Many developers worldwide have been or are active in the Jini Community. At the same time, further research at Sun coalesced around exploration of "something like Jini," ultimately leading to Project JXTA and the peer-to-peer (p2p) approach to GFNs, an approach that also boasts an active supporting community of thousands of developers. GFN concepts play at the framework-molding layer even as they provide a model ripe for commercial exploitation. With the fundamental strength and weakness of the assumption that JVMs are ubiquitous in the Jini network, the framework offers a reliability and penchant for GFNs that cannot be matched by any preceding NDC framework, including vanilla Web Services and CORBA.

# Peer-to-Peer Networks: The Project JXTA Example

Strictly speaking, both CORBA and Web Services provide a framework in which some p2p patterns can emerge. But GFN-style applications such as file sharing, instant messaging, collaborative frameworks, and even spaces computing models are simply easier to encode in what is fundamentally a highly interoperable p2p environment. Content delivery networks that use p2p protocols to push value to the network edge will find an increasingly wide array of devices to target, and distributed resource-sharing projects, as exemplified by SETI@Home, are also easily enabled. Imagine the possibilities for p2p in fields such as gaming, ecommerce, grid computing, and even wireless devices. Commercially successful p2p frameworks still await discovery, however, in the wake of the much maligned Napster.

Along with Napster came a realization that in a network that is sufficiently mature with respect to the Nth Laws, interesting properties gleaned with p2p approaches may have significant impact on a number of assumptions. Intellectual property rights notwithstanding, the more popular an item in a p2p network becomes, the easier it is to obtain. It is also true that a p2p network is naturally suited for dynamic group formation. On such a network, a simple p2p model, as shown in Figure 9.3, provides one of the least centralized, most flexible frameworks yet considered, and perhaps one of the most difficult to manage as well.

## Project JXTA and p2p

Another deflection-point-embracing technology closely associated with Bill Joy is Project JXTA. From the perspective of Reed's law, Project JXTA is without peer in the fitscape of frameworks that would compete for NDC dominance. While GFNs are at the heart and soul of JXTA, managing the p2p networks and applications that emerge is another matter.

Where Jini assumes JVMs everywhere, Project JXTA assumes nothing anywhere. A simple set of protocols, bound only to advertisements writ-

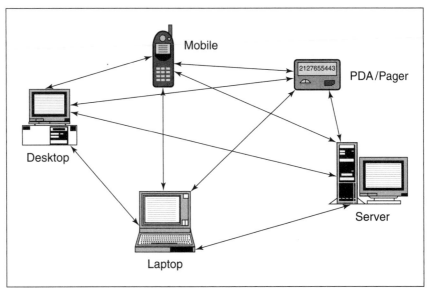

Figure 9.3  Peer-to-peer (p2p) network

ten in XML, form the basis for the JXTA p2p framework. The following five concepts are key to JXTA nomenclature:

- Advertisements—XML documents (like WSDL) that can describe any resource, node, or service
- Peers—Nodes on a JXTA network that implement JXTA peer protocols
- Peer groups—Dynamic groupings of peers that are not tightly specified and could be a group of services or nodes, a geographically similar grouping, and so on
- Messages—Communications in the datagram style (UDP) for use on unreliable, asynchronous or unidirectional transports (like IP)
- Pipes—Connection of peers in one-to-one, one-to-many, and many-to-many relationships for message passing
- Pipe binding—Runtime binding that allows rebinding if errors occur

Project JXTA defines scores of communication protocols that are independent of each other. That is, if an arbitrary application uses only one of the protocols defined to accomplish its aim, it may still find some homage in a JXTA network as shown in Figure 9.4.

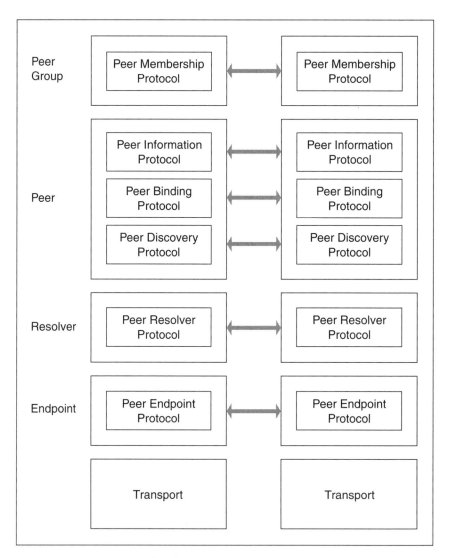

Figure 9.4. JXTA protocol independence

Project JXTA is open source, functionally equivalent to the Apache source license.[4] JXTA defines an application "stack" for p2p communication, which provides much of the underlying interoperable piping. While JXTA was originated by Sun Microsystems (and does begin with a J) it is not based on the Java platform, nor does it require a JVM to run. Although the reference implementation does target J2SE, some JXTA developers have implemented JXTA protocols using C, Python, and Perl as well. Advertisements in XML are specified, ensuring high interoperability.

## Peer Group Services

In p2p networks, peers tend to self-organize into peer groups. A peer group is a collection of nodes that implement the peer protocols and that may have a common set of interests. Each peer group is identified by a unique PeerGroup ID. The JXTA protocols do not mandate the circumstances for peer group creation but only specify how peers may publish, discover, join, and monitor peer groups.

A peer group can provide a set of services. JXTA specifies a core set, called peer group services, the on-the-wire data encoding for which it describes. But because of the community approach taken by the Project JXTA team, a much larger engineering group is involved in the effort, easily allowing additional peer group services to be developed, which add the following to the core set of peer group services:

- Discovery service: Used by peer members to search for peer group resources (peers, peer groups, pipes, and services)

- Membership service: Used by peer members to reject or accept a new group membership application

- Access service: Used to validate requests made by one peer to another

- Pipe service: Used to manage and create pipe connections between the different peer group members

- Resolver service: Used to address queries to services running on peers in the group and collect responses

- Monitoring service: Used to allow one peer to monitor other members of the same peer group

Not all the above services, or the JXTA protocols, must be implemented by a JXTA peer group. By the same token, other services can be envisioned and easily join the JXTA-enabled p2p network; something like the Jini LUS comes to mind, or p2p spaces computing, which too is being explored by a small community worldwide.

## Peer Horizons

Recall that with Jini enabled networks, a device can know nothing about any identified repository and still manage to join a network. With JXTA, at the very least, the identity of something that exercises at least the peer protocol must be known. Once bootstrapped, however, either multicast may be used, usually on a LAN, or unicast to a repository of peers. In JXTA, such repositories are called "rendezvous servers"; these can cache

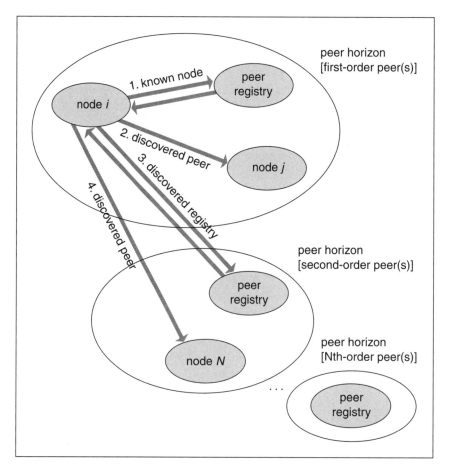

Figure 9.5. JXTA peer horizons

data from and about other peers and offer peer advertisements and proxies and are structured much like a directory from the Client-Registry-
Service conceptual model.

Searching for services in a JXTA-enabled network begins with a query
of first order peer(s), including known rendezvous servers, a step that begins the exploration process for the network resources in question. First-
order peers are those whose existence is known, who are operating in com-
pliance with the JXTA peer protocol, and who are assumed to be available.
This constitutes a peer horizon from the perspective of the node initiating
the query. Rendezvous servers may ask other rendezvous servers within their
horizon if they know of the service, a query that may repeat from server to
server, increasing the scope of the search horizon exponentially with each
layer, as shown in Figure 9.5. Because of cascading rendezvous requests, a

peer must wait some reasonable amount of time before repeating a search. But the power and potential of a p2p network should be apparent.

### Pipes to Layers

One of the interesting features of Project JXTA is where on the OSI 7 stack JXTA pipes can play. With greater flexibility than any previously considered framework, p2p application patterns may consider exploitation of potential at each layer. While the ability of an inappropriately encoded p2p application to ignore an arbitrary firewall may at first give developers pause, the opportunity to bake in security at the network or transport layer is also exposed, even while a free ride on HTTP is ensured.

## Spaces Computing

There are a number of motivations for taking a spaces computing approach to NDC application development:

♦ Simplicity: For the most part, steep learning curves are not required. A handful of simple operations provides access to the typical tuplespace.

♦ Expressiveness: Using a small set of operations, a large class of NDC applications can be produced without a lot of code written.

♦ Loosely coupled protocols: A tuplespace must uncouple senders and receivers, to facilitate the composition of large applications. Components can be easily added without redesign of the entire application.

In discussing spaces computing, it is useful to attempt to define the term *organic software*. In truth, it is not meant to be a candidate for specification as much as it is an allusion to attributes that an NDC framework should exhibit if it is to be vital, in light of Deutsch's Eight Fallacies. A list of such attributes, which apply to any NDC framework, includes the following:

♦ Dynamic service and peer discovery
♦ Self-healing network attributes
♦ Distributed transaction capability
♦ Workflow automation and integration capability
♦ Agent collaboration

Any NDC framework that demonstrates these organic attributes can be tuplespace-capable. Conceptually, applications launch objects to and retrieve them from a space, as shown in Figure 9.6.

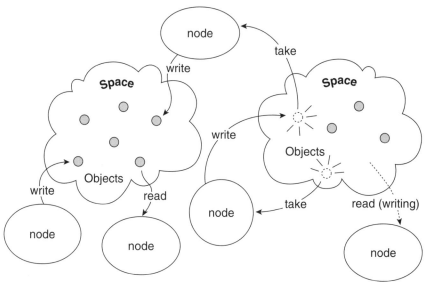

Figure 9.6 Spaces computing simplicity

## JavaSpaces Technology

JavaSpaces, like other spaces computing approaches, provides a simple mechanism for dynamic communication, coordination, and sharing of objects between JVMs. In an NDC application, a space acts as a virtual space between providers and requesters of network resources or objects. This allows applications participating in a spaces computing solution to exchange tasks, requests, and information. Object persistence is also standardized with JavaSpaces.

JavaSpaces assumes that users are all linked to a JVM. Transport between differenct languages can be implemented through the Java Native Interface (JNI) specification, and if a node is not linked to a JVM, programming links can be made through RMI/IIOP or CORBA transport systems. Although there are conceptually similarities to a database on one level, there are many differences between a spaces computing persistent object and one logged in a database. To be useful, databases require a tremendous amount of overhead in structured programming, interface design, type matching, and indexing. A database client must send specific queries to the server and receives specific answers to those queries. A spaces computing approach is a much more loosely coupled repository of data. The identity of a client or a server in a space is not relevant; data packets are treated just like any other object posted to the space—as an anonymous service.

With JavaSpaces, a system can be thought of as an event-driven distributed cache with behavior transfer capabilities—something not available with CORBA—with functionality well beyond that of a simple messaging system. An application running on a JavaSpaces implementation typically runs in the middle tier of a three tier client-server model (although it can run anywhere).

## Tuplespaces

The essence of spaces computing is the tuplespace (from Gelernter's original Linda sytem): a multiset containing tuples, which can be thought of as objects with exposed attributes. A *multiset* means that a tuplespace can contain an arbitrary number of identical tuples, which are treated as discrete objects. Some tuplespace implementations provide the ability to nest tuplespaces. The tuplespace can be implemented in a number of ways; both Jini network technology and Project JXTA have framework proponents of a spaces computing implementation for NDC applications.

Most tuplespace systems assume one or more spaces running on one or more nodes; the concept of distributing a single tuplespace over multiple nodes is less common. JavaSpaces supports multiple local and remote shared tuplespaces, but does not explicitly support distributed tuplespaces. IBM's TSpaces has similar limitations.

True distributed tuplespaces offer many advantages in terms of scalability and availability—attributes that would ideally be available in all spaces computing implementations. The Projext JXTA community is pioneering jxtaSpaces,[5] which is intended to provide scalable shared memory services for networks of heterogeneous peers. In large p2p networks, a global tuplespace can be used in many ways to simplify the building of complex NDC applications.

## Summary

From the perspective of GFNs, a spaces computing approach to NDC application development provides a simple, extensible, organic means of achieving results. To the extent that the attributes of organic software become more important over time, spurred by Nth Law-driven growth and the proliferation of networks of all kinds, spaces computing represents a tractable choice that will bring medium-term competitive advantage to its adherents. Indeed, as sedimentation and consolidation continue, in time a tuplespace too will become a commodity. At the moment, however, Gelernter's vision remains a largely untapped commercial resource.

## Notes

1. www.reed.com/Papers/GFN/reedslaw.html
2. While an IIOP flavor of RMI is specified for the Java platform, it does not provide the necessary protocol underpinnings to adequately support the Jini vision. Java Remote Method Protocol simplifies communication between JVMs and is the protocol of choice for RMI with Jini.
3. www.jini.org
4. www.jxta.org/project/www/license.html
5. jxtaspaces.jxta.org/

# Fallacies and Frameworks

From the perspective of developers, an NDC framework must either acknowledge or ignore each of Peter Deutsch's Eight Fallacies of Distributed Computing. A comparison of how the competing NDC frameworks approach each fallacy serves to illustrate the relative strengths, weaknesses, and opportunities inherent in each of the fitscapes they engender.

The dean of the business school I attended told this story:

---

A large, extended family that saw each other only on special occasions were joyously attending a dinner celebrating the 65th birthday of the matron of the tribe. Nearly 50 family members had gathered, renting formal attire and a large room at the best hotel in town; they chatted away as waiters served fine wines and exquisite hors d'oeuvres while a classical music ensemble played in the background. The birthday matron's 12-year-old granddaughter, sitting next to her grandmother, reached over to take a delicacy from the hors d'oeuvres platter when her elbow inadvertently knocked over the matron's glass of deep-red merlot, spilling its contents on the eggshell-white cotton tablecloth, leaving a crimson stain, and causing a sudden hush among the assemblage.

The waiters, who were actually actors trying to earn money between auditions, were stunned. Both busboys had called in sick earlier that evening in protest over a dispute, and the stunned actors didn't know exactly what to do about the spilled wine.

But one person knew: the matron. At length, she broke the silence with a carefully crafted statement: "The wine is on the table." It was exactly the right thing to say; the only statement that could have been made without offending, denying, blaming, or ignoring the reality of the situation. The context of the mishap required ritual elegance and adroitness.

A moment passed. Then a sense of relief permeated the air; the actors started behaving like waiters again, carefully removing dishes around the soiled area and covering the blemish with another tablecloth; the classical musicians began to play again; the matron smiled at her granddaughter and offered her another selection from the hors d'oeuvres tray.

---

# Deutsch's Eight Fallacies Re-viewed

The wine is on the table! Reality must be acknowledged if we would heal. To that end, recall Deutsch's Eight Fallacies:

1. The network is reliable
2. Latency is zero

3. Bandwidth is infinite

4. The network is secure

5. Topology doesn't change

6. There is one administrator

7. Transport cost is zero

8. The network is homogeneous

To acknowledge a fallacy is akin to the matron's statement; the reality of the network is wine that is spilled. But the truth is that there are eight problems here, not just one; each fallacy can be separately acknowledged or ignored. Existing NDC frameworks address some of the inherent problems articulated by Deutsch's Eight Fallacies by ignoring others. Invariably, some network realities are ignored until designs start to fray at the edges when implementations are actually built; the particular patterns of acknowledgement and denial are the basis for comparison between frameworks. In fact, it would be unwise to design any reasonably complex NDC application without first reviewing the development and deployment framework of choice in relation to the fallacies.

Each fallacy relates to others within the set, but each expresses a particular network nuance that may manifest in a particular manner. Indeed, each exposes an opportunity for NDC frameworks to add value by acknowledging a fallacy and taking steps to measurably reduce the innate risks to correct application execution. The key point here is measurability; each fallacy can be quantified.

## Measurement View

Consider the First Fallacy: in fact, the reliability of a network can be measured. While edge-to-edge reliability cannot be easily assured in something as fluid as the Internet, LAN and WAN reliability measures are routinely tracked and expressed in percentage of downtime. By the same token, the speed of light can be measured, as can switching speeds, opto-electric conversion speeds, and other inflators of latency. Bandwidth too can be measured (see Fig. 10.1), as can transport cost, network administration and application porting costs.

In fact, all of Deutsch's fallacies—or rather the extent to which the assumptions that constitute them turn out to be untrue—can be measured. And any process that can be measured presumably provides opportunities for process improvement, hence added value. Consideration of the way in

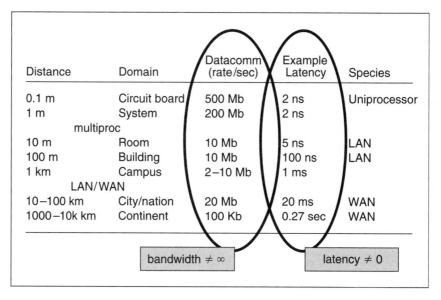

| Distance | Domain | Datacomm (rate/sec) | Example Latency | Species |
|---|---|---|---|---|
| 0.1 m | Circuit board | 500 Mb | 2 ns | Uniprocessor |
| 1 m | System | 200 Mb | 2 ns | |
| | multiproc | | | |
| 10 m | Room | 10 Mb | 5 ns | LAN |
| 100 m | Building | 10 Mb | 100 ns | LAN |
| 1 km | Campus | 2–10 Mb | 1 ms | |
| | LAN/WAN | | | |
| 10–100 km | City/nation | 20 Mb | 20 ms | WAN |
| 1000–10k km | Continent | 100 Kb | 0.27 sec | WAN |

bandwidth ≠ ∞          latency ≠ 0

Figure 10.1 Bandwidth and latency

which a given middleware approach would reduce the impact of sometimes onerous reality, as specified by Deutsch, is therefore of value to software developers.

## Simplification View

As "A Note on Distributed Computing" suggests, NDC developers may choose to ignore some aspects of reality in order to make simplifying design assumptions. So too can NDC frameworks. A framework can acknowledge a reality in one of two ways: either by masking the constraint or by exposing it through interfaces. If a framework masks the constraint, it must provide an extensible means of engineering around the constraint. If it exposes the constraint, developers are made aware of the need for mindful application adaptations.

For example, take the Eighth Fallacy: the network is homogeneous. The architects of Jini network technology initially made the simplifying assumption that a JVM with RMI would be everywhere. The problem of network heterogeneity would be masked from developers, even as the Jini approach acknowledged the fallacy. While the assumption may have been flawed from a (then) small-footprint-device perspective, it was reasonable for some applications and would allow work on a pioneering network platform to commence. And acknowledging the fallacy with a meaningful design choice meant that a more organic platform could emerge.

## Risk View

But note too the inherent risk. Even though we may acknowledge every fallacy at some juncture, as we must, there is no guarantee that the application will actually succeed in acknowledging the fallacy as the fitscape around it evolves. To the extent that WUS-style interoperability can give rise to an essentially homogeneous environment on the message level, the Jini approach to homogeneity, which is presumed to be orthogonal to XML wrappers, seems more brittle. So even while Jini would acknowledge the reality of a heterogeneous environment by assuming the homogenizing presence of a JVM everywhere, it ignores the reality of the early 21st century network, in which this homogenizing presence does not exist. By relative comparison, WUS acknowledges that reality where Jini ignores it, and this is reflected in relative levels of investment.

## Security View

It is often unclear exactly where a framework may draw a line with respect to Deutsch's fallacies. Security is an area that must evolve as rapidly as increasing processor capabilities require; the more computing capability available to any random user, the more likely that computing capability will be used to inappropriately compromise current encryption mechanisms. So while solutions may currently exist or are envisioned, none of the cited NDC frameworks offer long-term clarity in regard to the false assumption that the network is secure. Nor can it be argued that any of the frameworks effectively mask this fallacy.

The hard lessons of network security have become of utmost importance to our evolving global community in the early 21st century. One such lesson is that the viability of a service depends as much on the relationship between service provider and user as it does on the nature of the service itself. Another is that security and trust are at the top of every company's list of obstacles, slowing broad adoption of all NDC frameworks.

# Web Services Framework

From an investment perspective, the reality of Web Services is the most prominent feature of the NDC software fitscape. The extent to which the vast majority of software development is beholden to one of the oligopoly players and the forces represented by those players is evident when the fit-scape evolves. Regardless of whether my business is a pure Microsoft play, a real-time operating system shop, an ERP provider, a governmental agency, a retail chain, or one of a growing list of knowledge management players, Web Services will have impact on my work because of the weight and activities of the oligopoly proponents of Web Services in the NDC space—Microsoft, IBM, and Sun Microsystems.

## Network Reliability and Bandwidth

If we would examine WUS from the perspective of network reliability, we must examine how WUS interfaces behave in the absence of it. Recall that WUS would essentially transform standard Internet pages into messages. Messaging in general and asynchronous messaging in particular are critically important to network reliability. A loosely coupled distributed architecture, like one expressed in an asynchronous messaging system, is ideal because it allows nodes on the network to fail without disrupting the overall correctness of NDC operation or the viability of an arbitrary message.

In NDC communications among enterprises and across business entities, the use of vanilla Web Services over HTTP does not yet suffice, because of the absence of a standardized asynchronous messaging capability. Nodes are sometimes temporarily unreachable, the reality of which we cannot ignore. In this sense, Web Services will benefit from a union with Java API for XML Messaging (JAXM) and its asynchronous messaging capabilities (discussed in Chapter 6). Interfaces will always need data transformation and end-to-end guaranteed delivery, along with all the other enterprise needs such as scalability and security. If the lack of rigor in vanilla Web Services is not addressed by more powerful mechanisms, such as JAXM-based messaging providers, the framework will ultimately flounder.

Vanilla Web Services effectively ignore the first of Deutsch's fallacies. When modified by extensions, such as JAXM or those envisioned in the ebXML community, the fallacy is acknowledged and mechanisms may be offered. But not so with vanilla WUS.

This is true of bandwidth considerations as well; XML is not terse. The same footprint arguments that marginalized the early Jini efforts apply in full measure to WUS XML data streams and parsing requirements.

## Security

The vanilla WUS stack is vulnerable; as a result, developers that produce applications based on Web Services must rely upon collaborative security solutions, composed by hand from existing technologies such as SSL and IPSec. While these approaches may secure messages exchanged within SOAP, they undermine the dynamic potential of Web Services precisely because they demand a high degree of static coordination and collaboration between partners and among nodes. It is likely that a more robust set of standards will emerge to address WUS security concerns, but it is not clear that any extension to a framework that is based entirely on the demands of interoperability between platforms can ever really offer baked-in security.

## Topology

Asynchronous messaging capabilities are key to reliable networking, which provides the opportunity to manage a changing network topology on some level. To the extent that early WUS suffers from a synchronous view, its ignorance of the Fifth Fallacy (Topology doesn't change) is also betrayed. Any notion of self-healing must then become platform specific, which is not as interesting or as cost effective, as one that is more open.

## Administration

The false assumption of a single administrator is also ignored by vanilla WUS. It is expected that simple, SOAP-wrapped messages can be effectively knitted together through a repository of independent components; this assumes either terribly adaptable software (something akin to a clever computer virus) or a certain level of hands-on production, albeit through accommodating point-and-click tools.

Think of the Semantic Web, which would harvest meaning from information dynamically. Now take away RDF, ontologies, and any notion of a standardized general-purpose agent mechanism; what remains is XML, SOAP, and the promise of Web Services with all the work we've taken away to be done by hand, page by page, by NDC workers. Do you believe the output of all those human-bound fitscapes will always play together well? The more interesting a Web Service is from a business-value perspective, the more likely it is to require significant effort to implement. Witness the activities in various quarters which would provide a Web Ser-

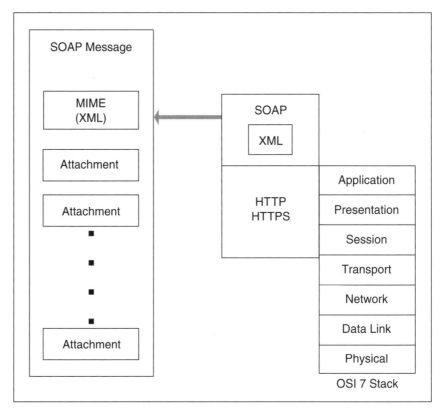

Figure 10.2  WUS and the OSI 7-layer stack

vices interaction layer on top of existing legacy interfaces. This will take time, resources, and commitment to design, implement, test, release and promote, and will often require extensive testing with partners.

## Transport

When it comes to transport cost, the Seventh Fallacy, recall that vanilla Web Services use HTTP, which rides TCP, which serves in the Transport layer of the OSI 7-layer conceptual model. Recall further the relationship of WUS to the OSI model, as shown in Figure 10.2.

    If there are no transport issues beyond those resolved by TCP, the model is fine. But what happens when there is an application-level need for other kinds of transport services? The cost of those services, in processing time, network chatter, and the absence of asynchronous reliability,

| | vanilla WUS | WUS ++ |
|---|---|---|
| 1. The network is reliable. | NAK | ACK |
| 2. Latency is zero. | NAK | ACK |
| 3. Bandwidth is infinite. | NAK | NAK |
| 4. The network is secure. | UNC | UNC |
| 5. Topology doesn't change. | NAK | ACK |
| 6. There is one administrator. | NAK | NAK |
| 7. Transport cost is zero. | NAK | ACK |
| 8. The network is homogeneous. | ACK | ACK |
| NAK = effectively ignores; ACK = acknowledged; UNC = unclear | | |

Figure 10.3  Vanilla Web Services and WUS plus ebXML/JAXM

are high. Once again, in order to actually move beyond the reality barrier of transport cost at the Application layer, we require significant extensions. Whether proprietary, such as Microsoft's BizTalk, or community-driven, such as ebXML and JAXM, transport issues at a higher conceptual layer must be economically resolved at an NDC application layer. And HTTP is not the answer.

## Homogeneity

When it comes to interoperability, WUS technology has set the standard. As long as XML is agreed to be the means by which data can be described, the combination of a simple, extensible wrapper for networked objects with XML as the descriptive mechanism is a powerful metaphor. Add base-level repository functions, and interoperability is fully encompassed. To that extent, vanilla Web Services as shown in Figure 10.3 pay homage to Deutsch's Eighth Fallacy, even as they sidestep many of the others.

## Web Services Futures

Web Services must evolve. Perhaps (as in e-commerce) a few new companies will emerge, lured by the range of temporary niches exposed by the behemoth battles of a fitscape characterized by a highly competitive oligopoly, but the bulk of the business will ultimately go to existing service providers. Those with pockets deep enough to endure the large investments and slow ramp-up times that are likely to be typical of new Web Services will be the only winners in the end.

# Jini Network Technology Framework

The magic of Jini networking bestrides the brilliant platform envisioned and pioneered by James Gosling. The assumption of a JVM everywhere dramatically reduces development and porting costs, ensures security and high-quality applications and is supported by the largest software development community in the industry. So it is reasonable to assume that networked applications will find harbor in those waters. That fundamental assumption is both the strength and weakness of Jini networking, due not to the technical implications but to other competitive selection criteria encountered in an often fickle fitscape.

## Homogeneity and Topology

The first iteration of the Jini vision required RMI-enabled JVM implementations, bound to the first standard release of J2SE. Non-JVM devices might be proxied into the Jini network and were enabled as such, but a JVM was required at some juncture and there was no standardized proxy structure. Later work on a surrogate interface that would enable Jini services to and from non-JVM nodes found a home in the PAN space with Bluetooth devices. But at their heart, Jini networks dance to a JVM beat, and Deutsch's Eighth Fallacy is both acknowledged and ignored.

To the credit of the Jini community, the vision of a surrogate architecture and its potential for surrogate hosts that would extend to limited devices an organic interconnected world, addresses any Eighth Fallacy exposure. The same is true for network topology, because the surrogate design acknowledges wireless behavior at the level of the surrogate host.

### Leases

Jini's leasing programming interfaces provide access to a resource or a request for some action that is not open ended, but access is granted only for some particular interval of time. This interval is generally determined by negotiation between the object asking for the resource (the lease holder) and the object granting access (the lease grantor).

In its most general form, a lease associates a mutually agreed-on time interval with an agreement reached by these two objects. The kinds of agreements that can be leased are varied; they include agreements on access to an object (references), agreements for taking future action (event notifications), agreements to supplying persistent storage (filesystems or JavaSpaces systems), or agreements to advertise availability (naming or directory services).

While a lease can provide exclusive access to a resource, exclusivity is not required. Objects that provide access to resources which are intrinsically sharable can accommodate multiple concurrent lease holders. Other resources might decide to grant only exclusive leases, combining the notion of leasing with a concurrency control mechanism.

If the time interval expires and the lease grantor has not heard back from the lease holder, programmatic actions can be taken to ensure resource recovery. Utilization of leasing, combined with the Jini discovery, join, and LUS protocols, is the magic that gives rise to self-healing capabilities in Jini networks; Deutsch's First Fallacy is clearly acknowledged.

## Latency

In addition to the speed of light, network gnomes, and routing bingo, the latency of messages is bound to messaging infrastructure. Just as vanilla Web Services can sidestep latency issues with the addition of an asynchronous messaging provider approach like JAXM, the more synchronous RMI protocols provide the pipe to what is effectively a messaging provider in the Jini network LUS. Between RMI, leasing, and the LUS, an asynchronous, distributed transaction model emerges, belying its synchronous dependency. And if we're asynchronous, why do we care about latency?

In general, latency is the time wasted by one component in a system as it waits for another component. In NDC, the amount of time it takes a packet to travel from one node to another is included. Together, latency and bandwidth define the speed and capacity of a network. Leases provide the means to transcend the constraints of network latency.

## Bandwidth

With respect to bandwidth, Java bytecode is relatively terse even when marshaled, and while it may not be fair to compare portable behavior with portable data characteristics, interoperability must include both. The extent to which Jini LUSs expose services that are bound to extensible Java objects speaks well to bandwidth considerations. Leasing, with dynamic time increments, allows for a self-tuning network when it comes to bandwidth utilization. The Third Fallacy too is acknowledged by the Jini vision.

## Security

Even while the Java platform is inherently more secure than previous approaches to NDC, applications cannot play in the wild with some abandon unless aspects of security are baked in at the protocol level; this, at least, is the view of some of the efforts that would spoof-proof the Jini environment.

The Davis project is an effort by the Jini team at Sun to address the need for a Jini technology security architecture and will ultimately result in a Jini Technology Starter Kit release from Sun. This kit will include a network security programming model allowing applications written in the Java programming language to make use of network security mechanisms in conjunction with RMI. It will also contain other components to support remote object export and configuration programming models and will provide a security policy for dynamically granting permissions at runtime. A secure version of a customizable implementation of the RMI programming model, called *Jini extensible remote invocation,* will also be provided. These facilities will form the basis on which security will be added to Jini technology-enabled applications and services.

But as we have said, security is always a moving target. While the efforts of the Jini community with respect to the fallacies are laudable, the inherently nonsecure environment that flows and congeals with GFN aplomb around the network metaphor presents one of the fundamental challenges to NDC developers today. No matter which framework or approach is chosen, security matters will continue to require application evolution.

# Project JXTA Framework

The "Jini or something like Jini" theme emerged after it became clear that perceived constraints of the Jini approach were technology-adoption barriers in what is otherwise a superior conceptual model for NDC. Just as the brilliance of the Jini approach is the simplifying assumption of a JVM everywhere, the brilliance of Project JXTA is the simplifying assumption of nothing anywhere, at least insofar as computing capabilities are concerned. Bound only to advertisements in XML, the heterogeneity of the network is acknowledged even as it is exposed for developers to augment.

## Reliability

An inherently unreliable network is expected with a p2p approach. As with vanilla WUS, there is no general mechanism for reliable messaging, but the general topology of each framework suggests how it will be achieved. WUS will most likely use centralized mechanisms to create highly available systems, such as clustered application servers with load balancing and hot-swappable services. Peer systems will use distributed peers running the same service in a redundant manner, with the first available peer that receives the message responding to the request. Generally, a p2p approach gives rise to organic attributes akin to the Jini approach, but with an entirely different architecture. Recovering from partial network failure is a capability exhibited by both. Hence, Deutsch's First Fallacy is acknowledged by p2p.

## Bandwidth and Latency

Systemic behavioral patterns frequently emerge in p2p networks. Consider the phenomenon of access, for example, the "the more popular an item is, the easier it is to obtain" pattern is routinely observed in p2p-enabled approaches. Another is the previously cited phenomenon of cascading searches, which has an implication in the time domain as well as the value domain. Latency, which is already nonzero, can be magnified by the messaging requirements of search ripples, which may exponentially bloat lightweight network chatter. But this is not to suggest that the platform ignores Deutsch's Second Fallacy. Quite the contrary; it is *understood* that network latency exists, and the search ripples may take time to settle, so a certain level of latency should be expected. The JXTA specifications reflect this reality. By the same token, chatter is chatter; Project JXTA ignores Deutsch's Third Fallacy.

## Security

One of the interesting developments in the p2p space is the growing of "webs of trust"; in essence, one peer can loan its credentials to another peer. This innovation may be significant in a general NDC security sense and may one day find its way into other frameworks, like Web Services. But for our comparison, it is unclear if p2p realistically has advantages for or offers insights into security beyond those of any other approach.

## Topology

As with the Jini network, p2p systems expect intermittent nodes, dynamic network links, and essentially changing topologies. Indeed, to the extent that Project JXTA protocols can ride HTTP through firewalls, much in the way of putative network topology can be ignored. Couple this aspect of Project JXTA with an incubator-ready GFN bias and the network can potentially take on forms not yet envisioned with respect to value. From a developer's perspective, p2p understands the fluid nature of network topology, but there is as much danger as there is potential for yet more ephemeralization in the topology-busting p2p vision.

## Administration

To the extent that organic software attributes give rise to self-healing capabilities in networks, the need for arbitrary system and network administration is theoretically reduced. Deutsch's Sixth Fallacy is interesting in that regard. This assumption is false both because there are many administrators and because there are none. If the future is to include myriad personal, intelligent devices, all of which interact with myriad networks, the software that binds them must also be capable of adapting to an unpredictable world of users. The alternative is a ballooning of help-desk requests well beyond the limits of any cost-effective business model.

It can be said that Project JXTA acknowledges Deutsch's Sixth Fallacy even as it winks at the firewall, allowing JXTA peers to discover JXTA services well-hidden otherwise. When it comes to administrators, there are always either many or none; take your pick. Interoperability is an application-level choice. The first wave of Web Services will emphasize moving information from one company's server to another's, but WUS will fail to capture mission-critical information at vital touchpoints—employee desktops, EmNets, and wireless nodes. This is prime p2p real estate.

## Transport Cost

With respect to transport cost, recall that JXTA can play at a variety of layers on the OSI 7-layer stack. Project JXTA provides an inherent flexibility in regard to the OSI 7 model, as shown in Figure 10.4, that is not available with any other NDC framework.

It is difficult to generalize about transport costs, because the needs of NDC applications invariably require the ability to intercede on some issues historically identified as germane to that datacom layer. Clearly, it is not viable to replace legacy protocols with each new application. But by the same token, as new services are envisioned, the repackaging, reliability, security, marshalling, and routing of application data will be of interest to those services. If, for example, my framework of choice relies entirely on HTTP or a similar protocol, any transport work my application may need to undertake must be within the session constraints of the underlying protocol. Network chatter and performance impact is the result. The distinct advantage of Project JXTA is the absence of assumption with respect to the Transport layer; it can be bound to HTTP as easily as to UDP,

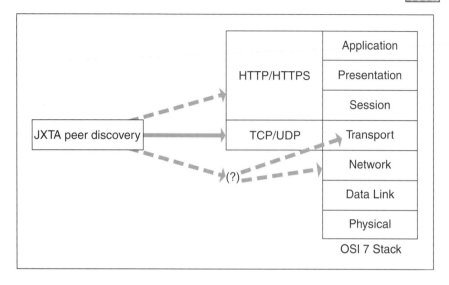

Figure 10.4  Project JXTA and the OSI 7 stack

or even replace TCP if application demands are such as to require those lengths, without breaking JXTA protocols. To that end, Project JXTA acknowledges the cost of transport with a flexible design; vanilla WUS does not.

## Homogeneity

If all we did was examine the basis for messaging in Project JXTA, we would conclude that the pipe metaphor was insufficient for a truly reliable NDC system to emerge, due in no small part to the essentially synchronous nature of the pipe. But the JXTA protocols bring other potential dimensions to bear, and those accord more asynchronous benefits. A messaging provider approach based on JXTA peer, peer group, and rendezvous protocols is something we can imagine as easily as we can a JAXM-based service attached to a WUS network—or even to a JXTA network.

# Other Perspectives

There is clear potential for more sophisticated NDC-enabled business flow models, which will incorporate all assets of an organization, including employees, into the process. As intrabusiness workflow systems and interbusiness processes converge, the marriage of complementary capabilities in NDC frameworks is inevitable.

| | vanilla WUS | WUS ++ | Jini | JXTA |
|---|---|---|---|---|
| 1. The network is reliable. | NAK | ACK | ACK | ACK |
| 2. Latency is zero. | NAK | ACK | ACK | ACK |
| 3. Bandwidth is infinite. | NAK | NAK | ACK | NAK |
| 4. The network is secure. | UNC | UNC | UNC | UNC |
| 5. Topology doesn't change. | NAK | ACK | ACK | ACK |
| 6. There is one administrator. | NAK | NAK | ACK | ACK |
| 7. Transport cost is zero. | NAK | ACK | ACK | ACK |
| 8. The network is homogeneous. | ACK | ACK | ACK/NAK | ACK |

NAK = effectively ignores; ACK = acknowledged; UNC = unclear

Figure 10.5 Comparing fallacies and frameworks

From a technical perspective, this means that Web Services and p2p networks will begin to swap messages. Web Services may expose an organizational view of data, while p2p networks serve as the collection mechanism on an entity basis. Web Services will elicit information from each entity's peer services and then roll it up to make it available as appropriate. To some extent, the strengths of each approach can be leveraged as some of the weaknesses are amended, assuming the end-to-end framework can afford to sacrifice much in the way of organic attributes. Goff's axiom applies.

To my reckoning, there is an inverse relationship, as shown in Figure 10.5, between the actual business investment that a framework may enjoy or demand and the degree to which it acknowledges reality in an NDC programming sense. Clearly, other considerations must apply.

Strictly speaking, measures can be applied not only to the myriad connections and cooking-point opportunities that software explores in an evolving fitscape but also to enabling costs of that fitscape, short and long term. One approach may enjoy competitive advantage over another as a result of a resource-friendly development cycle or a more legacy-constrained, incremental pattern of adoption (or both); legacy systems represent a barrier as much as they do an asset and an opportunity. Such governing factors will always figure significantly in the success or failure of a framework within in a fitscape; any framework may be fit for the moment or while certain conditions apply. But in the end, only those systems that are most adaptable—that is, fit for the broadest possible range of circumstances as the fitscape evolves—will survive to engage the inherently unpredictable unfolding demands of networks to come.

# Commentary

If a framework ignores a reality, one of two general outcomes can be envisioned: the developer must do the work necessary to acknowledge it, or the user must pay for the result. All too often, both are true, and the range of possible outcomes represents some combination of the two. Ultimately, it is the fickle user who acknowledges, by his choices, that which we would all agree is a viable measure of economic reality. As developers, we can choose at any juncture to acknowledge reality or ignore it; NDC framework decisions offer many such opportunities. There is no choice that is without long-term cost, regardless of origin, teleology, customer, or vendor.

Any claim to competitive advantage should therefore be carefully considered from a long-term perspective, with one eye on the realities of NDC programming and the other on the realities of NDC perceptions, which may not necessarily coincide. Our third eye, which should never be used without mindful application of the Kopetz principles of composability (see Chapter 11), should be focused straight ahead at what appears to be an iceberg the size of Singapore—which is by no means a metaphor. The reality of our changing planet, hostage to the failures of our past and our present, also encroaches on the larger fitscape that is NDC development.

# Composability: Real-Time, Grids, and the Rise of an NDC Meta-Architecture

Even as new frameworks emerge, NDC is beginning to embrace computing at the edge of the network: increasingly smaller devices, wireless datacom capabilities, and real-time EmNets represent a fundamental shift in networking. The closer to the edge we get, the greater the extent to which real-time network sensibilities will have an impact on NDC frameworks and programming.

Real-time computing is orthogonal to NDC; at least, that's been the traditional view. With latency issues, speed of light constraints, and indeterminacy, as noted by Deutsch's fallacies, the needs of real-time computing, especially hard real-time, cannot be met in such an environment. And yet it can be argued that some real-time systems research is leading the way in network innovation.

Very tiny processors can now be used in a variety of applications, networked by a broad menu of wireless datacom choices that potentially drive Internet connectivity several orders of magnitude beyond current measures. When it comes to technology consumption, however, the ultimate determinant of fitness for any product is competition within an economic landscape, which itself is altered by technology. As the Internet expands, we will find that the integration of the kinds of networks characterized by real-time EmNets will alter both our use and our view of evolving Internet technologies, including protocols and standards.

## Real-Time Systems

Historically, real-time systems grew from the need to control complex, mission-critical processes. Managing a nuclear reactor, for example, requires a good measure of systems control. Other kinds of applications, like the gathering of data from real-time sources (such as ticker updates for a stock market) also constitute real-time systems, albeit of a different kind. A *hard* real-time system, such as one controlling critical processes in a nuclear reactor, is one that would fail if its timing requirements were not met; the system is deterministic. A *soft* real-time system can tolerate significant, variations in the delivery of services like events, messages, interrupts, timers, and scheduling. A soft, nondeterministic real-time approach works for our stock market ticker if we're not concerned with short delays and the occasional missed message.

Real-time systems are bound, by definition, to temporal constraints. As such, the inherent indeterminacy of the Internet represents a fundamental barrier to broad adoption of Internet technologies by hard real-time systems, or at least by those aspects of such systems that are bound to hard real-time requirements; not every aspect of every application is so bound. Nonetheless, a line is drawn. Without a quality of service (QoS) assurance, from the Internet, that guarantees deterministic message delivery, a real distribution of a hard real-time application logic is not likely soon. Soft real-time systems are an entirely different matter.

## Soft Real-Time Applications

In general, soft real-time applications do not fail if a deadline is missed. Some soft real-time applications may process large amounts of data or require a very fast response time, but the key differentiator is whether meeting timing constraints is an invariant condition for success.

A number of NDC applications employ soft real-time approaches. Soft real-time computing is the general and most frequent case of real-time applications because in most cases, timeliness and predictability are not cost effective, or even possible. Indeed, the relevant characteristics of an execution environment may not even be deterministic. In soft real-time systems, an acceptable predictability of timeliness takes on other dimensions: the mean tardiness, the number of missed deadlines, or a particular probability distribution.

Soft real-time computing, as such, is more difficult to perform than hard real-time computing. Often, intrinsically soft real-time computing problems are abstracted into hard ones that can be analyzed and solved with techniques that developers may find to be simpler and more familiar than those for soft real-time computing, but that ultimately require additional resources and result in a reduction of overall system flexibility.

## Throughput Issues

Some real-time applications require high I/O throughput and fast response time to asynchronous external events, requiring continuous processing of large amounts of data. High throughput requirements are typically found in signal processing applications such as telemetric analysis, radar analysis, sonar, and speech analysis.

If an application needs to handle multiple data channels simultaneously, the result is high aggregate throughput. Some real-time systems, such as medical diagnosis applications, need a response time of about one second while simultaneously handling data from a growing array of external sources. But just as important as high throughput and fast processing is the ability of a real-time application to respond to asynchronous events, as well as its ability to schedule and provide communication among multiple tasks.

Some real-time applications require a response time of microseconds while simultaneously handling data from a large number of external sources. Consider a flight simulator, which might acquire hundreds of input parameters from the cockpit controls even as it computes position, orientation, and speed and sends several hundred output parameters to the cockpit console and visual display subsystem.

Requirements for real-time applications may vary; Goff's axiom applies. Some portion of an application may consist of hard, mission-critical tasks, all of which must meet deterministic constraints. Other portions may require heavy I/O throughput, even while other components may easily run at a lower priority, requiring no special real-time functionality. A successful real-time application is bound to the developer's ability to accurately define application requirements at every point in the flow, allocating resources and real-time priorities only when necessary.

# Component Composability

As noted in our discussion in Chapter 2, the composability of components is analogous to the musical etymology of the word itself. Just as a symphony is more than each instrument playing its respective part, a composition of independent entities must exhibit attributes of context awareness from both the value domain and the time domain in which all the entities play. Our clarinet player participates in the ensemble, bound by a peer horizon and interface specifications, and functions within that shared context.

True composability enables larger and more complex behaviors to be built or assembled from smaller, simpler components or objects, resulting in an orchestration based on context. The importance of composability is not new, but no general capability guarantee currently exists in any software environment that would ensure composability without careful analysis.

## Components in Context

*Components,* in the context of composability, can be thought of as units of development and deployment that have been designed to be constructively integratable into larger set of services. They provide standardized functionality, have well-defined application interfaces, and can be assembled with other components for specific functional purposes. A component may or may not be bound to a particular instantiation of hardware but must include, by definition, at least one unit of software. A constructively integratable component may comprise other components. (Interestingly, this definition of components, borrowed from real-time R&D, closely parallels that of Web Services.)

A specification of components is important to some real-time computing applications. The automobile industry, for example, which happens to be the largest aggregate consumer of embedded devices on the planet, depends heavily on clear specifications of COTS components, which can be cost-effectively utilized in the manufacturing of the modern ground transportation device as well as embedded within it.

Once a specification of components arises, the composability of those components becomes a layer at which value can be derived. Indeed, the promise of composability drives much current industry investment in a Web Services approach to NDC, vanilla and otherwise. But just as the spectrum of real-time is as broad as it is specific, which in turn enables an array of standard components, the very systems that would be built from those components must honor myriad constraints. Constructively integratable components are implied.

## The Kopetz Principles of Composability

Characteristics of a composable architecture for real-time systems have been identified by Hermann Kopetz of the University of Vienna.[1] Such an architecture is germane to technology trends in real-time systems being developed in the automotive industry today. While an examination of the hard time-domain attributes may not seem relevant to NDC, some characteristics identified by Kopetz are clearly germane to current distributed computing models; these would utilize the public networks to deliver commercially viable services that are less real-time-critical but nevertheless mission-critical from the perspective of the businesses relying on them. NDC too would require sensible architectural foundations if a composable architecture is of interest. The relationship to massively parallel systems and NDC may be less obscure.

Kopetz has cited a number of trends in the automobile industry, many of which are today shaping modern business (and therefore software) design considerations. Among them are systems on a chip (such as a 32-bit CPU VLSI with 1+ MB of memory), smart sensors, and COTS components. These trends are analogous to many of those that impact NDC software designs as well. Commodity servers running commodity operating systems marry to provide a COTS trend in many Web Services implementations, which—when containerized to expose components in a larger NDC system—would claim to give rise to composable and composed entities. As such, some of the sensibilities in the real-time world are germane to NDC, which too is subject to similar economic pressures.

To meet the demands of an increasingly competitive environment, Kopetz has proposed four principles of composability, all of which are in some sense applicable to NDC, and specifically to Web Services:

- Independent development of components
- Stability of prior services
- Constructive integration of the components to generate emerging services
- Replica determinism

Derived from the sensibilities of research done in distributed real-time computing and EmNets, these principles may be relevant to a composable architecture in the NDC environment. If the Kopetz model for a composable architecture does extend from real-time to NDC, it may be that only the WUS interfaces need support all four principles for the model to be viable. But even if more is required, these principles at least provide a basis for understanding the nature of component composability in NDC, and the problems that must be solved if such *guarantees* are to ever be forthcoming.

These principles, when applied to NDC application development, provide a basis from which to consider NDC frameworks and the interfaces exposed therein, as described below.

### Independent development of components

Components can be designed independently of each other only if the architecture supports a precise specification of all component services at the level of architecture design. This implies that a composable architecture must distinguish between architecture design and component design. It also implies that there must be a model of *cooperation*, that is, how various entities constituting an NDC application are to cooperate with each other. There is no paradigm within which we can talk about cooperation of entities such that we can compose cooperative scenarios; consequently, NDC programmers must deal directly with communication primitives to produce an ensemble-aware cooperation model. Without a standard cooperation model that incorporates (nontrivial) cooperation protocols, NDC applications are stymied, at least as far as dynamic, self-assembling, ad hoc ensembles are concerned.

### Stability of prior services

This principle ensures that validated services are not refuted by the integration of the component into an NDC ensemble. For example, the integration of a self-contained component (such as a composite entity that includes a business delegate pattern) into the service ensemble will not inadvertently consume a business service resource upon which the ensemble would otherwise rely. An unintended interaction between components can cause sporadic failure, which would be difficult to identify and which would reduce NDC application vigor in the WUS model. This is especially true for implementations that do not offer at least some other assurance of composability attributes.

### Constructive integration of components

Integration of a component into a system should normally follow a step-by-step procedure. Constructive integration requires that if $n$ components are already integrated, the integration of component $n + 1$ may not disturb the correct operation of the $n$ components already integrated. Note that unless interfaces are designed such as to provide assurances of both stability of prior services and constructive integration, any hope of ensuring that a component will exhibit characteristics mindful of those principles remains just that. Once a component becomes available in an environment in which an unknown set of ensembles can and will occur, it should be obvious that without exposing interfaces that facilitate such assurances, only adaptable implementations (or other approaches, subject to conjecture) can remedy such interface shortcomings.

### Replica determinism

This principle, when applied to NDC software design, is less concerned with the deterministic properties of an entity than it is with a level of fault tolerance. A set of replicated NDC components is *replica derminate* if all members of the set have the same externally visible state, and produce the same output messages at points in time that are sequentially bound as appropriate (as opposed to specified intervals of time, which are requirements in hard real-time systems). While it can be argued that NDC systems do have time-domain boundaries (that is, that a component must execute in less than infinite time), end-to-end sequence is far more important to program correctness than is a bounded time interval, given the temporally indeterminate nature of NDC.

## Extensible Interfaces

If we would honor the principles of stability of prior services and constructive integration in WUS-specific NDC development, either a hands-on remedy (such as an integration lab) is required or component interfaces must be extended to expose dynamically composable attributes. In light of the trend of decomposition and the drive to components, this realization must give us pause because the componentization exponential of that trend rivals that of its metatrend genealogy. Clearly, we must at some juncture ensure NDC component composability that does not require the intercession of a human being. Dynamic, self-assembled, ad hoc ensembles of components must somehow be encouraged for a truly ambitious composability to be realized, one which would acknowledge the age of ubiquitous computing to come.

When it comes to ensembles, as you may have discerned, the term "ad hoc" is not pejorative, but rather implies a desirable adaptive capability at the component level, allowing for dynamic interactions with other components, the fitscape of which cannot be finitely prestated. As such, extensible interfaces are of utmost concern if such a framework is to be viable.

## Closing Thoughts

In NDC development, strictly speaking, interfaces must always be of concern. Regardless of implementation, interoperability framework, messaging infrastructure, or application vendor, a plethora of interface questions must be addressed. User interface, data representation, messaging, logging, transaction semantics, security, QoS, and fault recovery capabilities are all germane to composability if we would extend the Kopetz principles to NDC development.

# Grids

Grid computing, first considered in Chapter 2, is another area that might shed light on potential directions for the exploration of composable NDC software development. As soon as it was demonstrated, in early NDC development, that a number of nodes could be connected to allow datacom, the utility of harnessing multiple nodes to solve problems was also clear. Grid computing is distinguished from NDC by its focus on large-scale resource sharing. Indeed, coordinated resource sharing and problem solving in dynamic, multi-institutional, virtual organizations is one focus of grid computing that differentiates it from the more general NDC arena.

The development of grid concepts at various technical levels (computational, data, and agent) reflects the fact that simple interconnection technologies at these levels are becoming relatively mature (although there is still much work to do), which will affect and likely begin to converge with NDC going forward. While earlier grid implementations were problem specific or discipline specific, generalization of grid computing emphasizes techniques for combining interconnected resources to solve increasingly complex classes of problems, including the following:

♦ Composability of resources in these systems

♦ Dynamic aspects of systems

♦ Seamlessness

♦ Greater generality, ubiquity, and mobility

Composability in the grid-computing sense is not the same as constructive integration of components in the real-time or NDC sense. However, the need for composable entities in grid computing does prompt considerations of the kinds of problems that must be solved in a general network sense and may therefore be applicable to NDC component composability. Indeed, as grid computing and NDC converge, the composable aspects of the grid system will naturally be expected of the components upon which the services on the grid will be built. Grid computing should therefore be viewed as a complementary fitscape in which composable components on a network are being explored in earnest, although not necessarily from the perspective of component interfaces.

In the case of grid computing, application transparency is a goal, meaning composability must be ensured not at an interface level but rather at an operating system or meta-architecture level, to mask or ignore application-level interface shortcomings. Grid computing, therefore, represents a very different approach, when compared to the real-time and embedded work, to providing constructive integration capabilities in NDC environments. Leveraging the approaches of grid computing and its methodologies for constructively and seamlessly integrating lower-level components may be of long-term value to a guarantee of NDC component composability at a Web Services level.

## Meta-Architectures

There are well over 100 million desktop computers and servers on the planet. Within the next few years, there will be over 100 billion Internet-enabled cell phones, automobiles, television set-top boxes, game consoles, home appliances and other devices. Today, the edge of the network is made of such devices. And we can expect about 100 trillion Internet-enabled thermostats, mail packages, cameras, articles of clothing, and other objects in a more remote future, as the edge of the network continues to expand. The problems inherent in managing components in such a world, let alone composing them, should be obvious. Each ensuing layer of networking touches increasingly interesting challenges in NDC. From the desktop to networked trousers, software development space swells to create opportunities several orders of magnitude greater than all that have come before. Edge computing is where innovation explores that opportunity.

## N1 from Sun

At Sun Microsystems, a combination of efforts in distributed grid computing, server and storage virtualization, and network resource optimization has engendered a meta-architecture approach to solving problems exposed by the unfolding edge. This approach is known as *N1,* a single term intended to address Sun's vision of the future of network computing.

Start with the idea that all compute resources on a network are like a public utility, electricity, for example. When you need it, it's there. You pay for what you use. Compute cycles, storage, bandwidth, software components, databases, etc., would all be available from a unified network interface. What would be required for an anytime, anywhere, any device network to become such a utility?

In addition to a grid computing engine shipped by Sun, N1 designers envision functionality from approaches like Jini network technology and Project JXTA technology to announce the presence of devices and users on a network. Ease of deployment should be a given. A developer could write a new version of an application and then make numerous copies of the software available, distributed to users worldwide, by utilizing the best of p2p coupled with the best of security assurances. Ideally, this application would sense the presence of other software already on the network and link into those existing applications with ease—which is the essence of composability.

Essentially, N1 describes what happens when a network of nodes and storage is assembled into a larger whole, much like what an operating system does for a node. A meta-architecture, which transcends any arbitrary node, provides the means for network orchestration.

## Other Approaches

Sun has not yet released a public specification for N1, but other approaches to a composable meta-architecture help illustrate some key points. In the June 2002 edition of Communications of the ACM, Nalini Venkatsubramanian of UC Irvine describes a composable architecture enabled by reflective middleware and a meta-architecture.[2] Venkasubrama-nian's strategy requires identification of certain key system services that are typically involved in nontrivial interactions between applications, or base-level objects, and the system, or meta-level objects. These core services are then used in the specification and implementation of more complex functions within the framework, as pure meta-level interactions. Three core services have been identified:

- ◆  Remote creation: reification of data at target
- ◆  Distributed snapshots: node and network state information
- ◆  Directory services: data and service repository

This short list of services may provide a basis on which a composable middleware architecture can be designed—if security and mobile requirements are considered and reliability presumed. But Venkasubramanian also cautions that any viable meta-architecture design must be based on formal semantics and formal reasoning methodologies.

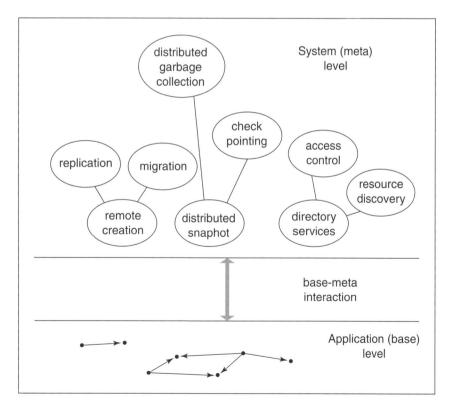

Figure 11.1  Core service classification

Essentially, the base-meta interaction layer, as shown in Figure 11.1, provides a means of ensuring some concurrent execution opportunities across nodes as appropriate, a network approach to what historically has been a function of a solitary node's operating system. At the same time, abstracting these services from any platform or framework provides a composable middleware layer that may make for a more dynamic system.

While representative of such an approach, Venkasubramanian's description of a meta-architecture for middleware is by no means the first or most profound. Strictly speaking, CORBA does much the same thing. What's interesting with this approach, and meta-architectures in general, is the quest for ultimate interoperability, which implies an ultimate wrapper at the level of component composability.

# Composability and Languages

Another approach to consider with respect to general NDC component composability is that of the languages used to generate components.

## The Fox Project

One example is the previously discussed Fox Project, whose objective is the development of language support for building safe, highly composable, and reliable systems. The project's designers would accomplish this with programming language technology, including examination of fundamental design principles, compiler technologies, and the mathematical basis of programming languages and logic. Their current emphasis is on applications for ensemble composition in embedded systems. It is a comprehensive program of research, applying theoretical foundations of programming languages (including ideas in type theory, formal semantics, and logic) to the development of tools and techniques for system software in general and embedded system software in particular. Closely linked focus areas include the following:

- Typed intermediate languages, which extend the benefits of type safety enjoyed by high-level source programming languages to the intermediate and target languages of a compiler
- Certifying compilers, which provide a foundation for trust-free code dissemination, in which code can be shared in an untrusted environment without sacrificing safety
- Proof-carrying code (PCC), a technique by which a host computer system can verify automatically that code provided by an untrusted agent is safe to execute

Type-directed certifying compilers support heterogeneous component integration. Since typed object code comes equipped with types, its safety can be relied upon without assuming that it arises from any one compiler or any one language. The same typed object code may arise from several different compilers for several different (type-safe) languages; this type information can then be used to mediate component integration to ensure the safety of composite ensembles. A type-safe linker can then ensure that the typing requirements of individual components are satisfied when they are linked, either statically or dynamically, in a running system.

The Fox Project pioneered the development of type-directed compilers. One observation of its designers is that type-directed compilers support the generation of efficient object code; the designers assert that most existing compilers seriously compromise efficiency to support automatic storage management or to permit the decomposition of programs into independent modules or components. By exploiting type information during compilation and at execution time, their type-directed compiler can avoid these compromises while preserving the benefits of storage management and modularity.

Another concept being investigated under the auspices of the project is the aforementioned proof-carrying code (PCC), which allows systems to automatically verify that code provided by an agent, which may be untrusted otherwise, will execute securely.

Obvious applications of PCC involve safe mobile code. However, PCC's significance in computer systems designs may go well beyond mobile-code applications, because PCC allows a measure of trust to be established between any parties that want to share executable content. Interestingly, the Fox Project researchers claim that the PCC approach eliminates the need for components like just-in-time compilers and bytecode verifiers (which may introduce a level of unreliability, generally speaking) from the trusted computing base, thereby increasing the level of assurance in the system as a whole.

The key idea behind PCC is to require the code producer to produce easy-to-check evidence that "explains" why the code is safe and then to attach this evidence to the code itself. When the code consumer receives the code, the evidence can be extracted and easily validated. The theoretical foundation of the project's current implementations of PCC is the notion of a formal proof of program safety. By precisely specifying the formal operational semantics of the programming language (typically, a native machine code language) and a set of rules for proving the safety of every machine instruction, they can obtain checkable encoding of safety proofs, designed so that the existence of the proof absolutely implies that the code meets all safety requirements. Precise details of the proof encoding are determined by engineering considerations, with the overall goal being the simple and fast validation of code binaries.

Certifying compilers, often based on typed intermediate languages, are used to produce PCC proofs automatically. This allows programmers to write programs in a typed high-level language (such as with Java semantics) and then automatically compile those source programs into highly optimized PCC binaries.

The Fox Project may provide additional opportunities for a lower level of composability from the NDC component perspective. Just as real-time sensibilities and grid computing provide insights into the inherently difficult problem of guaranteed component composability in a Web Services environment, language research may yield such insights as well.

## Darwinian Software

Unrelenting exponential growth, in practical terms, has given rise to a need for NDC frameworks that can exhibit organic software attributes. Any approach that honors composability also reflects such attributes. Realistically, the long-term solution will likely involve meta-architectures, which abstract key services, coupled with PCC, all exposed by extensible WUS-enabled interfaces. Under the covers we'll find a bevy of legacy systems, p2p caches, and sedimented distributed servers. But the potential for organic software is implied in its name: growth, adaptation, selection, and replication. Only when software evolves, in and of its own teleology and agent by agent, will we remove human hands from the process and allow our systems to simply disappear—joined with our minds, as it were, in a ubiquitous milieu of information fields and extremely ephemeralized products.

The concept of a fitscape implies evolutionary forces at work; even as Darwinian selection criteria reward the fit, the landscape itself changes as a result of that selection. Agents that are fit today will very likely not be so tomorrow, unless they themselves are adaptable. This is as true for NDC developers as it is of the frameworks within which they would work. All measures of software rigor are, by definition, a summation of adaptability; the more easily a component can adapt to existing conditions, the greater the reliability, fault tolerance, and (to some degree) security of that component.

Having access to information is not the same thing as having information to access; in the end, our networks are only as good as their con-

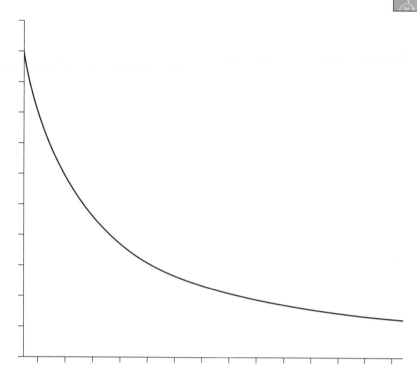

Figure 11.2 Power-law distribution: $Pn \approx 1/n$

tent. The branching out of increasingly mobile user interfaces represents an order of magnitude of additional torque in our metaphorical fitscape engine, but as with any product, species or idea, extinction events are as prevalent as are any arbitrary groupings. Extinction events over time follow a power curve distribution, by Kauffman's measure, that correlates quite nicely with Shannon's power curve distributions as shown in Figure 11.2 for stochastic processes in ergodic systems; all of which correlates as nicely with semantics. Meaning, then, a function of the observer, will paradoxically grow in a fitscape of data devoid of inherent meaning, intentionally designed to self-explore and to find meaning itself to be an extensible framework.

If we consider the classification of component communications as stochastic processes, research into the analysis, quantification, and classification of components based on their probable behavior could yield insights that would allow reliable component composition to occur independently of source. These might be similar to Zipf's law,[3] which is the observation that frequency of occurrence of some event (P), as a function of the rank

($n$) when the rank is determined by the above frequency of occurrence, is a power-law function (Pn $\approx$ = $1/n^\wedge a$ with the exponent $a$ close to unity). As has been empirically verified, Zipf's law successfully describes the probabilities of word occurrence in (for example) the English language and the sentences and paragraphs derived thereof.

If component communications do exhibit stochastic characteristics, a probabilistic approach to component communication analysis could provide a foundation for ensuring further guarantees of component composability that does not rely on any of the other potential approaches considered so far.

## Summary

Sired by Internet protocols and bounded only by an unfolding edge, innovation—real-time, embedded, mobile, wireless, optically stretched, and personalized to choice—will blossom as fast as learning curves are achieved by NDC developers worldwide. For example, real-time and fixed embedded systems representing real-time building services will at some point want to engage with network interfaces. Components at that level, classified by extensible properties, can make complex systems management in such environments much more economical, providing a niche opportunity for any group so motivated to act upon it. A product or service may emerge and eventually yield to fickle market selection forces, and then to consolidation, standardization, commoditization and, ultimately, sedimentation. That is, of course, if the idea is even viable.

But as Kauffman asserts, any reasonably complex adaptive system is nonergodic by definition, due to innovative pressures. While our frameworks would assure us predictable fitscapes in which to compose, neither our ideas nor our components can be exclusively bound by them.

### Notes

1. Hermann Kopetz, *Composability in a Time-Triggered Architecture* (Vienna: Technische Universitat Wein, 2000).

2. Nalini Venkatsubramanian, "Safe 'Composability' of Middleware Services," *Communications of the ACM*, 2002, 45(6), 49–52.

3. http://linkage.rockefeller.edu/wli/zipf/

# CHAPTER 12

# Innovation and Convergence

The promise of technology is realized only when the needs of agents within the fitscape are met. Beyond discovering, joining, and dynamically consuming services from a reliable NDC framework on which they can depend, applications are fundamentally bound to those agent needs. Just as the Nth Laws promise intelligence everywhere, the needs of these fitscape agents, both organizations and individuals, are served only when that abundance of intelligence is properly planted, husbanded, harvested, and processed; consumption cannot otherwise grow.

If our species is to survive, we must evolve from a Hunter-Gatherer Age of software development to an Agricultural Age, in which biological metaphors, farming discipline, and agribusiness sensibilities lead to abundant harvests. The threat of global warming; soaring populations in regions with the highest rate of illiteracy and the increasingly uneven distribution of global wealth that is the consequence; the increasing threshold of violence around the world, which overshadows all else—these are functions of human activity. The groups we have formed to date have created this dangerous reality.

Our scientific, commerical, military, political, and religious activities are all a manifestation of our shared belief systems, which too evolved, affected by all the information that is ours to assimilate. It's no wonder we forget the large shelves of ice breaking away from the Antarctic mass, icebergs much larger than that which settled the dispute between man and nature through the sinking of the *Titanic* in the early 20th century. The unsettling realities we face, coupled with the demands of early 21st century device proliferation, represent a software deflection point from which there is no retreat. If we would continue on the path of ephemeralization, which promises to help mend the "have/ have not" economic reality incumbent in most of our problems today, software that can adapt to changing environments is our only realistic choice.

There are no guarantees that the Nth Laws will continue their exponential vectors, at least not as they may have in the past. Long suffering from global economic malaise, technology investments have been severely punished in recent years, with particular emphasis on telecom stocks. World leaders in global telecom have watched investment capital evaporate since the turn of the century, a change that may considerably impact Gilder's law. The same may be said of Moore's law, if semiconductor equities are any measure (although this law has remained constant, if not accelerated, over three decades, despite other despondent moments in that sector). While it is not likely that Moore's law will expire within the next few years and that wireless and fiber optic infrastructure deployment enthusiastically continues, there are no guarantees.

The same must be said of any NDC framework that would harness opportunities bound to those laws—perhaps not as risky a wager as dropping three dollars in the MegaBucks machine at your favorite casino, but risky nonetheless, especially in view of the level of investment required to fully utilize any potential value. Alas, we cannot stand still. The fitscape evolves around us, due to us and despite us, and we, who make a living in that fitscape, are forced to innovate in order to compete.

To the extent to which wealth arises from increasing productivity, which is highly correlated with IT investments, a bet on NDC in a general sense is still a good one. But the developers of applications in any given framework who remain cognizant not only of Deutsch's Eight Fallacies but also of the innovation and convergence that must inevitably occur within a fitscape, will benefit thereby, as will their customers.

## Synergistic Convergence

The promise of technology, the Internet, and networks in general is one of increasing productivity—doing more with less. The Nth Laws ensure that IT will continue to economize a path toward total proliferation, commoditizing hardware and software in the process in an expanding, ephemeralizing spiral. As IT permeates other activities, they too become ephemeralized. When human value inputs, which are increasingly digitized, are joined in networks, GFN dynamics allow for dramatic increases in output over time. The promise of hyperproductivity is that the satisfaction of virtually all aspects of human needs—food, water, transportation, communication, and so on—will be all but guaranteed for everyone, at very low or no cost. On one level we are all working ourselves out of jobs, or at least we should be. But unless we decide to revisit some of the assumptions that seem to afflict some NDC frameworks today, future employment is all but guaranteed in application composition and system and network management at least.

*Convergence* means many things in the context of NDC. Generally, it is the coming together or joining of two formerly distinct things. In mathematics, convergence implies the property or manner of approaching a limit, such as a point, line, function, or value, which too is a theme in the opus of computing. Likewise relevant is the biological meaning: the separate, adaptive evolution of superficially similar structures, such as the wings of birds and insects or the eyes of humans and octopi. Unrelated species, subjected to similar environments, converge on similar structures over time; the same phenomenon occurs in NDC fitscapes.

Recall the 24 NDC R&D fitscapes discussed in Chapter 3, repeated here as Table 12.1.

Table 12.1    NDC research and development areas revisited

| | | |
|---|---|---|
| cluster concepts | distributed storage | peer-to-peer |
| collaborative computing | grid computing | pervasive computing |
| dependable systems | languages | real time and embedded |
| distributed agents | massively parallel systems | security |
| distributed algorithms | middleware | Semantic Web |
| distributed databases | mobile and wireless | spaces computing |
| distributed filesystems | network protocols | ubiquitous computing |

The obvious potential for synergy, based on shared interests among these areas of R&D, will result in convergence in related areas over time. Consider grid computing. As an umbrella for any number of other areas, the idea of a grid implies the entire list of distributed efforts (agents, algorithms, databases, filesystems, media and storage) as well as massively parallel systems, dependable systems, operating systems, cluster concepts, and even p2p. Indeed, if the attributes of an information grid are akin to those of a utility network, a meta-architecture is also implied, especially when wireless and mobile computing nodes are candidates for participation.

## NDC Attractors

Grid computing represents one of a small set of strange attractors in the evolving fitscape of NDC. A *strange attractor* is simply the visibly rendered pattern of the pathways produced by graphing the behaviors of a system. Since many nonlinear systems are unpredictable and yet patterned, work in complexity research calls such patterns "strange"; and since many such patterns tend to produce a fractal geometric shape, the processes involved are said to be attracted to that shape. Thus, the attractor is actually a set of points such that all trajectories nearby converge toward it. If we may make the strange attractor a computing metaphor, grid computing is definitely one such in NDC, as many distinct R&D fitscapes are on trajectories toward supporting or enabling the network resources implied therein.

There are four distinct, interdependent future paths toward which NDC will soon evolve, it seems to me, at least if the observable Nth Laws remain constant for a few more years to come. Each attractor represents both a different set of convergences in the NDC fitscape and a different set of potential outcomes. Each of these areas will attract considerable investments in applications to come, drawing on increasingly rich intellectual innovations while fundamentally bound to increasingly competitive economic constraints.

These four general attractors can be characterized as follows:

♦ Grid computing: The utility model, in which Lego-like components plug into a standard, highly available infrastructure spanning the entire taxonomy of networks, ultimately including mobile and wireless nodes.

♦ The Semantic Web: Web Services phase four, in which an intelligent infrastructure providing a means whereby dynamic, ad hoc ensembles can grow is fully defined and standardized.

♦ Spaces computing: The Mirror World model from edge-to-edge, providing for and expecting a near-real-time flow of all pertinent world data over self-healing networks and systems.

♦ Ubiquitous computing: The inevitable implication and promise of the Nth Laws, with network-aware, application-specific, edge-to-edge computing everywhere and resource utilization in the aggregate optimized to the extreme.

These convergence points are not mutually exclusive; indeed, the vision of ubiquitous computing requires all three of the other attractors in order to be complete. Nor are they independent of each other; a grid may just as easily host a space as it does the repository for a WUS component. But these convergence points represent the distinct channels of utility through which R&D investments will generally flow in the coming era. That is, of course, if computer science is even relevant.

Is software a commodity? If so, does the commoditization of software imply convergence in a more mathematical sense, toward an intrinsic limit on an industry which too is bound to growth constraints? One of the dangers we face is the marginalization of NDC resulting from perceptions left in the wake of the dotcom collapse, increasing security concerns, and a general global economic downturn. For technology to be adopted, there must be willing adopters, and that ultimately implies edge-user demand and satisfaction.

If, and only if, our networks continue to provide increasingly innovative and useful services will computer science remain relevant to business concerns. But commoditization itself is a dual-edged sword. The threat of an evolutionary dead end, coupled with inevitably increasing cost pressures, reduces the likelihood of continuous R&D investments in a commodity altogether, and software is no exception.

While it is not likely that the commercial exploitation of the software space will eliminate R&D budgets any time soon, the increasing competitive pressures that are felt in all quarters will likely drive R&D convergence toward umbrella concepts, from which to draw resource as needed. The four NDC attractors may represent such umbrellas. With an ultimate grid to bind all devices, a Semantic Web to facilitate a growing spiral of meaning and commerce, a huge space to mirror all that we would see in real time, and the proliferation of intelligent networked entities at all levels, the teleological vector of ubiquitous computing seems almost viable, almost within reach, almost certain. The hope, it seems to me, is the promise of that vision and all its inherent positive implications; the challenges are legion, and can be addressed only by processes and people over time. But if these attractors do indeed represent convergence points for innovation, NDC developers well-versed in the technologies of each will inherit both the opportunity and the responsibility that come with defining the future. Find a home in one of those fitscapes and provide all possible energy toward making a living to that end, and you may help the hope and promise of ubiquitous computing to be realized.

## The Future of NDC

In the mathematics of multidimensional spaces, the volume of a spherical figure is the product of its radius raised to a dimensional exponent and the transcendental value of pi ($\pi$). For example, in two-dimensional space, the volume of a circle is $\pi r^2$, where r is the value of the radius. The area of a circle, which in two-dimensional space is equivalent to its volume, has interesting properties with respect to that proportion of the total which is represented by the area of a circle of exactly half its diameter.

The area of the outer circle is $\pi$ and the area of the inner circle is $\pi(1/2)^2$, which is equal to $1/4\ \pi$; only a quarter of the area of the larger circle lies within a circle of half the diameter. Now consider spheres similarly arranged as shown in Figure 12.1.

The volume of a sphere is $(4/3)\ \pi r^3$; the ratio between the volume of a smaller sphere that is 1/2 the diameter of the larger sphere to the volume of the larger sphere is reduced to 1/8. If we add more dimensions, the relationship between the number of dimensions and the volume ratio between inner and outer hyperspheres continues as $1/2^n$, where $n$ is the number of dimensions. So hyperspheres in four dimensions would exhibit

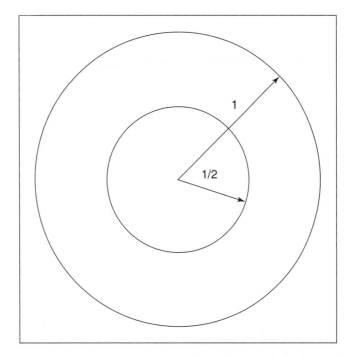

Figure 12.1  Comparing properties of areas of circles

of ratio of 1/16, for example, and so on. The surprising result is that the more dimensions we add, the greater the percentage of volume that lies near the surface. As a metaphor for NDC growth, the opportunities exposed by deflection point events represent increasing dimensionality; computing on the edge is the inescapable result.

The proliferation of NDC devices is adrift in sea of legacy assumptions and driven by global-economy innovations, which create a fitscape of constantly shifting opportunities. The future of NDC depends as much on capital investment as it does on technological innovation. Thus, factors beyond the attributes of any framework have as much an impact on convergence as does any well-founded vision. But from what we know, much is implied, as shown in Figure 12.2.

Computing on the edge suggests dozens and, one day, hundreds and even thousands of concurrent personal devices, all of which must somehow find interface harmony in a networked environment. The interaction of personal devices with information fields represents only one challenging aspect of user interface evolution to come. Take the concept of virtual reality, in which worlds filled with agents, either real-time representations

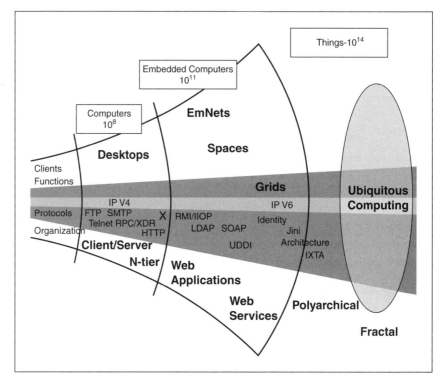

Figure 12.2  Future of NDC

of actual entities or computer-generated, Turing-Test-busting game bots, become the most cost-effective means of dynamic interaction. Join this prospect with a growing array of wireless choices, and the emergence of an augmented reality becomes both possible and perhaps even commercially viable.

## Augmented Reality

Imagine "see-through" devices, as described by Stephen K. Feiner of Columbia University, which superimpose computer graphics on the user's view of the world.[1] His current designs incorporate prisms that reflect network-derived data on a liquid-crystal display within the user's line of sight. This approach allows light from the surrounding world to pass through, thus augmenting reality rather than obscuring or replacing it. In Feiner's prototype, a system of sensors keeps track of the position and orientation of the user's head, which helps ensure that graphics display appropriately with respect to landscape.

Work in augmented reality (AR) represents a revolution in user interface as much as it does evolutionary growth in wireless, Nth Law-derived capabilities. Once integrated, a head-top device may be indispensable for all network interface needs, including even the once sacred space of desktop computing. If AR fields begin to riddle metropolitan centers, applications well beyond desktop capabilities will emerge. Transportation, shopping, entertainment, and group events and interactions of all kinds will find innovative uses in these systems. Even an old-fashioned stroll down the sidewalk could be something akin to wearing 3D glasses in a holographic amusement park. To the extent that the broadcast of information can be utilized to add value to processes of all kinds, a head-top box may be in a future near you.

Serving those new eyes will be a multitude of systems, all of which must somehow find conversation in an assemblage of legacy protocols. Interoperable by choice, competitive by design, the platforms we build today will become the basis for those new eyes; what we ultimately see tomorrow will be a function of the platform choices we make today. As our visions of NDC—once bound almost exclusively to client-server relationships, which meant a desktop focus by virtue of sheer volume—evolve to contain a new reality, we find that we are constrained by more than Deutsch's Eight Fallacies. We must also confront the ultimate fallacy of geographically contained nodes, an assumption that still riddles wireless protocols, as does the fallacy of composable objects on a network. These new realities, exposed by wireless, Nth Law-derived fitscape vectors, must be acknowledged lest frameworks and fancy make us fools.

## Information Management Metaphors

David Gelernter of *Mirror Worlds* fame, one of the early visionaries of network potential, has described the kind of transformations that will occur if our work in NDC continues to be fueled by exponential growth phenomena. In a rambling online tome provocatively entitled "The Second Coming—A Manifesto,"[2] Gelernter's own recovery and growth, as well as that of the Internet, hint at the transformations to come. Let's ramble with him.

I want information, not a computer. The latter is just the means of enjoying the former. If I can obtain the information I need without a traditional computer, today's operating systems and browsers are obsolete. The NDC future Gelernter envisions is based on cyberbodies drifting in the computational cosmos, which he also calls "the Swarm"—self-contained, neatly ordered collections of information, like immaculate giant gardens. A user will walk up to any "tuner" (connected device) and slip in a "calling card," which identifies a cyberbody. Once the tuner tunes it in, the cyberbody arrives and settles, like a bird perching on a tree limb.

Your entire electronic life could be stored in such a cyberbody. The ability to summon it to any tuner at any time creates a utility of information that will fine-tune transactions of all kinds. Presumably, the AR vision segues neatly into such an infrastructure.

Gelernter also envisions user-interface evolution, albeit metaphorically. Modern user interfaces are based on a file-cabinet metaphor; we store "files" on disks, organize files into "folders," and so on. Computers, however, especially networked computers, are fundamentally unlike file-cabinets in that they can take action. To the extent that metaphors affect computing, the file-cabinet metaphor prevents a more active view of information management, promoting instead a passive understanding that is fundamentally wrong for computers.

The standard file-naming policies of a file-cabinet approach to information management have far-reaching consequences. These policies don't merely force us to make up names where no name is called for; they also impose limits on our ability to classify exogenous documents, those that arrive from the outside world. For example, a fresh email message cannot stand on its own as a separate document, nor can it show up alongside other files in searches, nor sit by itself on the desktop, nor be opened or printed independently; it has no "filing system" name, so it must be cached on arrival inside an existing file (that is, the mailbox) that does have a name (albeit one the email interface allows us to routinely ignore). The same holds for incoming photos, faxes, browser bookmarks, scanned documents, and so on.

According to Gelernter, the file-cabinet metaphor is broken. We shouldn't have to put files in directories; the directories should reach out and grab them. If a file belongs in ten directories, all ten should reach out and take a reference, automatically and simultaneously. Moreover, a file should be allowed to have no name, one name, or many names, and many files should be allowed to share one name. A file should be allowed to exist in no directory, one directory, or many directories, and many files should be allowed to share one directory.

The organization of information should, in short, mimic that of our own minds. Information components stored in minds do not have names and are not organized into folders; they are retrieved not by name or folder but by content. For example, if you hear the voice of someone you know and the voice triggers the memory of a face, you've retrieved a visual memory that contains the voice as one component. Everything in your memory can theoretically be seen from a temporal perspective: past, present, and future. Our network storage metaphor should be so flexible and so determined.

If Gelernter's Swarm and hungry directories are to emerge, the concept of polyarchical systems must be embraced. Literally meaning "multiple rule sets," a polyarchical system is one that can respond meaningfully to messages of unknown content or origin. Document classification and transformation are germane to this concept.

# Polyarchical Systems

Imagine an Internet appliance that can meaningfully process documents from any platform. A Microsoft Word document and a game executable targeting some flavor of Linux, for example, would be equally easy to process. In polyarchical systems, such capabilities would not depend on embedded intelligence as much as on network intelligence. The ultimate promise of Web Services, rooted in document transformation, hints of such capabilities.

Polyarchical systems can achieve the ultimate in platform interoperability with a number of approaches. Polyarchical intelligence might well be part of an evolving local operating system, which grows in capability as it processes unrecognized messages requiring network resolution. When receiving a document of unknown structure, such a system would query known document-class repositories for platform knowledge germane to the new class of document. A "magic cookie" approach to document-class recognition (that is, one based on unique document header information) would be one useful approach. Indeed, polyarchical chips at the edge might even rewire themselves as needed, like a field programmable gate array (FPGA), which can dynamically overlay chip logic to improve performance of a known algorithm or even to achieve interoperability.

Alternatively, polyarchical document transformations could just as easily be tied to service providers, a proxy-like approach in which documents targeting edge systems are always correctly transformed, using the inherent capabilities of the edge node. As long as edge devices have access to messages that are well formed from their perspective, a polyarchical network can be envisioned.

As with the grid computing attractor, a meta-architecture is needed if polyarchical system capabilities are to fully inhabit edge-to-edge application space. This represents a convergence in NDC framework design as well; by abstracting operating system services, messaging, resources in general, and even datacom protocols, the opportunities for dynamic composability at a component level may yet be explored as a convergence toward an NDC meta-architecture evolves. Polyarchical systems will be a feature of that progress.

## Autonomic Computing

Organic software is required if the billions of intelligent devices that will be manufactured and networked within the next few years have any hope of realizing their potential value. Human bandwidth is limited; our ephemeralizing work can continue only if we relinquish control over systems that may have required regular human intervention in the past. Autonomic computing, which IBM has launched as a key initiative, describes a vision of self-managed computing systems requiring a minimum of human interference. The term is derived from the autonomic nervous system, which controls key bodily functions without our conscious awareness or involvement.

The explosion of information concurrent with the integration of IT into everyday life has led to new demands in the management and maintainenance of computer systems and networks. In fact, demand is already outpacing supply when it comes to expertise in managing increasingly complex networked systems. Open IT jobs in the United States alone number in the hundreds of thousands, even during economic perturbations, and demand for skilled IT workers will double in just a few years. Furthermore, as we boldly move toward ubiquitous computing, the stability of current infrastructure, systems, and data will face increasingly greater exposure to outages, disrepair, and general network indeterminacy. IBM believes that we are rapidly approaching a deflection point in the evolution of the industry's views toward computing in general and the associated infrastructure, middleware, and services that enable it; in short, that increasing system complexity will soon demand skills beyond human ability to muster. This increasing complexity, coupled with a shortage of IT professionals, exposes an inevitable need to automate many of the functions associated with system and network management today. Autonomic computing is IBM's answer to that need.

What do fickle users want from computing systems? In my view, Gelernter's view makes sense: users want to interact with systems intuitively and to be far less involved in running them. Ideally, we'd all like computing systems to pretty much manage themselves and essentially disappear even while providing us with the information we require. The autonomic nervous system, which sends messages that regulate life-enabling functions such as temperature, respiration, and heart rate without the need for conscious processing or even awareness, provides an apt metaphor. The cyberequivalent is clear: a network of organized, "smart" computing components that provide needed services and support without conscious human effort.

The IBM approach also represents a more general shift to a computing approach defined by data. Access to data from multiple, distributed sources, in addition to traditional centralized storage, will allow users to transparently access information when and where they need it. At the same time, this view will necessitate changing the industry's focus on processing speed and storage to one attempting to develop distributed networks that are largely self-managing, self-diagnostic, and transparent to the user.

According to the IBM autonomic computing vision, computer systems, software, storage, and support must exhibit three fundamentals attributes from a user perspective:

- ♦ Flexibility: The system is able to sift data by taking a platform- and device-agnostic approach.
- ♦ Accessibility: Like the autonomic nervous system, the system is always on.
- ♦ Transparency: The system performs its tasks and adapts to a user's needs without dragging the user into the intricacies of its workings.

On the surface, there are many similarities between the autonomic computing vision and that of a spaces approach married with polyarchical concerns. Again, a design convergence at the NDC framework level is implied. Thus, the attributes of autonomic computing are useful to consider in a broader context.

While the definition of autonomic computing will evolve as contributing technologies mature, IBM has suggested the following list of characteristics of an autonomic computing system:[3]

1. **Self-aware:** A system needs to "know itself"—its components must also possess a system identity. Since a "system" can exist at many levels, an autonomic system must have detailed knowledge of its components, current status, ultimate capacity, and all con-

nections to other systems to govern itself. A system must also know the extent of its "owned" resources, those it can borrow or lend, and those that can be shared or should be isolated.

2. **Self-configured:** A system must configure and reconfigure itself under varying (even unpredictable) conditions. System configuration or "setup" must occur automatically, as well as dynamically adjust that configuration to best handle changing environments.

3. **Self-improved:** A system never settles for the status quo—it always looks for ways to optimize its workings. A system must monitor its constituent parts and fine-tune workflow to achieve predetermined system goals.

4. **Self-healed:** A system must perform something akin to healing—it must be able to recover from routine and extraordinary events that might cause some of its parts to malfunction. A system must be able to discover problems or potential problems and then find an alternative way of using resources or reconfiguring the system to keep functioning smoothly.

5. **Self-defended:** A virtual world is no less dangerous than the physical one, so an autonomic computing system must be an expert in self-protection. A system must detect and identify various types of attacks and protect itself against them to maintain overall system security and integrity.

6. **Neighborhood aware:** A system must know its environment and the context surrounding its activity, and act accordingly, finding and generating rules for how best to interact with neighboring systems. A system must tap available resources, even negotiate the use by other systems of its underutilized elements, adapting both itself and its environment in the process.

7. **Open:** A system cannot exist in a hermetic environment. While independent in its ability to manage itself, a system must function in a heterogeneous world and implement open standards. In other words, an autonomic computing system cannot, by definition, be a proprietary solution.

8. **Self-determined:** A system must anticipate the optimized resources needed while keeping its complexity hidden. A system must marshal IT resources to shrink the gap between the goals of the user and the IT implementation necessary to achieve those goals—without involving the user in that implementation.

These characteristics, which define organic software attributes from the perspective of the edge user, also represent the great potential of NDC framework convergence going forward. A Semantic Web, a grid, and a space can all lend themselves to the realization of autonomic computing characteristics on the edge of the inflating universe that is NDC.

## Amorphous Computing

When James Lovelock published his Gaia hypothesis in 1969, which we discussed in Chapter 1, a reductionist approach to knowledge acquisition was in vogue (and to some extent remains). The reductionist approach involves building descriptions of systems out of the descriptions of their subsystems, yet remaining ignorant of the relationships between them.

Once the positions of atoms in a molecule are specified, for example, the relationships between the atoms are also specified. Similarly, once the relative locations of molecules within a biological system are specified, the relationships between these molecules are also specified. Taking such relationships into account as an independent concern, as NDC (for instance) must do, goes beyond a purely reductionist approach.

Alas, there is more to a system than the specification of its parts and their relationships. In complex adaptive systems, behaviors that do not lend themselves to such analysis emerge. Cells cooperate to form multicellular organisms, a function of a genetic program that is shared by all neighboring cells. Colonies of ants cooperate to construct their hills, based on simple rule sets and messaging systems. Humans form cooperative groups to build towns, cities, nations, and IT infrastructures, with cultural constraints shaping the results.

This type of behavior raises fundamental questions about the organization of computing systems and the fallacy of composable components. How can we enable coherent behavior from the cooperation of large numbers of unreliable, architecturally distinct components? Ubiquitous objects can be networked in unknown, irregular, and elusive ways. What approaches are viable in instructing this horde of programmable entities, enabling them to cooperate to achieve particular goals?

These questions have been of fundamental theoretical interest for years; only now, as we face the inevitable implications of exponential growth, must they be addressed. Now is the most opportune time to begin to engineer emergent order. Unless we identify the engineering principles and languages that can be used to observe, control, organize, and exploit the behavior of the tidal wave of intelligence building at the edge of the network, the growth of IT will be thwarted.

Research into amorphous computing at MIT[4] has as its objective the creation of the system-architectural, algorithmic, and technological foundations for the exploitation of programmable materials—that is, those that incorporate vast numbers of programmable elements that may react to each other and to their environment. Such materials, which can be fabricated economically, are key to the amorphous computing vision, provided that computing elements are amassed in bulk without arranging for a precise interconnection architecture or testing. To exploit programmable materials, we must identify engineering principles that enable a more organic approach to the organization of cooperative entities.

# Emergence

In Chapter 1, a discussion of the genesis of computer science cited Babbage, Turing, and Von Neumann as potential candidates for fatherhood. Given the emergence of NDC and the paradoxical implications discussed herein, however, we may be better served to ask John Holland to take responsibility, as it may ultimately be his child after all. The importance of Holland's role should be clear given the context of the future of NDC. Consider the implications of amorphous computing.

If we are to imagine amorphous computing systems, the reductionist habits that brought us here must be broken, and a more integral view of system behavior adopted. Stephen Wolfram recently published a near-1200-page tome entitled *A New Kind of Science*[5] in which he describes the behavior of some 256 simple rule sets that drive interesting behaviors in cellular automata (CA), as well as giving rise to Wolfram's Principle of Computational Equivalence.

The problem of emergence is related to the problem of components. Instead of asking how we, or other creatures, behave in context, we should ask why nature exhibits particular patterns, or even has patterns at all, and is not a single undifferentiated mass. Wolfram suggests a beginning set of rules. Regularities exist, manifested in recognizable patterns, but where do these regularities come from? They're connected to the fundamental physics somehow, just as the flapping of butterfly wings and thunder storms are connected, but how do we get from one to the other?

## Cellular Automata

Like the Church-Turing thesis, Wolfram's principle speaks of equivalence between computing engines, but it goes much further, suggesting that computational equivalence applies to processes of any kind, natural or artificial. The behavior of the cells that replicate and cooperate to form a leaf on a tree, for example, is a function of a set of rules, presumably encoded in each cell's DNA. To the extent that the same set of rules can be encoded in silica, there is a computational equivalence. Thus, not only is it possible to reach a more complete understanding of cellular behavior in the context of an organism, it is also possible to mimic the phenomena of biological information management and cellular cooperation.

The study of emergent behavior in computer science began with John Von Neumann in the infancy of our industry. He chose to study self-reproduction, hubristically ignoring everything biologists knew about the way existing organisms actually reproduce themselves. He was able to prove that a certain class of CA can have a "general constructive automaton," a configuration of states that can construct almost any configuration of states. Since his work predated the widespread availability of computing nodes and the Internet, Von Neumann accomplished all this with pencil and paper, a practice still honored in theoretical computer science. He didn't label states with colors, as is the case in many CA experiments today, but with little wiring-diagram-like icons, to help show the function of each cell. His constructor is told what to build by a "tape," a string of cells whose states the constructor read as instructions—a theoretical Turing machine.

## Genetic Algorithms

John Holland, a pioneer in machine learning and the world's first Ph.D. in computer science, is most famous for the invention of genetic algorithms (GA). These algorithms are based on a strategy of recombination of instructions, rather like nature's evolutionary strategy of genetic recombination in sexual replication. Proposing a subtle form of machine learning and optimization, quite consciously based on evolutionary biology, Holland's *Adaptation in Natural and Artificial Systems* is a classic.

One of the things Holland has been studying for many years is the problem of components and the reuse of categorical parts. Any sighted human being can easily parse an unfamiliar scene into familiar objects like buildings, streets, automobiles, trees, other humans, and so on. This quick decomposition of complex visual scenes into familiar components is something that we cannot yet mimic with computers, because we have almost no idea how it is done. The problem of finding and using good building blocks recurs in all intellectual domains: scientific theories, for example, require as building blocks entities or variables that are subject to simple, reliable, findable laws. This problem is related to the problem of induction or, more precisely, of hypothesis. Kaufmann's observation that it is impossible to finitely prestate the configuration space for any complex adaptive system is at odds with the scientific method. The schema theorem for genetic algorithms is Holland's attempt to address the problem in that better-behaved domain, in essence specifying the kind of building blocks a GA can't fail to find, and how quickly it is likely to find them.

This we can call *emergence*, a mystery we routinely observe without explaining, short of Holland's and Wolfram's work. How can we harness the power of emergence in NDC? As GA approaches explore the fitscape of NDC, some of the answers are likely to be discovered.

GAs, inspired by Darwin's theory of evolution, solve problems through the evolution of algorithms. An algorithm starts with a set of solutions (like digital chromosomes), which form a population. Solutions from one population may be selected, according to their fitness within their environment, for use in forming a new population, which may be fitter than the old one. The more suitable solutions are, the more likely it is that they will successfully reproduce. This is repeated for multiple generations until some fitness-testing condition is satisfied.

During reproduction, recombination occurs, as genes from parents form in some way the whole new digital chromosome. The newly created offspring can also show mutations, as the elements of the digital chromosomes are slightly changed during reproduction. In biological systems, mutations are most often caused by errors in copying parental genes; similar mutations can be introduced in digital systems. The fitness of a biological organism is measured by success of its life or its ability to successfully compete in its fitscape, and our digital organisms are similarly measured.

The work on GA's has generally been orthogonal to NDC. A single node is all that is ever required for GA research to continue. But imagine the potential for GAs, unleashed in an NDC environment, that continually learn to improve system and network interactions. At the heart of GAs is the reality of the unpredictable exploration of state space, which encodes adaptable behavior into a fitness strategy. The exploration of increasingly complex network configurations as well as the problems inherent in any vision of composable components will certainly benefit from the emergence of GAs in NDC. Indeed, it should be clear that adaptable software of some kind, with or without a recombinant strategy, will be required if ubiquitous computing is to remain our teleological vector.

## Fractal Patterns

As shown in Figure 12.3, a *fractal* is a rough or fragmented geometric shape that can be subdivided into parts, each of which approximates a smaller copy of the whole. In addition to this general self-similarity, fractals are independent of scale—they look similar, no matter how close you zoom in. Many mathematical structures are fractals, such as Sierpinski's triangle, the Koch snowflake, the Peano curve, the Mandelbrot set and Lorenz attractors. Fractals also describe many real-world objects that do not have simple geometric shapes, such as clouds, mountains, turbulence, and coastlines.

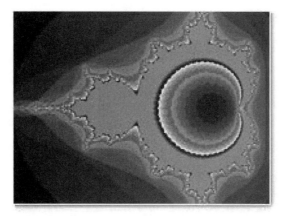

Figure 12.3  The JavaSpaces fractal

Within NDC, fractal patterns do not represent merely the implementation of applications to calculate fractal objects; while interesting and sometimes useful, the mathematics and ultimate visual display of an object with fractal properties are of less interest than the implications of fractal patterns that may emerge on the network. Of interest too is the evolving embrace of the chaotic sciences in NDC, à la Kauffman, Wolfram, Holland, and others, which would describe the properties of complex adaptive systems without traditional constraints.

In short, fractal patterns on the network imply the marriage of chaos and NDC. Self-similarity and independence of scale mark NDC fractal pattern attributes. A client-registry-service conceptual model is an example of such a pattern. This model is applicable within a given node, on a private LAN, across a WAN and the public network in general, a self-similarity that we can envision throughout the network at almost all levels, independently of framework or platform. If autonomic computing is to ever be edge-user viable, something like the Recovery Blocks technique from software fault-tolerance research (as shown in Figure 3.6 and discussed in Chapter 3) may also be utilized as a fractal pattern to ensure not just application correctness, but polyarchical attributes as well.

Even as the properties of fractal mathematics are useful in the exploration of such diverse fields as quantum computing, economics, and art, the essence of fractal patterns as an NDC computing metaphor is powerful. If we can harness the properties of fractal patterns in NDC, recognizing the insights of Kauffman and Wolfram in the process, amorphous computing may yet emerge, in the nick of time, to assuage the intense pressures we must now face.

## Relentless Innovation

In the course of our exploration of NDC potential, we have added at least two fallacies to Deutsch's original eight: first, that nodes are geographically bound and second, that components are composable. These two additional fallacies represent the bulk of the issues that must be solved as innovation gives rise to consolidation in NDC. While some frameworks are stronger than others in regard to the extended list of fallacies, no framework is completely untenanted by ignorance. For ubiquitous computing to be realized, the fluid nature of a wireless network must be polyarchically engaged at some level. Composable components must also be facilitated at some level if we would avoid a decline in network usability due to increasing edge intelligence and inevitably decreasing edge-user competence as the population of users swells.

All R&D efforts in NDC exhibit similar properties with respect to a fitscape: autonomous agents who, in their efforts to make a living, persistently explore Kauffman's adjacent possible and modify the fitscape in the process. The dynamics of a fitscape—interestingly giving rise to novelty, which is unpredictable by definition—represent our evolving understanding of Darwinian systems. Given the remarkable efficacy and rich differentiation exhibited by natural systems, we could do a lot worse than to adopt an organic model for NDC software. The properties of such natural systems, which may sometimes be computationally equivalent to NDC endeavors, can provide inspiration for our designs as well as strategies for algorithmic adaptation, both of which will be required in large measure if NDC promise to be realized.

Innovation must relentlessly occur, regardless of fitscape constraints. Indeed, a fitscape requires innovation from competing agents. But unabated novelty is as dangerous to life as is stasis; the rate of innovation cannot exceed the ability of the fitscape to test it. Thus, NDC in the aggregate faces a deflection point of a magnitude greater than any we may have imagined to date, if current NDC framework approaches are any measure. To confidently proceed, we must paradoxically give up control to maintain control and implement systems based on the attributes of organic software. Just as our participation in fitscapes gives rise to innovation, software agents making a living in virtual fitscapes must innovate. Just as our economic fitscapes force us to explore niches and novelty, software must do likewise, and adaptive software will be the result. For software to evolve to its full potential, software fitscapes that most effectively promote evolution must be created; a marriage of a spaces computing approach and agent-aware GAs provides a rough approximation of what such fitscapes might look like.

# Conclusion

We have no choice but to evolve from a Hunter-Gatherer Age of software development to an Agricultural Age, if indeed we would take the metaphorical leap to a new civilization. In *After the Clockwork Universe,* Sally J. Goerner asserts that early 21st century zeitgeist modalities are as transitional and as painful as those that marked the turning from the Dark Ages to the Enlightenment some 500 years ago. In the pre-Copernican world, the mindset that placed God, and therefore mankind, at the center of the universe also required that the earth itself be that nexus. Then science came along, surfing the killer waves of information born of the printing press, and a new view was born. Newtonian reductionism, the adoption curve of this new mindset, peaked sometime toward the end of the 20th century, although the fruits of that perspective continue to abound. Another integral mindset, characterized by a network metaphor, is now in ascendance, one that paradoxically connects both of its predecessors within a larger container.

Computer science has bootstrapped an ephemeralizing deflection point unique in human history. If there is hope for humanity, it is in software. And if there is hope for software, it lies paradoxically in our humanity, and in all the messy, organic, sometimes irrational fitscape-specific attributes humanity may exhibit. The extent to which we decide to engineer organic software attributes into NDC frameworks is the long-term basis for that hope. There is no other option.

Somewhere between Einstein's relativity, Heisenberg's uncertainty, and Gödel's incompleteness, all of which so sweetly describe our space, patterns emerge in complex adaptive systems for which descriptive mechanisms do not yet exist. And it is the floor of connections upon which such patterns must dance, a dance we glimpse even now with our portals. If ubiquitous head-top AR ever meets ad hoc NDC component ensembles, which grow intelligently, elegantly, and immediately from seeds to cash crop, tailored to their contexts, . . . a new human civilization is all but guaranteed.

## Notes

1. Steven K. Feiner, "Augmented Reality: A New Way of Seeing," *Scientific American* (April 2002), 48–55.

2. http://www.edge.org/3rd_culture/gelernter/gelernter_p1.html

3. http://www.research.ibm.com/autonomic/overview/elements.html

4. http://www.swiss.ai.mit.edu/projects/amorphous/

5. Stephen Wolfram, *A New Kind of Science* (Champaign, IL: Wolfram Media Inc., 2002).

# Index